The Impact of Human Rights Prosecutions

The Impact of Human Rights Prosecutions

Insights from European, Latin American, and African Post-Conflict Societies

Edited by
Ulrike Capdepón and Rosario Figari Layús

LEUVEN UNIVERSITY PRESS

The publication of this work was supported by the Balzan Foundation and Universität Konstanz

International Balzan Foundation

Universität Konstanz

ISBN 978 94 6270 249 3
eISBN 978 94 6166 353 5
https://doi.org/10.11116/9789461663535
D / 2020 / 1869 / 42
NUR: 828

Typesetting: Crius Group
Cover design: Daniel Benneworth Gray
Cover illustration: *Justicias* (*Infojus Noticias*, 2014) © Kiti López

GPRC
Guaranteed
Peer Reviewed
Content
www.gprc.be

Table of Contents

About the Contributors

Kristine Avram co-edited a special issue of the *Journal of International Political Theory* on Marcel Mauss in International Studies (2018). Her research interests include international criminal law and justice, philosophy and sociology of law, theories of collective violence and conflict, and narratives and narrative approaches. She is a Research Fellow and Lecturer at the Centre for Conflict Studies, Philipps University Marburg. Her current research project deals with the ascription of individual criminal responsibility in the aftermath of collective violence and repression.

Ulrike Capdepón holds a PhD in Political Science from the University of Hamburg and the GIGA German Institute for Global and Area Studies (Germany, 2011). She is currently a research fellow at the Institute for Advanced Study, University of Konstanz, where she acts as coordinator of the "Reconstructing Memory in the City" project. In 2017 and 2018 she was a Lecturer in the Program in Latin American Studies (PLAS) at Princeton University (USA). She has been a Marie Curie Fellow at the Spanish National Research Council (CSIC) in Madrid, and a postdoctoral researcher at the University of Konstanz working on the ERC project "Narratives of Terror and Disappearance in Argentina." From 2014 to 2016, she was a postdoctoral research scholar affiliated to the Institute for the Study of Human Rights (ISHR) at Columbia University in New York City. Her research interests include human rights, memory studies and transitional justice in Latin America and the Iberian Peninsula. She is the author of *Vom Fall Pinochet zu den Verschwundenen des Spanischen Bürgerkrieges: Die Auseinandersetzung mit Diktatur und Menschenrechtsverletzungen in Chile und Spanien* [From the Pinochet Case to the *Desaparecidos* of the Spanish Civil War: Coming to Terms with Dictatorship and Human Rights Violations in Chile and Spain] (Transcript, 2015).

Rosario Figari Layús is a postdoctoral researcher at the Justus Liebig University of Giessen in Germany. She holds a PhD in Political Science from the Philipps University Marburg. Her areas of work and research are transitional justice, human rights, and political violence. She has worked as a researcher and teacher at various institutions, including the University of Buenos Aires, the Free University of Berlin, University of Heidelberg, the Institute for Interdisciplinary Research on Conflict and Violence (IKG) at Bielefeld University and the University of Konstanz in Germany. She is the author of several books, among them *The Reparative Effects of Human Rights Trials: Lessons from Argentina* (Routledge 2017), for which she received the prestigious Doctoral Studies Award of the Philipps University Marburg in Germany. Additional publications include: *The Role of Transitional Justice in the Midst of Ongoing Armed Conflicts: The Case of Colombia* (Potsdam University Press, 2010) and *Los Juicios por sus protagonistas en Argentina* [The Trials for Crimes Against Humanity from the Perspective of their Main Actors] (Eduvim, 2015).

Boris Hau is a Chilean lawyer who holds a Master's degree in human rights and governance from the Universidad Autónoma de Madrid, Spain. He is a research associate of the Transitional Justice Observatory of the Universidad Diego Portales, Chile, specializing in issues of memory and human rights policy. He previously served as a researcher and testimony-taker for both iterations of Chile's second Truth Commission, the "Valech Commission," which documented cases of dictatorship-era political imprisonment and torture. He currently teaches on a range of human rights related courses at Chile's Alberto Hurtado University. His undergraduate thesis focused on the work of Chile's best-known dictatorship-era human rights defense organization, the Catholic Church's Vicariate of Solidarity.

Iris Jave is based at the National University of San Marcos and at the Pontifical Catholic University of Peru, where she is a researcher at the Institute of Democracy and Human Rights and a member of the Research Group on Memory and Democracy. She has published several books and articles on memory studies, human rights and political communication, and has contributed to the development of human rights policies at various state institutions, among them Peru's Ministry of Women and the Peruvian Truth and Reconciliation Commission. She teaches communications at the University of Lima and the Pontifical Catholic University of Peru.

Geoffrey Lugano holds a PhD from the University of Warwick, United Kingdom, where he wrote a thesis on the domestic and regional impacts of the International Criminal Court's (ICC) interventions in Kenya, Uganda and the wider African continent. Some of the resulting research output has been published in the *International Journal of Transitional Justice*. From August 2015 to June 2016, he held a research fellowship at the International Nuremberg Principles Academy, Germany, where he researched attitudes to the ICC in Kenya. Lugano holds an MSc in Governance and Development from the Institute of Development Policy and Management at the University of Antwerp, Belgium, and a BA in Political Science from Kenyatta University, Nairobi, Kenya.

Joachim J. Savelsberg is Professor of Sociology and Law and Arsham and Charlotte Ohanessian Chair at the University of Minnesota. He teaches courses in the sociology of law and human rights, crime and punishment, sociological theory, and sociology of knowledge. Publications include *Representing Mass Violence: Conflicting Responses to Human Rights Violations in Darfur* (University of California Press, 2015); "Global Justice, National Distinctions: Criminalizing Human Rights Violations in Darfur" (with Hollie Nyseth Brehm), *American Journal of Sociology* 121(2) (2015): 564–603; *American Memories: Atrocities and the Law* (with Ryan D. King, Russell Sage Foundation, 2011); and *Crime and Human Rights: Criminology of Genocide and Atrocities* (Sage, 2010).

Debbie Sharnak is an Assistant Professor of History and International Studies at Rowan University in New Jersey, USA. Her research and teaching explore the history of human rights, transnational networks, Latin America, and transitional justice. In her current book manuscript, *"Of Light and Struggle" in Uruguay: Contesting the International History of Human Rights,* she investigates the evolution of human rights discourse, particularly during Uruguay's transition back to democratic rule. Her work has been published in *Diplomacy & Statecraft,* the *Journal of Iberian and Latin American Studies, Taller,* and several edited volumes. She was previously a lecturer in the History and Literature program at Harvard University, and has done work for the International Center for Transitional Justice, Freedom House, and the Centro Nacional de Memoria Histórica in Colombia.

Valeria Vegh Weis is an Argentinean/German Lecturer of Criminology and Transitional Justice at Buenos Aires University (UBA) and National Quilmes University. She is an associate researcher at the Max Planck Institute for European Legal History in Germany and an Alexander von Humboldt Postdoctoral Researcher at Freie Universität Berlin, where she focuses on the role of human rights and victims' organizations in the enforcement of truth, justice, reparations, and guarantees of non-repetition. She is also an associate researcher at the Max Planck Institute for European Legal History in Germany where she co-directs the research group "Transnational Criminal Law in Transatlantic Perspective (1870–1945)." She holds a permanent position at the Argentinean Public Defender agency and has 15 years of experience working in different criminal courts and international organizations. She holds a PhD in Law and an LLM in Criminal Law from UBA and an LLM in International Legal Studies from New York University. She has held prestigious fellowships including the Fulbright and the Hauser Global Scholarships. She has published extensively on the topics of criminology, transitional justice, criminal law, and mental health law. Her book *Marxism and Criminology: A History of Criminal Selectivity* (Brill, 2017; Haymarket Books, 2018) was awarded the Choice Award by the American Library Association and the Outstanding Book Award by the Academy of Criminal Justice Sciences.

Annette Weinke, PD Dr. is associate professor and senior researcher at the Friedrich-Schiller-University Jena. She is also co-director of the Jena Center of 20th Century History and co-founder of the study group "History of Human Rights in the 20th Century," hosted and sponsored by the Fritz Thyssen Foundation. Her research focuses on the entanglements between international politics, international human rights law, and transnational legal advocacy in contemporary Europe and the United States. In her latest book, she explores the origins of transitional justice as a transatlantic intellectual field and its contribution to human rights discourses and practices of the 1990s.

Acknowledgements

This book is the product of several years of intensive work that would not have been possible without the support and collaboration of many people and institutions. First and foremost, we wish to thank Mirjam Truwant, our editor at Leuven University Press at the Catholic University Leuven (KU Leuven, Belgium). Thank you for giving us the opportunity to publish this edited volume and for the intellectual support that made its publication possible. It has been a pleasure to work with you. We would also like to express our gratitude to Silvana Mandolessi, Professor of Cultural Studies at KU Leuven for putting us in touch with the publishing house.

Many people have contributed in different ways to making the book possible. We appreciate their knowledge, ideas, patience and encouragement. First, our profoundest thanks to all the contributors who generously entrusted us with their valuable chapters and inspiring work, namely Annette Weinke, Kristine Avram, Boris Hau, Debbie Sharnak, Iris Jave, Geoffrey Lugano, Joachim Savelsberg, and Valeria Vegh Weis, as well as Aleida Assmann who wrote the Prologue to this volume. This book would not exist without your sharing your great insight and knowledge with us.

Crucial for this book was the support of Philip Derbyshire, Dafydd Roberts, and David Brenner, who copy-edited the text. Their detailed proofreading and precise suggestions greatly improved the manuscript, making it much more legible, clear and informative, and we especially appreciate Dafydd's work under pressure at the end. We also would like to thank the two anonymous peer reviewers for their helpful suggestions for improving the first draft of the manuscript. Furthermore, we would also like to thank the Young Scholars Fund of the University of Konstanz and the Balzan Foundation, which generously funded the publication.

A very special thanks goes to Kiti López, the artist who draw the beautiful image that appears on the book cover. This illustration was made in 2014 for the Argentine online news agency *Infojus Noticias*, which reported on judicial news and events. The agency operated between 2013 and 2015. The image shows a woman holding a scale, symbolizing justice in the courts. Kiti has drawn many different "justices" over the last years, always trying to give it a new, different and diverse aspect from the one we are used to seeing in statues. Thank you for sharing your art with us.

Our thanks go also to all the colleagues who very generously shared their ideas and gave us constructive feedback on parts of the manuscript. We would like to express our special thanks to Jill Strauss (BMCC, CUNY, New York

City) and Gruia Badescu (University of Konstanz). We are also very grateful to Annegret Krüger for her detailed and dedicated review and corrections to the book manuscript, to Paul Heinrich for his help in preparing the Index, and also to our friend and colleague Florencia Diaz, whose outstanding support in the final stages was crucial. Your expertise, enthusiasm and engagement with this difficult topic were a great inspiration to us in our research and writing of this volume.

Last but not least, we would like to express our grateful thanks to Profs. Aleida and Jan Assmann at the University of Konstanz and Prof. Stefan Peters at the Justus Liebig University of Giessen. Your constant support and encouragement have given us the freedom and confidence to develop our own ideas and projects. Without it, we would have not been able to produce this book.

Prologue

Aleida Assmann

The concept of human rights emerged as a latecomer in the history of civilization. Yet, even after they had been repeatedly proclaimed in the second half of the 18th century in the United States, in France, and in the French colony of Haiti during the slave revolution there, human rights did not immediately put an end to violence and suffering. In recent centuries, Western civilization has continued to be marked by racial dominance and unrestricted forms of violence against those who were exploited by or in the way of the Western will to power. After the Second World War, human rights were declared anew on a universal level by the United Nations. Nevertheless, it took another 50 years until – after the end of the Cold War – these moral norms finally achieved legal status and were enshrined in institutions and newly established international courts. This book, compiled and edited by two engaged female researchers, traces the short history of human rights laws in order to assess their social and political impact while comparing human rights trials across three continents: Latin America, Europe and Africa.

This comparative framework yields interesting evidence of the fact that cases of human rights prosecution often occur in multidirectional connections. Such prosecutions trigger and empower each other across national borders and geographic distances, thus revealing a network of models, impulses and imitations. This interactive dynamic is an essential insight as it allows us to observe precisely how new norms and standards are established and disseminated. Human rights trials are radically different from other trials because they are much more precarious. Their objective is to include what other legal systems had systematically excluded. Hence, they remain a historic innovation with only a brief tradition. Rather than being firmly grounded in the social fabric and cultural practice, such trials take issue with forms of violence that are built into political structures, lingering racism, and other patterns of institutional power. After a regime change, a transition process may introduce new values and norms, but people stay in office, careers continue, and attitudes and affects are not so easily replaced. And even those persons who are replaced do not easily give up their power but find manifest or latent ways to prolong their hold on the society.

Human rights trials therefore have a unique status. In them, the law provides a stage and platform for telling truths that have not yet gained general acceptance, and for presenting witnesses who had not yet been acknowledged or respected. Especially in societies in which there is little to no historical research or objective media communication about massacres, the torture of regime critics, or the perpetration of genocide, the law court becomes the arena for the story of otherwise unheard voices and the perspective of victims. Each case is yet another step in strengthening the human rights paradigm which at the same time forms the basis for these new types of trial. Their aim is thus innovation and moral transformation in societies that are always in danger of falling back into old habits.

The "justice cascade" that has been registered in recent years can either be attributed to more eruptions of mass violence or to the impact of the trials themselves in achieving a higher level of sensitivity and accountability vis-à-vis human rights violations. The transformation of a moral norm into a law is a significant step, but laws and trials alone cannot sustain a human rights paradigm. That paradigm has to be backed up by politics, education, research, and a civic culture of attention that values the other and protects the victim.

In 1939 Hitler is said to have asked: "Who speaks today of the extermination of the Armenians?" He was referring to the genocide in 1915 under the cover of the First World War in which a million Armenians lost their lives. This cynical question was a proud assertion of the principle of impunity. It was such impunity that encouraged him to start the Second World War and to pursue his project of murdering the European Jews under the cover of another global conflagration. The historic shift from impunity to accountability in the late 20th century is both the result of this rupture in civilization and evidence of its progress. This progress is irreversible, yet it is anything but a stable development. As the essays compiled in this volume demonstrate, there have been many setbacks and backlashes. Today, the civilizing process is measured by the degree to which the human rights paradigm is administered in courts of law in order to protect the rights of those who are most vulnerable. One thing is clear, however: the so-called "process of civilization" is not a principle that evolves on its own, once it has been established. Instead, this "process" takes the shape of a continuous struggle and readiness to fight for and recover these basic rights and values. In such a process, the legal apparatus cannot do the job alone. It also depends on the collective will in a democratic society that shares a victim-centered culture of attention and that appreciates institutions which support enlightenment and research, transparency and truth.

Introduction
Do Human Rights Trials Make a Difference after Conflict, Dictatorship and State-Sponsored Violence?

Rosario Figari Layús and Ulrike Capdepón

Do human rights trials make a difference? And if so, of what kind? What factors contribute to making that difference? These are the main questions this edited volume seeks to address by bringing together the insights from different country case studies that draw on substantial empirical research and engagement with relevant literature on the development, limitations, and impact of human rights prosecutions in Europe, Latin America, and Africa.

The right to justice, evoked in many international legal instruments, calls for states to investigate, prosecute, and sanction crimes against humanity, helping to ensure that similar atrocities never happen again. Similarly, criminal trials and other legal proceedings are often expected to re-legitimate the social order and state institutions by signaling a new commitment to human rights and democratic principles (Méndez 1997; Sikkink 2011). In instituting accountability for human rights violations, the state creates new legal frameworks, communicating to society, but also to state servants, what is allowed and what is not. This is why prosecutions following systematic human rights violations are usually seen as a promise of "never again" and a guarantee of non-repetition.

However, at a time when right-wing authoritarianism, anti-human-rights tendencies and exclusionary discourse are on the rise worldwide, human rights trials – and human rights norms themselves – have increasingly become a field of contestation, impacting not only the struggle against impunity and victims' fight for recognition but also historical narrative and memory. Although recent years have seen criminal trials become more common as a state-sponsored means to justice after war, dictatorship or mass violence, involving the investigation and prosecution of the individuals responsible for major human rights violations, such proceedings do face resistance, constraints and difficulties.

The Nuremberg trials are generally seen as having initiated a worldwide proliferation of human rights provisions and demands for accountability (Teitel 2003; Lutz 2009). The prosecution of 24 Nazi leaders between 1945 and 1946 represented a milestone in terms of the attribution of individual criminal responsibility for mass human rights violations. They marked an advance not only in bringing grave crimes to justice but also in developing the fundamental principles of human rights, laying the basis for today's international human rights law and institutions.[1] On an international level, the enforcement of individual criminal responsibility for mass violations of human rights could only be revived after the end of the East–West conflict in the 1990s, with the establishment of *ad hoc* special tribunals, such as the International Criminal Tribunal for Rwanda (ICTR), the International Criminal Tribunal for the former Yugoslavia (ICTY), the Special Court for Sierra Leone (SCSL) and the permanent International Criminal Court (ICC) established in 1998 to give effect to the prevailing international consensus on the obligation to prosecute the "most serious" international core crimes: war crimes, crimes against humanity and genocide (Donnelly 1999; Marks 2014). At the same time, the arrest in London of former Chilean dictator Augusto Pinochet on a warrant issued by a Spanish judge was widely perceived as an important move in the struggle against impunity and a step towards the global implementation of the principle of universal jurisdiction in matters of human rights violations and political repression (Roht-Arriaza 2005). However, as the contributions to this volume tend to show, more than 20 years after that promising event, the demand for international criminal justice and the application of human rights treaties does not seem to have achieved its expected goals (Hafner, Burton & Tsutsui 2005), notably in the case of the ICC, described as practicing a "distant justice" (Clark 2018).

An important contribution to the discussion of the consequences of human rights trials – domestic, international or hybrid – has been the notion of the "justice cascade," which describes the growth and expansion across national borders, in the 1990s and 2000s, of individual criminal accountability for human rights violations (Keck & Sikkink 1998; Lutz & Sikkink 2002; Sikkink & Booth Walling 2007). This swell of prosecutions has been described by Sriram as a "revolution in accountability" (2005).

1 Among them, the Genocide Convention and the Universal Declaration of Human Rights of 1948, the Geneva Conventions of 1949, the International Covenants on Human Rights of 1966, along with the creation of investigative and accountability procedures at the UN and regional intergovernmental levels.

These scholars see a normative shift from blanket amnesty or impunity to growing criminal accountability for human rights violations. This has often been attributed to the national adoption of international norms, a "domestication" of human rights provisions (Risse & Sikkink 1999; Lutz & Sikkink 2001). However, it is important not to underestimate the importance of such local factors as domestic power relationships and the often decades-long struggles against impunity conducted by activists, organizations and victims' associations (Collins 2006; Lessa et al. 2014), or the emergence of new transregional initiatives and modalities of collective action on the part of civil society actors seeking to promote memory and justice (Gready & Robins 2017), whose influence has become stronger over recent decades (Karstedt 2010). The establishment of global norms and human rights accountability initiatives can thus be seen as an aspect of a two-way process: they would not be possible without local struggles and demands for human rights prosecutions. Although the existence of international and regional human rights norms and courts, the pursuit of justice in third countries and the principle of universal jurisdiction have played a significant role as catalysts, in upping the pressure for domestic prosecutions (O'Sullivan 2017; Roht-Arriaza 2005; Lessa 2019), the progress in criminal justice for crimes against human rights would not have been possible without the local mobilization of victims' groups and relatives and the support of international human rights organizations in many countries of the world.

One has then to insist on the importance here of domestic accountability and local demands for human rights prosecutions – indeed, the Eichmann trial in Jerusalem in 1961, the Holocaust trials in France in the 1980s and 1990s and the trials of the Argentine military juntas in the 1980s all preceded the expansion of international justice (Lutz & Reiger 2009). While international trials act as an important reference and resource, they also serve as a complementary and auxiliary instance when local accountability mechanisms fail, as several chapters in this book demonstrate.

What this volume highlights is the variety of impacts and consequences that international but also domestic criminal trials can have at the local level. While in cases such as Argentina and Chile the action of European courts has been important for initiating domestic prosecutions, the cases of Uruguay, Kenya and Spain discussed here show that it is very difficult to identify any general trend in how these international processes contribute to the promotion of justice in local courts. While in some countries of the Southern Cone discussed in this book, actions in European third-state courts or the Inter-American Court of Human Rights have been crucial in triggering domestic prosecutions, the same dynamic has not been seen in such cases as Spain or Kenya, where the struggle against impunity seems even to have gone backward. As illustrated by the different chapters, the recourse to domestic or international criminal justice for violations of human rights following conflict, war or dictatorship varies widely in its effects on different societies with their differing legal and political systems. Bringing together contributions and case studies from three world regions – Europe, Africa and Latin America – helps to explore and understand the key factors and dimensions of accountability efforts, their varying consequences and the diversity of local experience. What has been the impact of accountability measures on victims, on political and institutional structures and access to justice, truth and memory, and on public and social acknowledgement of the crimes committed, and what are the factors that play a crucial role either in advancing or impeding accountability?

The chapters collected in this volume offer insights into different kinds of prosecutions for human rights violations in post-conflict or post-authoritarian contexts, both domestic and international, and how they affect the societies and political systems in which serious crimes and atrocities have taken place. Taken together, they document how accountability efforts and criminal prosecutions around the world have had a variety of effects and consequences for victims and for local politics and civil society. To account for this diversity, the selection here combines studies from recognized and well-documented country cases in criminal accountability for human rights violations (such as Germany, Chile and Argentina) with cases from less-studied countries (Peru, Uruguay, Spain and Sudan) and others that have as yet been scarcely studied in depth yet (such as Romania and Kenya).

Taken together, these contributions raise and engage with the following pivotal questions: Are human rights trials a relevant state-sponsored mechanism for European, Latin American and African societies to deal with a legacy of human rights violations and state-sponsored violence? Under what circumstances do domestic and international human rights trials have positive, reparative and social effects? What are the political, legal, social or discursive constraints on prosecution? Who are the central actors in human rights prosecutions in Europe, Latin America and Africa, and what challenges do they face? What is the specific role of domestic victims' and international human rights organizations or professional expert networks in seeking justice in the courts? And in what ways does the struggle against impunity and for prosecution change national narratives or the way that past atrocities are publicly remembered?

The transitional justice paradigm and the contribution of this volume

This book offers new perspectives on human rights prosecutions and relevant empirical data from a variety of contexts, providing the local illustrations and contextual detail that are critical to shaping scholarly debate. It relies on the authors' local expertise and familiarity with the pertinent political dynamics, which shape their analysis and findings.

Combining different theoretical approaches to the restorative and retributive dimensions of criminal justice, from political science, sociology and legal studies, the contributions to this volume analyze how and why human rights trials can have a variety of functions and effects. A cursory glance at the literature on human rights prosecutions reveals that studies on the effects of human rights courts are very rare and usually treat single cases only. Most analyses examine the characteristics and modalities of prosecutions (Blake 2014), the conditions that led to them (Roehrig 2009; Burt 2009, 2011), the actors in them and their political and legal strategies and contributions (Varsky 2011; Burt 2011; Collins, Balardini & Burt 2013; Payne & Pereira 2016), the political dynamics of trials (Collins 2010), developments in the kinds of crimes prosecuted – transnational crime (Lessa 2019), genocide and crimes against humanity (Feierstein 2008, Lorenzetti & Kraut 2011, Robinson 2016) – the jurisprudence developed (Mira 2017), or the relationship between prosecutions and the construction of memory and the changing of historical narratives (Adler ed. 2018, Wilson 2011, Laplante 2014, Jelin 2003). However, there are a number of significant works that discuss the consequences of trials on processes of dealing with a conflict-ridden history, such as Sikkink and Booth Walling (2007) and Sikkink (2011a, 2011b), which apply a more quantitative approach to analyzing the effects of trials in individual countries or the deterrent capacity of human rights prosecutions. Indeed, several of the contributions here make reference to Sikkink's concept of the "justice cascade." Important as these studies are, most of them, however, present an implicitly positive image of the effects of human rights prosecutions without considering what negative effects they may have when not conducted properly or from a victim-centered perspective.

Most of the existing scholarship has focused on the Latin American experience, because Latin America is the region where there have been more prosecutions for human rights violations than anywhere else. Although there have been many difficulties and setbacks, the constant struggle against impunity has given this region and its victims' and human rights movements a pioneering role of great importance to accountability activists in other regional contexts (Sikkink 2014). Analysis of the effects of human rights trials in other regions as well as Latin America allows this volume to offer a comparative perspective on not only their potentials but also their limitations, notably when they are felt not to have contributed to the social acknowledgement and empowerment of victims, or where they have been rejected by parts of the population. In Spain, for instance, the undoubted success of the Argentine Complaint in fostering awareness of the crimes of the Franco dictatorship has not led to a general acknowledgement of the victims of Francoism on the part of the Spanish state, nor has it triggered domestic trials.

One of the distinctive features of this volume is that in its consideration of human rights prosecutions it does not always make reference to the transitional justice framework. In recent decades it has become the received common sense in the scholarly literature that human rights trials, as an object of study, be framed within the transitional justice paradigm, under which accountability for past human rights crimes is pursued by a variety of means, among them domestic or international prosecutions, amnesties, the purging of perpetrators from security forces and civil service, truth commissions, monetary and symbolic reparation to victims, the establishment of memorials, and official public apologies (Kritz 1995; Teitel 2000). Within such an analytical framework, concerned with the impact of transitional justice mechanisms as a whole, criminal trials become just another instrument among many alternative options in the transitional justice toolbox (see for example Okafor & Ngwaba 2015; Olsen, Payne & Reiter 2010; Van der Merwe, Baxter & Chapman 2009; Hafner & King 2007; Forsberg 2001; Ratner & Abrams 1997).[2] In this, the distinction between transitional justice measures and ordinary criminal justice – the domestic institution responsible for judging human rights violations in any state that claims to be democratic and governed by the rule of law – tends to become blurred. Treated in this way, the prosecution of former heads of state or public appears as an extraordinary measure resorted to in the course of, or following, political transitions. However, it is necessary to question this tie between the transitional justice paradigm and the prosecution of human rights violations. Criminal justice preceded the transitional justice paradigm and should be viewed and analyzed on its own terms. Criminal proceedings are of vital importance, not only in so-called "transitional" or "post-transitional" contexts, but also for the ordinary functioning of any democratic state. While transitional justice mechanisms are seen as extraordinary, temporary measures, criminal prosecutions are

2 For instance, according to Forsberg, there is no ideal procedure to deal with the crimes of the past because "different cases require different measures" (Forsberg 2001, 66).

standard procedure in any regular justice system. The question thus needs to be asked: Where does the need to link human rights prosecutions to transitional processes come from? Why are they presented as typical of transitional situations (and thus as extraordinary *ad hoc* measures) and not as an integral element of the democratic rule of law? One answer may be that they are, in practice, extraordinary and *ad hoc* interventions. Indeed, demands for transitional justice mechanisms mostly arise when a country's regular institutions – such as the ordinary criminal justice system – do not fulfill their obligation to deal with human rights violations, failing the victims and the citizenry as a whole.

In this volume we offer a range of perspectives on the impact of human rights prosecutions following violent conflict and/or repression. While certain contributions analyze the conduct of trials in the context of other transitional justice measures such as truth commissions or reparations, others treat them as an ordinary mechanism of accountability typical of any state operating under the rule of law. By including both understandings – as instrument of transitional justice or ordinary mechanism of criminal justice – the book offers a broader perspective on their impact on the societies considered.

The impact of criminal justice in post-conflict and post-authoritarian societies

Considering the impact or effect of human rights trials calls for certain methodological clarifications. It is not easy to analyze the social and political implications of human rights trials or of any kind of justice policy, and this is perhaps why the literature is relatively sparse. According to the Oxford Dictionary, the noun "impact" has two meanings: "the action of one object coming forcibly into contact with another" and "a marked effect or influence" (Oxford Dictionary 2020). Whereas these definitions would be more adequate to analyze the impact on material things and objects, proper of the natural sciences, the use of the concept of "impact" is more complex when applying it to social relations and human beings. Thus, it is important to make clear that the use of the terms "impact," "effects" and "consequences" does not exclude the importance, heterogeneity and agency of actors involved and participating in prosecutions.

In assessing the effects of policy, it can be appropriate to look at the changes, the intended or unintended consequences, engendered by particular events or acts (Ergas & Eberbach 2010). The notion of "impact" itself presents many difficulties when one is dealing with human rights, victims, political systems, social relations and subjectivities. In turn, societies and individuals do not react in uniform or predictable ways to policy measures such as prosecutions. The ways in which human rights trials affect victims and societies depend on, to varying degrees, an array of factors, which are discussed in the conclusion: (a) the remaining power of perpetrators, (b) the part played by governmental institutions in prosecutions, (c) the legitimacy and independence of the instances responsible for prosecution and trial, (d) the role and agency of victims in the demand for justice, (e) social attitudes towards measures of accountability, and (f) the passage of time and the type and scope of violence, together with other more personal factors such as political history, social background and so forth.

The analysis of impact takes on an additional layer of complexity when it is considered as a dynamic phenomenon through time: on the one hand, assessment of the impact of government policy and/or human rights trials on individuals and societies may require years if not decades; on the other, people's own perceptions of a particular situation can change over time and political processes are dynamic. These considerations do not mean that the results presented here are invalid, but rather that they must be considered as partial, emerging from a particular historical moment and from specific political, geographical and biographical contexts. The effects of trials may change over time.

By impact is meant some kind of change, or the emergence of a new dynamic, in social, legal and political conditions. Changes may be superficial or profound, personal or social, temporary or permanent, material or symbolic, legal or informal, while the nature of change also depends on the perceptions and reality of those affected or touched by it. Impact is not limited to positive change but includes the negative consequences and reverses documented in some of the chapters. While human rights prosecutions can foster positive changes for victims and societies when judicial authorities have the will to bring them and trials take a victim-centered approach, the effects can be negative when prosecutions lack political, legal or economic support or when victims are marginalized. It is thus crucial to consider and distinguish between the different types of impacts of human rights prosecutions.

The impact of justice in the courts as a form of victim acknowledgement

The so-called "legal paradigm," which sees the law as the most appropriate tool to provide redress to victims of human rights violations and mass atrocities, has grown increasingly salient both nationally and internationally, as many survivors, activists and policy makers have come to see trials and the right to justice as crucial to social and legal reparation (Beristain 2009; Van Boven 2005; Roht-Arriaza 1990; Beckerman 2010). The social harms caused by state and political violence – among them fear, isolation and the destruction of social ties – do not spontaneously vanish with the end of violence or the fall of the regime (Kordon & Edelman 1986; Salimovich, Lira &Weinstein 1992; Robben 2007). The role of subsequent governments will be crucial in either reproducing or dismantling these effects over time. As is shown by several case studies in this collection, while the institution of criminal prosecutions, whatever their shortcomings, can provide a means for victims and others to deal with a conflictual past, the absence of any kind of institutional, legal redress tends to re-victimize victims and intensify strains within society, impeding the dismantling of many of the present consequences of past violence. As some scholars argue, the absence of any kind of intervention can even contribute to the expansion or escalation of violence, in a process referred to as "the spiral of violence" (Hacker 1973; Hurtado 2008). The legacy of violence can thus persist in the form of fear, repression, silence and trauma after the end of the violence or of the authoritarian regime, more especially when perpetrators remain in power and enjoy impunity (Cohen 2001; Zur 1994; Figari Layús 2017; Aguiar 1993).

Structure and overview by chapter

This collective work is structured chronologically and regionally, starting with the European cases, moving on to Latin America and concluding with the current efforts at accountability in Africa. The regional contexts and the nature of the conflicts and violence in question of course vary greatly. The geographical structure of the work does however reflect to some extent the geopolitics of accountability. The book offers three very different but exemplary European case studies – the case of post-Nazi West Germany, recent prosecutions in post-Communist Romania, and the making of a transnational legal complaint in Argentina as a means to obtain the justice denied in Spain to the victims of the Franco dictatorship. The cluster of chapters on Argentina, Chile, Peru and Uruguay show how certain Latin American countries, after a long period of impunity, pioneered the way for domestic and third-country prosecutions for human rights violations, while the African case studies that follow, looking at the ICC, Darfur and Kenya, are more concerned with proceedings before international courts, though the post-election violence in Kenya in 2008 also saw domestic human rights trials held there. The different chapters together not only provide new insights into the impact of human rights prosecutions and the difficulties they face in different contexts and regions, but also illustrate the development of these legal procedures over time.

The book begins with Annette Weinke's chapter on the prosecution of Nazi crimes in postwar West Germany. It describes a failure to comprehensively investigate and convict for such offenses, despite the precedent set by the Nuremberg trials in 1947. Retracing the development of prosecutions in the Federal Republic and the socialist GDR, it shows that in the East, after a spate of immediate postwar convictions of Nazi criminals, a culture of impunity was installed there too by the 1950s. The chapter also offers a survey of the changing public reception of such trials, from the Frankfurt Auschwitz trials of 1963–1965 and the Majdanek trial of 1979–1981 to the prosecutions in reunified Germany after 1989. Analysis of the legal basis on which cases were judged leads Weinke finally to conclude that a victim-centered human rights perspective was and remains absent from the German jurisprudence. In the following chapter Kristine Avram addresses domestic accountability efforts for crimes committed during the early years of Romania's Communist regime. The chapter focuses on a single trial in 2016, known as the "Romanian Nuremberg," in which Alexandru Vişinescu, former commander of the infamous R.S. detention facility, was convicted of crimes against humanity. It looks more particularly at victims' groups, their accounts of the violent past and how the trials triggered a process of truth-finding and story-telling. Ulrike Capdepón's chapter, which concludes the section, serves as a bridge connecting the European and Latin American case studies, as it looks at the effort to find justice abroad for the crimes of Spain's Franco dictatorship and the politics of victimhood that followed locally upon the assumption of universal jurisdiction by the Argentine courts.

The Latin American case studies draw a varied and complex picture of what is a key region for this volume. The experience of living under dictatorship and the ensuing struggles for accountability that so profoundly marked the second half of the last century in Chile, Argentina and Uruguay offer interesting comparative insights into the different legal mechanisms employed to overcome impunity. The section opens with the impact of the Pinochet case on Chilean domestic politics and the shifts from impunity to accountability triggered by this external event. Boris Hau analyzes the path from impunity to justice in the courts in post-dictatorship Chile by giving account of the current human rights prosecutions, the legal, social and political advances they have prompted and the obstacles they have faced. He particularly attends to the victims' long struggle against impunity and their insistent demand for prosecutions, focusing especially on relatives of the disappeared, who played a significant role in bringing the perpetrators of the Pinochet regime to justice. In the chapter that follows, Rosario Figari Layús offers an overview of the struggle for justice in post-dictatorship Argentina, attending in particular to the impact and consequences of different recent governmental attitudes – of support, indifference or disdain – to human rights prosecutions and their significance for victims. While the Argentine case offers an example of the abrogation of the so-called impunity laws that initially informed and constrained the post-dictatorship democratization processes in the three neighboring countries, in Uruguay, the object of Debby Sharnak's contribution in the next chapter, the conduct of human rights prosecutions is still being hampered by the Supreme Court considering the crimes committed during the dictatorship as common crimes and hence subject to statutes of limitations. Though in Uruguay there were some important human rights convictions of high-profile politicians in the past, in the face of the failure of the country's Supreme Court to proceed with prosecutions today, Sharnak shows how international developments, comparable in their impact on civil society to the effect of the Pinochet case in Chile, among them the Operation Condor trial in neighboring Argentina, have prompted renewed calls for justice. At the same time, the Uruguayan case evidences some setbacks to accountability efforts, including attacks on and death threats to civil society actors such as lawyers and human rights activists. Next, a distinctively victim-centered perspective is offered by Iris Jave's study of the post-conflict scenario in Peru. It examines, on the one hand, advances and setbacks in the quest for justice, and on the other the different senses of justice deployed by the mostly indigenous victims, addressing in doing so a crucial paradox in the recourse to legal process as a way of coming to terms with the past.

The third section of the book starts with Geoffrey Lugano's chapter, which discusses the selectivity of the internationalization of justice effected by the ICC. More specifically, it deals with what Lugano calls the ICC's "Africa problem." The fact that the ICC has only ever prosecuted defendants from African countries has, Lugano argues, not only fostered a widespread rejection of the ICC in Africa, it has also contributed to a de-escalation of the "justice cascade," perpetuating the continent's postcolonial condition in which external powers impose their top-down decisions. Lugano's critique of the role played by the ICC in Africa is followed by Savelsberg's chapter, which stands in distinct contrast to Lugano's in focusing on the discursive effects in Western countries of the ICC's interventions elsewhere. Savelsberg deals in particular with the ICC's intervention in the Darfur case, analyzing the debate it has prompted in international media. In his analysis of what he calls "the representational power" of international criminal justice, he particularly focuses on the cultural effects of such judicial interventions, which are – according to the author – too often disregarded by scholars and practitioners, but may well be of the greatest importance in nourishing the narratives that delegitimize mass atrocities. In the last chapter, Valeria Vegh Weis considers the post-electoral violence that occurred in Kenya in 2008, looking at accountability efforts at national and international level, focusing in particular on the circumstances of victims who are often marginalized, deprived not only of justice but of many other basic rights, and on the difficulties and tensions arising from the fact that the accused still hold positions of power.

We hope that this volume helps advance understanding of the impact of human rights trials. The different contributions provide new perspectives on the subject, together with detailed analyses of developments and assessments of the concrete impact of human rights prosecutions in the various regional contexts. The extensive empirical analysis of human rights trials and their effects on victims, perpetrators and societies as a whole offers lawyers, participants, justice system actors and policy makers insight into key, problematic aspects of current practice. Both human rights scholars and practitioners will, we hope, benefit from the analysis provided here, with better understanding helping remedy shortcomings and so improve outcomes for victims.

References

Adler, N. (ed.) 2018. *Understanding the Age of Transitional Justice.* New Brunswick: Rutgers University Press.

Aguiar, E., 1993. *Efectos psicosociales de la impunidad.* Paper presented at the International Conference of the Liga Internacional de los Pueblos. Session Impunity, Impunidad, Geneva, 1–10.

Alija-Fernández, R. A. & Martín Ortega, O., 2018. "Franco's Victims in Spain: The Long Road Towards Justice and Recognition." In Druliolle, V. & Brett, R. (eds.) *The Politics of Victimhood in Post-conflict Societies.* St. Anthony's Series. Oxford: Palgrave Macmillan, 53–76.

Beckerman, S., 2010. "Retraumatización: una nueva vieja historia." In Kordon, D., Edelman, L., Lagos, D. & Kersner, D. (eds.) *Sur, Dictadura y Después... Elaboración psicosocial y clínica de los traumas colectivos.* Buenos Aires: EATPI. Psicolibro Ediciones, 126–135.

Beristain, C., 2009. *Diálogos sobre la Reparación: Qué reparar en los casos de Violaciones de los Derechos Humanos.* Quito: V&M Gráficas.

Blake, J., 2014. "Should Domestic Courts Prosecute Genocide? Examining the Trial of Efrain Rios Montt." *Brooklyn Journal of International Law* 39(2): 564–611.

Bonacker, T. & Safferling, C. (eds.) 2013. *Victims of International Crimes. An Interdisciplinary Discourse.* The Hague: Asser.

Burt, J.-M., 2009. "Guilty as Charged: The Trial of Former Peruvian President Alberto Fujimori for Human Rights Violations." *The International Journal of Transitional Justice* 3: 384–405.

Burt, J.-M., 2011. "Desafiando la impunidad en tribunales nacionales: juicios por derechos humanos en América Latina." In *Justicia Transicional. Manual para América Latina*. New York: Centro Internacional para la Justicia Transicional, 209–228.

Capdepón, U., 2018. "Die späte Auseinandersetzung mit der Franco-Vergangenheit in Spanien." In Mihr, A., Pickel, G. & Pickel, S. (eds.) *Handbuch Transitional Justice. Aufarbeitung von Unrecht – hin zur Rechtsstaatlichkeit und Demokratie*. Berlin/Heidelberg: Springer, 275–294.

Clark, P., 2018. *Distant Justice*. Cambridge/New York: Cambridge University Press.

Cohen, S., 2001. *States of Denial. Knowing about Atrocities and Suffering*. Cambridge: Polity Press.

Collins, C., 2006. "Grounding Globalized Justice – International Networks and Domestic Human Rights Accountability in Chile and El Salvador." *Journal of Latin American Studies* 38: 711–738.

Collins, C., 2010. *Post-Transitional Justice: Human Rights Trials in Chile and El Salvador*. Philadelphia: Pennsylvania State University.

Collins, C., Balardini, L. & Burt, J.-M., 2013. "Mapping Perpetrator Prosecutions in Latin America." *International Journal of Transitional Justice* 7(1): 8–28.

Donnelly, J., 1999. "The Social Construction of International Human Rights." In Dunne, T. & Wheeler, N. J. (eds.) *Human Rights in Global Politics*. Cambridge: Cambridge University Press, 72–102.

Ellen, L. & Reiger, C. 2009. *Prosecuting Heads of State*. Cambridge: Cambridge University Press.

Ergas, Y. & Eberbach, K., 2010. *Human Rights Impact. General Issues and Sectoral Perspectives*. Symposium Proceedings. Institute for the Study of Human Rights, Columbia University.

Feierstein, D., 2008. "El carácter genocida del proceso de reorganización nacional." *Revista Digital de la Escuela de Historia. Universidad Nacional de Rosairo* 1(1): 149–164.

Feierstein, D., 2011. *El genocidio como práctica social: Entre el nazismo y la experiencia argentina: Hacia un análisis del aniquilamiento como reorganizador de las relaciones sociales*. Buenos Aires: Fondo de Cultura Económica.

Figari Layús, R., 2017. *The Reparative Effects of Human Rights Trials: Lessons from Argentina*. Transitional Justice Series. New York: Routledge.

Finnemore, M. & Sikkink, K., 1998. "International Norm Dynamics and Political Change." *International Organization* 52(4): 887–917.

Forsberg, T., 2001. "The Philosophy and Practice of Dealing with the Past: Some Conceptual and Normative Issues." In Biggar, N. (ed.) *Burying the Past. Making Peace and Doing Justice after Civil Violent Conflict*. Washington: Georgetown University Press, 57–72.

Gready, P. & Robins, S., 2017. "Rethinking civil society and transitional justice: lessons from social movements and 'new' civil society." *The International Journal of Human Rights* 21(7): 956–975.

Hafner Burton, E. & Tsutsui, K., 2005. "Human Rights in a Globalizing World: The Paradox of Empty Promises." *American Journal of Sociology* 110(5): 1373–1411.

Hafner, D. & King, E., 2007. "Beyond Traditional Notions of Transitional Justice: How Trials, Truth Commissions, and Other Tools for Accountability Can and Should Work Together." *International & Comparative Law Review* 30: 91–109.

Hurtado, M., 2008. "Breve exploración sobre la función del derecho penal en el proceso de reconocimiento de las atrocidades perpetradas en el marco de conflictos armados o de represión." *Judicialización de crímenes de sistema. Estudios de caso y análisis comparado*. Bogotá: Centro Internacional para la Justicia Transicional, 97–108.

Jelin, E., 2003. *State Repression and the Labors of Memory*. Minneapolis: Minnesota University Press.

Karstedt, S., 2010. "From Absence to Presence. From Silence to Voice: Victims in International and Transitional Justice since the Nuremberg Trials." *International Review of Victimology* 17(1): 9–30.

Keck, M. & Sikkink, K., 1998. *Activists Beyond Borders: Advocacy Networks in International Politics.* Ithaca, NY: Cornell University Press.

Kordon, D. & Edelmann, E., 1986. *Efectos psicológicos de la represión política.* Buenos Aires: Sudamericana Planeta.

Laplante, L., 2014. "Memory Battles: Guatemala's Public Debates and the Genocide Trial of José Efraín Ríos Mont." New England Law Boston Research Paper No. 15-02: 621–673.

Lessa, F., 2019. "Operation Condor on Trial: Justice for Transnational Human Rights Crimes in South America." *Journal of Latin American Studies* 51: 409–439.

Lessa, F., Olsen, T., Payne, L., Pereira, G. & Reiter, A., 2014. "Overcoming Impunity: Pathways to Accountability in Latin America." *International Journal of Transitional Justice* 8(1): 75–98.

Lorenzetti, R. & Kraut, A., 2011. *Derechos Humanos. Justicia y reparacion. La experiencia de los juicios en la Argentina.* Buenos Aires: Sudamericana.

Lutz, E., 2009. "Prosecuting Heads of State in Europe." In Ellen, L. & Reiger, C. (eds.) *Prosecuting Heads of State.* Cambridge: Cambridge University Press, 24–45.

Lutz, E. & Sikkink, K., 2000. "International Human Rights Law and Practice in Latin America." *International Organization* 54(3): 633–659.

Marks, S., 2014. *Human Rights: A Brief Introduction.* Boston: Harvard University Press, 1–23.

Méndez, J., 1997. "In Defense of Transitional Justice." In McAdams, A. J. (ed.) *Transitional Justice and the Rule of Law in New Democracies.* Notre Dame/London: University of Notre Dame Press, 1–26.

Mira, J., 2017. "Justicia sin fronteras: el impacto del ejercicio de la jurisdicción penal universal por España en la reapertura de los juicios por los desaparecidos en la Argentina (1996–2007)." *Revista jurídica de los derechos sociales* 7(1): 494–515.

Okafor, O. C. & Ngwaba, U., 2015. "The International Criminal Court as a 'Transitional Justice' Mechanism in Africa: Some Critical Reflections." *International Journal of Transitional Justice* 9(1): 90–108.

Olsen, T., Payne, L. & Reiter, A., 2010. *Transitional Justice in Balance. Comparing Processes. Weighing Efficacy.* Washington D.C.: United States Institute of Peace Press.

Orentlicher, D., 1991. "Settling Accounts: The Duty to Prosecute Human Rights Violations of a Prior Regime." *The Yale Law Journal* 100: 25–37.

O'Sullivan, A., 2017. *Universal jurisdiction in international criminal law: the debate and the battle for hegemony,* New York: Routledge.

Oxford Dictionary 2020. Meaning of Impact. Available at: https://www.lexico.com/definition/impact [Accessed June 11, 2020].

Payne, L. & Pereira, G., 2016. "Corporate Complicity in International Human Rights Violations." *Annual Review of Law and Social Sciences* 12: 63–84.

Robben, A., 2007. *Political Violence and Trauma in Argentina: The Ethnography of Political Violence.* Philadelphia: University of Pennsylvania Press.

Robinson, A., 2016. "Challenges to Justice at Home: The Domestic Prosecution of Efrain Rios Montt." *International Criminal Law Review* 16(1): 103–133.

Roehrig, T., 2009. "Executive Leadership and the Continuing Quest for Justice in Argentina." *Human Rights Quarterly* 31(3): 721–747.

Roht-Arriaza, N., 2005. *The Pinochet Effect. Transnational Justice in the Age of Human Rights.* Philadelphia: University of Pennsylvania Press.

Salimovich, S., Lira, E. & Weinstein, E., 1992. "Victims of Fear: The Social Psychology of Repression." In Corradi, J., Weiss Fagen, P. & Garretón, M. (eds.), *Fear at the Edge: State Terror and Resistance in Latin America.* Berkeley, CA: University of California Press, 72–89.

Sikkink, K., 2011a. "Policy, Theory and the Justice Cascade." In id., *The Justice Cascade: How Human Rights Prosecutions Are Changing World Politics*. New York: W. W. Norton, p. 225.
Sikkink, K., 2011b. "El efecto disuasivo de los juicios por violaciones de derechos humanos." *Anuario de Derechos Humanos* 7: 41–61.
Sikkink, K., 2014. "Latin American Countries as Norm Protagonists of the Idea of International Human Rights." *Global Governance* 20(3): 389–404.
Sikkink, K. & Booth Walling, C., 2007. "The Impact of Human Rights Trials in Latin America." *Journal of Peace Research* 44(4): 427–445.
Sriram, C. L., 2005. *Globalizing Justice for Mass Atrocities. A Revolution in Accountability*. London: Routledge.
Teitel, R., 2000. *Transitional Justice*. New York: Oxford University Press.
Teitel, R., 2003. "Transitional Justice Genealogy." *Harvard Human Rights Journal* 16: 69–94.
Van Boven, T., 2005. *Basic Principles and Guidelines on the Right to a Remedy and Reparation for Victims of Gross Violations of International Human Rights Law and Serious Violations of International Humanitarian Law*. United Nations Doc. E/CN.4/2005 L.
Van der Merwe, H., Baxter, V. & Chapman, A., 2009. *Assessing the Impact of Transitional Justice. Challenges for Empirical Research*. Washington D.C.: United States Institute of Peace Press.
Varsky, C., 2011. "Testimonies as Evidence in Criminal Prosecutions for Crimes Against Humanity." In Center for Legal and Social Studies & International Center for Transitional Justice (eds.) *Making Justice. Further Discussions on the Prosecution of Crimes against Humanity in Argentina*. Buenos Aires: Siglo Veintiuno Editores, 30–49.
Wilson, R. A., 2011. *Writing History in International Criminal Trials*. Cambridge: Cambridge University Press.
Zur, J., 1994. "The Psychological Impact of Impunity." *Anthropology Today* 10(3): 12–17.

Human Rights Trials without Human Rights Law

Prosecuting Nazi Crimes in Postwar Germany After Nuremberg

Annette Weinke

What had preoccupied some West German politicians, jurists, and clerics during the Allied occupation period developed into a permanent part of official government policy just months after the founding of the Federal Republic. Following the American verdict in the so-called "Ministries Trial" (case no. 11) and the subsequent British trial of Erich von Manstein, a lively diplomatic tug-of-war about the fate of convicted German war criminals began (Jasch & Kaiser 2017). Leaving aside the vehemence with which not only the West German government and the opposition but also renowned representatives of the civil service, jurisprudence, and media debated the "question of war criminals," what is astonishing in retrospect is the self-assurance with which critics insisted that international criminal law was on Germany's side. As early as April 1947, at the height of the series of American follow-up trials of representatives of the German elites, the re-established *Deutsche Gesellschaft für Völkerrecht* (German Society of International Law) had defiantly insisted that war had always led to violations of human rights. Instead of examining the crimes committed *by* Germans as they were being documented by the Allies in numerous large and smaller trials, the *Gesellschaft* complained about crimes supposedly committed *against* ethnic Germans as a result of "mass expulsions" from the former German territories in the East (Stahl 2015). To understand subsequent discussions and developments it is therefore helpful to see how those waging the political-legal campaign against the "Nuremberg system" presumed a claim to *(semi-)sovereignty* on the one hand while using human rights arguments *to reject* the binding character of Allied legal sanctions against Germans on the other. Thus, it was in these early West German debates that there emerged a highly selective and deeply ambiguous attitude towards international humanitarian law in general and the international protection of human rights in particular – with some long-lasting effects even beyond the end of Germany's partition. Taking this paradoxical finding as my point of departure, this chapter will give a long view of the legal prosecution of Nazi crimes in Germany and highlight some of its particularities. I will particularly focus on trajectories in the Western Federal Republic of Germany (FRG), where – in contrast to East German Democratic Republic (GDR) – the issue of prosecuting Nazi crimes had become a focal point of political, legal, and media discourses and controversies since the mid-1950s (Weinke 2002).

"Nuremberg" was followed by a host of legislative initiatives aimed at processing the legacies of Allied punishment and denazification policies, commonly referred to as *Kriegsfolgelasten* (war-related burdens), as quickly and quietly as possible. More specifically, in the early Adenauer era, government policy on dealing with the recent past consisted in overturning all Allied convictions and gradually closing all ongoing investigations into Nazi crimes. Laws guaranteeing exemption from punishment or amnesty passed in 1949 and 1954 respectively, and benefited several hundred thousand of those classified as "followers" (*Mitläufer*) and tens of thousands of those suspected of Nazi crimes, including major offenders (Eichmüller 2012).

Moreover, people are still hesitant to acknowledge that in Germany's Eastern part, too, a culture of impunity was established at the same time, albeit under entirely different circumstances. In contrast to the Western occupation zones, where the confrontation with the Eastern bloc led to a dramatic decrease in Allied pressure in the "question of war criminals" and to its eventual complete abandonment, the Soviets continued their practice of draconian punishments and internment until the early 1950s. For East German communists, this resulted in considerable legitimation problems since the existence of tens of thousands of special camp prisoners and convicted war criminals on German soil collided with their own claim to an "antifascist-democratic new beginning" (Meyer-Seitz 1998). Therefore, very early on, the leadership of the Socialist Unity Party (SED) attempted to convince the Soviet occupation authorities of the advantages of adopting a more moderate policy towards nominal Nazi party members. There also is much to suggest that SED leaders saw the upcoming closing of the last Soviet special prison camps in late 1949 as a chance to conclude the unpopular criminal prosecution of Nazis with a fanfare. Allied criminal law had previously been instrumentalized repeatedly in order to fight political enemies and for large-scale expropriations of middle-class business owners. Thus the convictions of about 3,400 internees awaiting sentencing during the Waldheim mass show trials in the spring of 1950 represented several watershed moments in the history of the East German prosecution of Nazi crimes: while these trials followed the tradition established by Soviet occupation law, their exceptional human rights violations and unsubstantiated charges also marked a break with the judicial "antifascism" of the occupation period (Weinke 2001). Moreover, in the eyes of the party and state leadership the trials symbolized the conclusion of East German war crimes prosecutions. Until the lifting of the occupation statute in 1955 this meant that the GDR also spent much less energy on investigating Nazi crimes; at just one conviction per year, the East German conviction rate reached a new low in 1956/57, almost simultaneously with the West German one.

After an extended phase of non-prosecution in both German states, the SED leadership in the mid-1950s increasingly began to publicly raise the subject of the Federal Republic's anti-totalitarian founding consensus and expose its inherent contradictions. The external circumstances of beginning propaganda and intelligence operations against "Nazi and war criminals" in the West suggest that they were by no means merely led by a vision of how to deal with the Nazi past politically, but that this change of course was in fact also based on cold, calculated decisions of realpolitik. While the institutional responsibility lay with the SED Central Committee's departments for *Westarbeit* (Work in the West), international relations, and propaganda, as well as with the GDR Staatssicherheit (Ministry for State Security, StaSi), it was Friedrich Karl Kaul (SED), a German-Jewish lawyer who had returned from Latin American exile, who functioned as the legal adviser and spokesperson for these East German political campaigns. Based on a wealth of captured files that had been gradually returned to the GDR by the Soviets since the early 1950s, they began to review materials from a "political-operative" point of view and use them in order to discredit West German decision makers. It was symptomatic of the legalistic style of politicized German past that they followed a pattern which obviously reflected the experience of legal discrimination in the Weimar-era system of "class justice." Political battles were re-staged in the legal arena with reversed roles: while the "victorious" East German communists played the role of prosecutor, the "re-nazified" Federal Republic appeared as the defendant or the convicted criminal. The most elaborate of all East German campaigns was the attack on "Hitler's hanging judges in Adenauer's service" that began in May 1957: until 1960 the "Commission for German Unity" presented new lists about every six months which contained the names of about 1,000 West German officials in the judiciary and government ministries who had played a part in the death sentences of people persecuted by the Nazi regime for political or ethnical reasons. Although they were usually based on authentic documents, these East German accusations initially caused little reaction in the West. This was not only due to a still widely intact self-immunization to such claims by an anticommunism that was shared across social strata and milieus, but also to the relatively coarse presentation of facts, something that the Central Committee also failed to agree on.

So, what caused the reliable protective shell of the FRG's self-exculpating society to finally start to crack? First, half a decade after the FRG's founding, controversial court decisions on Nazi cases and sensational legal scandals related to Germany's treatment of its Nazi past became ever more frequent. They often revealed anti-Semitic attitudes, which also raised doubts abroad about the German legal profession's adaptability to democracy. Additionally, the burdensome inheritance of West German civil service law, triggered by the surge of returning POWs in 1955 and subsequent administrative appeals, increasingly led to tensions regarding employees of the judicial and administrative authorities with a Nazi past. Broader social developments such as a noticeably greater sensitivity in dealing with the Nazi past further exacerbated the crisis of legitimacy within the judicial system. At times it became obvious that Germans projected onto the judiciary in charge of prosecution and compensation those issues resulting from the political-moral challenges of a more proactive way of coming to terms with the past. With their attacks against reinstated Nazi jurists, the GDR thus responded to the West German constitutional state's latent loss of credibility on the one hand while intensifying it in a manner barely controllable by legal policy on the other.

In the fall of 1958, the justice ministers of the federal states and the Bonn government agreed on a change of course in their policy of prosecuting Nazi crimes. From now on criminal investigations were no longer to be launched only in individual cases that had accidentally come to light; instead individual areas of crime were to be investigated systematically based on knowledge produced by historical research. On the advice of the Federal Ministry of Justice, it was decided to establish an inter-state authority for preliminary investigation without executive power. It was to focus primarily on the investigation of crimes which had occurred "where there was no place of jurisdiction within the territory of the Federal Republic." This mainly meant the crimes perpetrated in concentration camps and by *Einsatzgruppen* (Special Operations Units) in the occupied territories in the East. Each federal state pledged to second one justice ministry official to the *Zentrale Stelle der Landesjustizverwaltungen zur Aufklärung nationalsozialistischer Verbrechen* (Central Office of the State Judicial Administrations for the Investigation of National Socialist Crimes) based in Ludwigsburg for a limited term.

The "fever curve" of Nazi war crimes trials

The resounding success resulting from the centralization of responsibilities was mainly reflected in the rapidly rising number of investigations. In the first year of its existence the above-mentioned Central Office opened roughly 500 preliminary investigations (Weinke 2008b). By 1964 about 700 further investigations had been launched. In line with its legal policy brief to focus on investigating crimes committed outside of the German territory, the Office investigated, among other things, intentional killings committed in the extermination and concentration camps of Auschwitz, Chelmno, Treblinka, and Großrosen, in the ghettos of Lodz and Warsaw, in Polish forced labor camps, and during the so-called death marches towards the end of the war. Other crimes investigated included the massacres of eastern European civilians perpetrated by the *Einsatzgruppen* of the Security Police (Sipo) and the Security Service (SD), police battalions of the *Ordnungspolizei* (Order Police), and members of the *Volksdeutscher Selbstschutz* (Ethnic German Self-defense Units). Although the prosecutors at Ludwigsburg struggled with "leaks" in the State Offices of Criminal Investigation (*Landeskriminalämter*) and they were met with skepticism and resentment by law enforcement agencies, their work boosted the investigations. Federal Justice Ministry statistics show, for example, that the increased discussion of this topic in the federal and state parliaments, ministries, and the media led to public prosecutors now launching such proceedings independently of the Central Office.

As the example of Hessian General State Prosecutor Fritz Bauer shows, whether and how an investigation was carried out depended particularly on the personal interest and commitment of those heading the authorities in question. In part responding to information from Ludwigsburg, in part acting on his own accord, Bauer launched numerous significant Nazi trials in the 1960s: not only did he pick up on specifically Hessian postwar traditions with the investigation of "euthanasia" killings, with the three Auschwitz trials (1963–1966) and the Frankfurt trial of diplomats in 1967/68, he also initiated the first comprehensive and detailed judicial investigation of the bureaucratic mass murder of European Jews. As a novelty in West German legal history, Bauer practiced a blend of history and criminology by requesting expert opinions from historians at the Munich-based Institute for Contemporary History (IfZ) (Turner 2018). And it was Bauer who added a new nuance to West German Nazi trials – which usually relied on written evidence – by increasingly including the testimony of surviving victims.

While the trial of Adolf Eichmann, former head of the Reich Security Main Office section for "Jewish Affairs" (*Judenreferat*), held in Jerusalem was deliberately conceived as a trial based on the testimony of survivors (Weinke 2018), the Nazi trials held in West Germany relied mostly on written documents such as Nazi files. The reasons for this lay not only in the psychologically understandable reluctance of surviving witnesses to set foot on German soil again after the horrific events they had experienced during the war. Another crucial factor was the continued presence in the courtrooms of perpetrators who had either been acquitted or granted an early release. They were usually very well informed about complex legal details yet they claimed ignorance about historic events in which they had played a part. This so-called *Kameradenhilfe* (support for comrades-in-arms) was coordinated by Werner Best, former deputy to Sipo/SD chief Reinhard Heydrich and governor of occupied Denmark. Confronted with the "expert knowledge" of this coterie who took advantage of the then existing vacuum of specific historical research on the recent past, prosecutors from the 1960s began to back up their charges with copious documentary evidence. Another reason for the increased urgency to consult Nazi files was that when individual areas of investigation were intensified, they often shed light on previously unknown crimes that had to be investigated before the statute of limitations expired. In comparison to the 1950s, the political-legal interests had thus changed decisively: although the Federal Republic did signal an increased interest in captured archival materials to the Western Allies soon after its founding, its leadership never expressed any intention to use them for the purpose of criminal prosecution. About 10 years later the exact opposite was the case: when Nazi files were searched for or requested from abroad, this happened almost invariably because they were needed to prepare Nazi trials.

The original decision to establish an office for preliminary prosecution was burdened with a number of paradoxes, however, some of which over time turned out to be grave defects. Apart from the smoldering issue of the unpunished judicial murders and other atrocities, these primarily included the unresolved question of access to German files held in Eastern European archives. Towards the end of the 1950s the Ludwigsburg prosecutors under the leadership of their director, Erwin Schüle, had attempted to sidestep the existing absolute ban on contact stipulated by the "Hallstein Doctrine," with which the West German government sought to prevent third countries from recognizing the GDR diplomatically. They did so by using the Polish Military Mission in West Berlin in order to establish informal contact with the Main Commission in Warsaw. Half a decade later these contacts had become permanent in the sense that the documentary evidence held in Warsaw was now considered indispensable for investigative work carried out in the FRG. To the same extent that the number and significance of Nazi trials grew, so did public pressure on the political leadership to work out a reasonable compromise with regard to access to files held in Eastern archives.

That the limited access turned out to be highly problematic was due not just to the West German policy of non-recognition, but also to the specific part the GDR played. On the one hand, the East German campaigns had initially helped to prompt West Germany to take up the prosecution of Nazi crimes again. At the same time, the "antifascist" barrage from the East could also serve as a pretext for refusing closer cooperation on the matter of archival material by pointing to political interests concerning the relations between the two German states. It was this seemingly irresoluble conflict between politics and morals that the SED leadership took advantage of in the mid-1960s: while seeking to stabilize their own "antifascist" alliance with their eastern neighbor by spectacular propaganda campaigns against the "Bonn Ultras," they also hoped to make progress towards a *de facto* recognition by deliberately handing over evidence to select West German members of the judiciary. It revealed a dual strategy of confrontation through propaganda and ostensibly pragmatic rapprochement designed to gradually decrease their ideological opponent's room for maneuver.

Following an intense verbal exchange in parliament, the West German Bundestag on March 25, 1965 passed the "Law on the Calculation of the Statute of Limitations" (*Gesetz über die Berechnung strafrechtlicher Verjährungsfristen*) (von Miquel 2004). It pushed back the start of the 25-year statute of limitations for homicide by just under five years, so that respective investigations could still be opened until January 1, 1970. Thus, the previous decision made by the government coalition partners, the Christian Democrats and Christian Social Democrats (CDU/CSU) and the Free Democrats (FDP), to let the statute of limitations for severe Nazi crimes expire on May 8, 1965 for reasons of constitutional law had been *de facto* revoked. At the same time, the Bundestag considered as outdated the announcement, unrealistic from the beginning, that all evidence on crimes committed by Germans during the occupation existing in Eastern archives would be systematically reviewed before this date in order to ensure an interruption of the statutes of limitation. This complete revision of a cabinet decision is notable for two reasons: first, it occurred within just a few months, and second, it represented the result of a compromise that the parliamentary group leaders of the Social Democrats (SPD) and CDU/CSU had negotiated to the disadvantage of the smaller coalition partner. A few months before the controversy about the statute of limitations culminated, the right-wing Nationale Partei Deutschlands (NPD) (German National Party) announced at their founding party convention that they would fight for a "true representation of history." Their triumphal election success that won them seats in the state parliaments of Hesse and Baden-Württemberg was mainly carried by the mobilization of all those mostly male, middle-aged voters who were tired of German "self-castigation" and the supposed "constant discussion of the Nazi past."

Even after the extension of the statute of limitations for Nazi murders, the beginning of official cooperation with the GDR's eastern neighbors, and the expansion of West German investigations to include "desk-murderers" in the highest party and government offices, the legal prosecutions continued to be marked by grave deficits and ruptures. The unequal treatment of defendants who had been either subordinates or high-ranking officials and were therefore culpable to different degrees primarily manifested itself in the fact that those judged to be responsible to a lesser degree were overwhelmingly categorized as "accessories" to mass murder. The Federal Court of Justice was split on the legal practice of sentencing defendants as accomplices. However, it continued to be applied by the lower courts not least because it seemed to open up the only legal path to evade the legally prescribed punishment for murder.

In addition to these functional reasons there were also actual distortions of perception in play. For example, the legal practice of qualifying those belonging to the "core group(s) of the genocide" (Ulrich Herbert) as subaltern subordinates without any proper intention to exterminate victims goes back to the historical misjudgment that the numerous executors of National Socialist racial policy had neither room for maneuver nor genuine motive for killing Jews, Soviet POWs, and Sinti and Roma. In the 1960s there had been hardly any academic research that could have questioned this interpretation, so criminal prosecutors had to rely on the information provided by witnesses who were themselves culpable as perpetrators and who played the role of eyewitnesses in court – such as the above-mentioned Werner Best. By no means do I intend to reduce the part the Ministry of Justice, the Bundestag, and especially the Federal High Court played in the retroactive, scandalous statute of limitations for accessory to murder. However, it was primarily the absurd application of the accessory rule to fanatical Nazis and all-too-eager civil servants that created the prerequisites for the "cold amnesty" of 1968/69 in the first place. The hypothesis that this had been a coup planned well in advance by Eduard Dreher, head of the criminal law division in the Federal Ministry of Justice in Bonn, seems plausible considering that his predecessor, Josef Schafheutle, lent his support to a 1965 draft for just as wide-ranging a partial amnesty for "minor accessories" submitted by the CDU. Moreover, Dreher had recommended the adoption of his concept of a retroactive amnesty for accessories to murder in Nazi war crimes cases to his former supervisor and judge at the European Court of Justice, Walter Strauß, with barely disguised inventor's pride. Previously, he had sneaked his idea into the Introductory Law to the Administrative Offenses Act (§ 50, section 2 StGB), which went into effect in 1968 (Görtemaker & Safferling 2015).

Among the international public, such occurrences only amplified existing doubts about the German government's willingness to deal with the Nazi past. The French newspaper *Le Figaro*, for example, combined its criticism of the half-baked compromise on the statute of limitations with the prognosis that one could not exclude the possibility that the German government in 1969 "will once again find itself in a situation similar to that in which it held its debates in the past weeks" (quoted according to von Miquel 2004, 317). What many critics had feared did in fact happen: once the next expiration date for the statute of limitations came closer, pressure on the grand coalition of CDU/CSU and SPD mounted to find a more reliable solution that did justice to the political-moral significance of the issue. After the SPD had once more demonstrated its good will by submitting a request to abolish the statute of limitations for genocide, the governing parties on June 26, 1969 with a vote of 297 to 128 passed their joint draft law for the Ninth Criminal Law Reform Act, which stipulated both the exclusion of genocide from the statute of limitations and a 10-year extension of the statute of limitations for Nazi murders. While this new parliamentary compromise barely made itself felt in the practice of criminal prosecution, the consequences of the inconspicuous § 50, section 2 of the Criminal Code (StGB) were all the more grave. One year after it came into effect, criminal prosecutors reported that charges against at least 300 defendants were dismissed. They especially criticized the tendency among many public prosecutor's offices to use § 50 II to "embellish" other reasons for dismissing charges, meaning they were using it as an instrument of judicial economy. The controversial clause by no means only benefited "desk criminals," for so-called "minor accessories" profited from this concealed amnesty to the same extent, including members of police battalions and nurses. Therefore, it can be said that the approval the FRG had won by extending the statute of limitations was undone by this "cold amnesty." Its ideological opponent in the East especially sought to make use of this to its own advantage. After not responding for several years to requests by West Berlin's office of the public prosecutor to hand over evidence for crimes committed by the Reich Security Main Office (RSHA), GDR authorities used this wave of dismissed charges against "Eichmann's men" once again to polemicize against the West German "nature reserve" for war criminals. Apart from its sporadic participation in larger West German Nazi trials, the other German state noticeably toned down its propaganda about the Nazi past after the change of the Bonn government from Kurt Georg

Kiesinger (CDU, 1966–1969) to Willy Brandt (SPD, 1969–1974). Of course, this did not mean that they would cease to keep West German politicians busy with targeted provocations (Weinke 2008a, 151–172).

Attempts to correct the course

It was symptomatic for the changed awareness of history in West Germany following the broadcast of the US TV series *Holocaust* that those delegates who in the Bundestag debates on March 29 and July 3, 1979 voted for the abolition of the statute of limitations for murder were backed by a slim majority of voters for the first time. To the supporters of a stricter prosecution of Nazi crimes, who had witnessed the often arduous debates during the 1960s, it must have seemed all the more strange that the general shift in public opinion against a statute of limitations for Nazi crimes occurred at a time when the number of trials actually decreased.

At the beginning of the 1970s, West German Nazi trials had already passed their zenith. This development was mainly caused by two factors. First, most of the accused had already reached an advanced age at this point. Therefore, they could usually find a physician who would declare them unfit to stand trial should they be charged. Secondly, as I mentioned earlier, especially due to the introduction of § 50 II of the Criminal Code a number of larger investigations that were just about to go to trial in the late 1960s had suddenly collapsed. Among those were the ambitious RSHA crimes case pursued by a Berlin special team of investigators and the investigations of the planners and organizers of the Nazi murders of the chronically ill ("Operation T 4"), which Fritz Bauer had launched in the final years before his death in 1968. Yet a decreasing number of investigative proceedings and trials did not mean that the prosecution of Nazi crimes had become socially irrelevant. On the contrary, media representatives, filmmakers, critical intellectuals and scholars, including some (legal) historians, repeatedly demonstrated their willingness to engage with the issue. In fact, it was the seeming hopelessness of the possibility of legal convictions at such a late date that kindled their criticism, usually expressed in the context of sensational acquittals or dismissal of proceedings. Both the momentum gathered by the investigative authorities created for the purposes of dealing with the criminal legacy of the Nazi past and the interplay between the German public, politics, and judiciary played a part in ensuring that a series of important large-scale investigations and trials of Nazi criminals were held in the final two decades of the old Federal Republic as well. Comparable to the first Frankfurt Auschwitz trial (1963–1965) in terms of its historical significance, the trial of the SS members in charge of the concentration and extermination camp Majdanek was held at the Düsseldorf district court from November 26, 1975 until June 30, 1981. The trial of former deputy commander Herrmann Hackmann and 16 other defendants, including members of the Political Section and SS camp guards, turned into the longest Nazi war crimes trial in the history of the FRG. Enough victims were willing to testify, subjecting themselves to the strain of giving testimony despite small prospects of success. One of the questionable side aspects of this trial was that the defense attorneys, most of whom belonged to right-wing circles, succeeded to a considerable degree in using the judicial forum as a stage for their own propaganda. Almost daily the witnesses who had traveled to Germany from abroad were denigrated by Nazi and anti-Semitic slogans. In March 1978 even the Israeli parliament felt the need to criticize those conducting the trial for its prolonged duration and the unrestrained agitation of the defense attorneys.

Twenty-one years after the official start of the investigations, only one defendant, Hermine Braunsteiner-Ryan, was sentenced to life imprisonment in June 1981. Seven other defendants were given prison sentences between three and 12 years, one was acquitted, and four female camp guards had already been acquitted in 1979. The acquittals and overall mild sentences were met with incomprehension and outrage among the public. Commissioned by the chairman of the Norddeutscher Rundfunk (NDR) public broadcasting service, Hans Brecht, Frankfurt-based filmmaker Eberhard Fechner shot a documentary on the Majdanek trial with a running time of several hours, which was titled *Der Prozeß* (The Trial) and broadcast on German public television's Channel Three from November 21 to 27, 1984.

While the Majdanek trial and its echo in the media generally contributed to the marginalization of Nazi victims, the 1979/80 trial by jury of former BdS/KdS (*Befehlshaber der SiPo und des SD/Kommandeure der SiPo und des SD*) members Herbert Hagen, Kurt Lischka, and Ernst Heinrichsohn held in Cologne had the opposite effect. Some of these former members of the Sipo and SD had already been sentenced in absentia by French military tribunals in the late 1940s, but these sentences were not carried out in the FRG and, based on a rather idiosyncratic interpretation of the Transition Agreement between Germany and the Allies by the Federal High Court, their cases were not reopened either. It was only in 1971 that this prosecution gap was closed by the German–French "Supplement to the Transition Agreement." However, another five years would pass before the first witnesses were heard in what was to become the "Lischka trial." Ernst Achenbach, a politician and amnesty lobbyist from North Rhine-Westphalia belonging to the right wing of the FDP, who himself had been involved in the deportation of Jews as the former head of the political section at Nazi Germany's embassy in Paris, was able to use his influential, politically almost uncontested position as rapporteur to the Bundestag's foreign policy committee in order to delay the ratification of this agreement until 1975. The opening of investigations against the former Paris Sipo-SD chief Kurt Lischka und two other SS officials was eventually forced by a group of French activists around Paris lawyer Serge Klarsfeld and his German wife Beate Klarsfeld. By a spectacular attempted kidnapping of Lischka and the trial it provoked, in which Lischka, still walking free, testified against the Klarsfelds, they at least briefly managed to interest the German media, who by now were focusing almost exclusively on the "RAF complex," in the prosecution of Nazi crimes. In a trial lasting only a few months, all three defendants were given long prison sentences in February 1980; meanwhile the remaining 21 defendants in the so-called "France complex" who had been tracked down were acquitted.

In the West the 1980s were mainly shaped by efforts to correct the grave deficits in the handling of Nazi judicial murders and other atrocities. In October 1979, roughly 25 years after investigations had first been launched and more than 11 years after the controversial acquittal of the former Nazi judge Hans-Joachim Rehse, for the first time in the history of the FRG a systematic investigation of the judges at the former People's Court (*Volksgerichtshof*, VGH) was begun. It was prompted by a new criminal complaint brought by Frankfurt attorney and former Nuremberg prosecutor Robert M.W. Kempner. He had come across a copy of the Nazi propaganda film *Verräter vor dem Volksgerichtshof* (Traitors Before the People's Court), which had been believed lost and seemed to clearly disprove the Federal High Court's claim that the VGH had been a legitimate court. Berlin Senator for Legal Affairs Gerhard Meyer (FDP) instructed the public prosecutor at the superior court to prove that the People's Court had not been a "legitimate court" according to § 1 of the Judicature Act (GVG). Not only were they instructed to put the last People's Court judges and prosecutors still alive on trial, but they were also expected to set aside their own justification for closing the investigation into the People's Court that had been sent to Kempner eight years earlier. To further deepen the prosecuting authorities' dilemma, 40 West German university professors spoke out in the *Frankfurter Rundschau* newspaper three months after the investigation was reopened. Using rhetoric that rather overshot its target, they demanded that the People's Court not be acknowledged as a legitimate court (and thus the judge's privileges not be applied) since this was an institution that stood "blood-soaked and despised before the sense of justice of all nations." Motivated by the apparent hope that a history of systematic amnesty that had lasted for more than 30 years could be reversed at the last minute, they also issued the following alarmist appeal: "Democratic justice … has a reputation to lose if it spreads protective laws over the murderers who wore the robes of the People's Court and the special courts" (quoted after Stolleis 1994, 244). In the end, the investigations lasting for almost five years remained unsuccessful. Twenty-seven of the 110 individuals charged died during the course of the investigations and there was no proof that the remainder either worked for the People's Court (for a time) or played a role in death sentences passed by the court. The only person brought to trial on September 6, 1984 was 82-year-old superior court councilor Paul Reimers. Before the court had ruled on the trial opening, Reimers committed suicide in November 1984.

Criticism of the Berlin prosecutors' time-consuming investigative strategy was rejected by future Berlin SPD Senator for Legal Affairs, Jutta Limbach, who claimed that it had been necessary to disprove the Federal High Court's ruling on the legitimacy of the People's Court. Yet there had been broad consensus among the judiciary since the early 1960s that the People's Court was no longer a legitimate court as of August 1942.

When the Green Party parliamentary group in March 1986 filed an inquiry into the handling of Nazi judicial murders, this set a new course in the debate on the criminal prosecution of Nazi crimes and war crimes. For one thing, this initiative aimed to introduce the controversies about the Kohl administration's course of a "normalization of the past" that had simmered since the early 1980s into parliament. The same year, the debate about Ernst Nolte's theses and Jürgen Habermas' criticism of them culminated in the *Historikerstreit* (historians' debate). The phenomenon of "legocentrism" (Günter Frankenberg) also came under scrutiny: it refers to the tendency common in West German discourses on the past to discuss questions of the historical, political, and moral treatment of the Nazi regime's perpetrators and victims primarily through legal categories. In a certain sense, this foray by the Green Party itself suffered from the "predominance of the jurist's view" of which it accused the government. For in the time-tested manner of left-wing social critics, it refused to connect with the scholarly debates among historians. Nonetheless it had the merit of inspiring a fundamental debate about the priorities and blind spots of a statist "coming to terms with the past" by means of criminal law.

Limits of the (national) law

With the so-called "third phase of coming to terms with the past" that began in 1990 when the SED dictatorship collapsed, the long overdue conversation about the West German prosecution of Nazi and war crimes finally began. Contrary to the hopes of left-wing West German critics of the judiciary however, it unfolded against the backdrop of prosecuting GDR state crimes. Incidentally, legal practitioners were once again having a moment: they were now tasked with evaluating records in Eastern and Central European archives in a search for undiscovered evidence and reviewing investigations launched by the Stasi before 1989 that had been mostly inconclusively dropped. The justice ministers specifically instructed the Central Office in Ludwigsburg to review a total of 88 "Central Investigative Proceedings" (Zentrale Untersuchungsvorgänge, ZUV) from the period between 1964 and 1989 with the parameters of criminal law in mind. In some cases, the preliminary investigations that had resulted from this review were referred to the public prosecutor's office in whose jurisdiction they fell, and in some cases, they were closed. To this day there have been no legal convictions. Crimes committed by the armed forces in the former occupied territories became another focus of public prosecution. Previously, these investigations had hardly played a role at all in the criminal prosecution of Nazi crimes, but in the course of the public debate about the Hamburg "Wehrmacht" exhibition some new investigations were launched while others were reopened. As the Federal High Court's sensational "Caiazzo" verdict of 1995, resulting in the impunity of the main culprit for mass shootings of Italian civilians, and the conviction of 93-year-old Friedrich Engel in 2002 showed, these prosecutions did not produce any results that could satisfy the demands of a democratic legal culture: in 2004 the Federal High Court dismissed the charges against Engel, the former head of the SS Security Service in Genoa, by ruling that while the shooting of 59 Italian hostages had been cruel objectively, it was impossible to prove retroactively that the defendant had acted with subjective cruelty.

The final question that remains is how the criminal prosecutions of Nazi crimes were received by the public in both German states. While we still know very little about public opinion in East Germany, concrete information about responses in West Germany is now available. US legal historian Devin Pendas has made the case that the efforts to solve and prosecute Nazi crimes had reinforced existing antagonistic mental barriers rather than removing them (Pendas 2006). First, there is the fact that even important trials such as the Auschwitz trial were either judged negatively or apparently ignored by a large share of the public. By way of contrast, the media interest was greater than average. The polarizing effects of Nazi war crimes prosecution divided critics into two camps. Representatives of both the political left and right rejected the trials on principle. Thus right-wing conservative journalist Winfried Martini, who before 1945 had worked for Paul Carl Schmidt in the press section of the Reich Foreign Ministry, reverted to the biologistic vocabulary of times past by speaking of a "process of putrefaction" to which the state and society were exposed through the Nazi trials (Martini 1969). Meanwhile Martin Walser, at this time on the left of the political spectrum, thundered in Teutonic furor: "The trial of the Auschwitz foot soldiers has gained a meaning that no longer has anything to do with the legal process. The historical profession toes the line; exposure, moral and political education of a population who apparently could not be brought to remember past events by any other means" (Walser 1965, 189). In general, left-wing critics exhibited a tendency to highlight the prosecution's biased motives, thus portraying them as an alibi for West German decision makers with a Nazi past. *Spiegel* journalist Gerhard Mauz, for example, referred to the testimony of "desk murderer" Friedrich Karl Vialon before the Koblenz district court in 1963 as the beginning of an "infection" while he described Federal Chancellor Kurt-Georg Kiesinger's 1968 testimony in the Frankfurt diplomats' trial as the "peak of the fever curve," which had obfuscated awareness of his "involvement" (Mauz 1971). While critics outside the mainstream expressed sustained doubts about the legalistic form of dealing with the Nazi past, opinion leaders in the national daily and weekly papers highlighted the stabilizing effects of the Nazi trials. As Pendas has shown by using the reporting on the Auschwitz trial as an example, they did so by employing various rhetorical strategies. As might be expected, the *Frankfurter Rundschau* and *Süddeutsche Zeitung* both particularly emphasized the moral-didactic objectives set by the trials, which were understood as a work of remembrance for future generations. Conservative papers such as the *Frankfurter Allgemeine* or the *Ruhr Nachrichten* took a defensive yet also constructive stance. Their warning to avoid a politicization of the Nazi trials by conducting them according to the well-proven rules of a constitutional state based on the rule of law was also meant to implicitly deny the extraordinary character of these trials. The price paid for this strategy of normalization, Pendas concludes, were ruptures in the political culture and collective memory of West German postwar society. Yet it also is undeniable that it was these very socio-psychological mechanisms of self-delusion which had launched these trials in the first place and kept them going for more than 60 years.

Conclusion

On July 15, 2015 one of the last trials about crimes committed at Auschwitz concluded. The Lüneburg district court sentenced 96-year-old SS-*Unterscharführer* Oskar Gröning to a four-year jail term for being an accessory to murder in 300,000 cases. Despite the defendant's advanced age, it took more than a year before the Federal High Court confirmed the sentence in September 2016.[1] This makes Gröning one of a small number of about 1,600 individuals who were effectively sentenced for Nazi and war crimes by the West German court system on the basis of national penal law since 1949. He also belongs among the much smaller circle of former SS men who were prosecuted for the crimes they committed in concentration and extermination camps. The crimes of Gröning and other SS members had been known to the West German justice system for decades. Prompted by the initiative of Frankfurt Chief Public Prosecutor Fritz Bauer, the Frankfurt public prosecutor's office in the 1950s had opened a file for a centralized investigation named "Auschwitz concentration camp" that contained several hundred suspects (Nestler 2017, 41–68). Yet regardless of this knowledge and a case law of the highest courts that had since 1969 at least theoretically created the possibility of charging members of SS guards in Nazi extermination camps with functional complicity in mass murder, neither the Central Office in Ludwigsburg nor West German public prosecutors took action. It was only in 2011 with the sensational sentencing of former Trawniki police auxiliary John Demjanjuk by a Munich court that the old case files from the 1960s and 1970s were reviewed and a handful of former SS men were put on trial. Since most of the defendants are in their late 80s or even older, it is foreseeable that very few of them will ever stand trial (Douglas 2016).

Prompted by these most recent sentences against former Nazis, there currently is a debate about the extent to which the West German judiciary bore responsibility for the overall failure to prosecute the perpetrators of Auschwitz. Today the Central Office admits that an understanding of the law that was "not always accurate" had led to the large-scale dismissal of proceedings since the early 1970s (Rommel 2017, 104). Meanwhile its critics claim the Central Office had run a "judicial blind flight" which had been caused by a lack of overview and autonomy among the administrators in charge (Nestler 2017, 67). Thus, even more than 70 years after the Genocide Convention was passed and 60 years after the Central Office was established, the debate on the judicial handling of Nazi and war crimes is conducted within a framework which – based on the individual case or certain groups of crimes – reproduces the system and complicated dogmatic ramifications of German criminal law. Yet this not only distracts from the larger historical context, it also fails to consider the characteristic features of West German criminal prosecution since investigations were reopened.

1 The verdict is printed in *Neue Juristische Wochenschrift* 2017, 498 ff.

For one of the fundamental constants of this large-scale project was that it was based on a fateful underrating of the task at hand and a simultaneous overrating of the judicial system's effectiveness in which politicians, the judiciary, and the public repeatedly reassured one another over long periods of time. Most of all, the challenge involved in prosecuting the crimes of a century that were of previously unknown character and scope was seriously underestimated. As I have shown in this chapter, it was this very misconception, however, that provided the decisive momentum required in 1958 to create a political majority for the establishment of the Central Office. By contrast, those involved tended to overrate the prosecution work already accomplished by the Allies as well as the possibility to prosecute Nazi injustices with the means of German criminal law. Even in the 1990s and 2000s, when the limits of this practice were plainly obvious to most of those involved and the courts reverted to a human rights-friendly interpretation of GDR law in their simultaneous prosecution of SED injustices, nothing changed.

Despite all its achievements, the legacy of 60 years of West German prosecution of Nazi crimes also includes the fact that to this day not a single perpetrator has been convicted of genocide or crimes against humanity. It is important to keep in mind that the FRG Criminal Code has included its own article on genocide since 1954.[2] But as Lawrence Douglas has emphasized again recently, the predominant legal opinion to not apply this article retroactively to Nazi crimes for reasons of constitutional law was no more binding in the past than it is today (Douglas 2013, 754). In a certain way, the 1947 resolution of the German Society for International Law seems to extend its problematic effects even into the present. Back then human rights were invoked for the German victims of communist expulsions while they were denied to the German and non-German victims of the National Socialist policy of plunder and extermination. But can the fact that international humanitarian law is not applied today really be explained by this long-lasting historical precedent or is it not rather that a break with a legal practice that has prevailed for more than 60 years would lead to a dramatic loss of face for the German criminal justice system and criminology? While it is probably impossible to give definite answers to questions such as these, it is high time for German legal historians to turn towards the more fundamental problems of prosecuting Nazi crimes instead of continuously getting embroiled in trifling discussions about where to lay the blame.

2 On the history of § 220 of the Criminal Code, see Weinke (2019).

References

Douglas, L., 2013. "Was damals Recht war ... Nulla poena und die strafrechtliche Verfolgung von Verbrechen gegen die Menschlichkeit im besetzten Deutschland." In Priemel, K. C. & Stiller, A. (eds.) *NMT. Die Nürnberger Militärtribunale zwischen Geschichte, Gerechtigkeit und Rechtschöpfung*. Hamburg: Hamburger Editionen, 719–754.

Douglas, L., 2016. *The Right Wrong Man*. Princeton: Princeton University Press.

Eichmüller, A., 2008. "Die Strafverfolgung von NS-Verbrechen durch westdeutsche Justizbehörden seit 1945. Eine Zahlenbilanz." *Vierteljahrshefte für Zeitgeschichte* 56(4): 621-640.

Eicmüller, A., 2012. *Keine Generalamnestie. Die Strafverfolgung von NS-Verbrechen in der frühen Bundesrepublik*. Munich: De Gruyter.

Görtemaker, M. & Safferling, C., 2016. *Die Akte Rosenburg. Das Bundesministerium der Justiz und die NS-Zeit*. Munich: Beck.

Jasch, H.-C. & Kaiser, W., 2017. *Der Holocaust vor deutschen Gerichten. Amnestieren, Verdrängen, Bestrafen*. Leipzig: Reclam Verlag.

Martini, W., 1969. *Die NS-Prozesse im ost-westlichen Spannungsfeld*. Pfaffenhofen: Ilmgau Verlag.

Mauz, G., 1971. "Was hätte ich vermuten sollen?" *Der Spiegel*, May 3.

Meyer-Seitz, C., 1998. *Die Verfolgung von NS-Straftaten in der Sowjetischen Besatzungszone*. Berlin: Berliner Wissenschaftsverlag.

Nestler, C., 2017. "Warum erst jetzt?" In Lüttig, F. & Lehmann, J. (eds.) *Die letzten NS-Verfahren. Genugtuung für Opfer und Angehörige – Schwierigkeiten und Versäumnisse der Strafverfolgung*. Baden-Baden: Nomos, 41–68.

Pendas, D. O., 2006. *The Frankfurt Auschwitz Trial, 1963–1965: Genocide, History, and the Limits of the Law*. Cambridge: Cambridge University Press.

Rommel, J., 2017. "Der Beitrag der Zentralen Stelle der Landesjustizverwaltungen zur Aufklärung nationalsozialistischer Verbrechen." In Lüttig, J. & Lehmann, F. (eds.) *Die letzten NS-Verfahren. Genugtuung für Opfer und Angehörige – Schwierigkeiten und Versäumnisse der Strafverfolgung*. Baden-Baden: Nomos, 81–109.

Stahl, D., 2015. "Entschließungen deutscher Völkerrechtler." In *Quellen zur Geschichte der Menschenrechte, Arbeitskreis Menschenrechte im 20. Jahrhundert* (ed.), May 2015. Available at: https://www.geschichte-menschenrechte.de/entschliessungen-deutscher-voelkerrechtler/ [Accessed April 12, 2020].

Stolleis, M., 1994. "Die „Weiße Rose" und ihre Richter". In id., *Recht im Unrecht. Studien zur Rechtsgeschichte des Nationalsozialismus*. Frankfurt am Main: Fischer, 233–246.

Turner, M., 2018. *Historians at the Frankfurt Auschwitz Trial: Their Role as Expert Witnesses*. London: I. B. Tauris.

von Miquel, M., 2004. *Ahnden oder Amnestieren? Westdeutsche Justiz und Vergangenheitspolitik in den sechziger Jahren*. Göttingen: Wallstein.

Walser, M., 1965. *Unser Auschwitz*. In Kursbuch 1, 189–200.

Weinke, A., 2001. "Die Waldheimer 'Prozesse' im Kontext der strafrechtlichen Aufarbeitung der NS-Diktatur." In Haase, N. & Pampel, B. (eds.) *Die Waldheimer "Prozesse" – fünfzig Jahre danach. Dokumentation der Tagung der Stiftung Sächsische Gedenkstätten am 28. und 29. September 2000 in Waldheim*. Baden-Baden: Nomos, 27–48.

Weinke, A., 2002. *Die Verfolgung von NS-Tätern im geteilten Deutschland. Vergangenheitsbewältigungen 1949–1969 oder: Eine deutsch-deutsche Beziehungsgeschichte im Kalten Krieg*. Paderborn et al.: Schöningh.

Weinke, A., 2008a. *Eine Gesellschaft ermittelt gegen sich selbst. Die Geschichte der Zentralen Stelle Ludwigsburg 1958–2008*. Darmstadt: Wissenschaftliche Buchgesellschaft.

Weinke, A., 2008b. "The German-German Rivalry and the Prosecution of Nazi War Criminals During the Cold War (1958–1965)." In Friedländer, H. & Stoltzfuss, N. (eds.) *Nazi Crimes and the Law*. Cambridge: Cambridge University Press, 151–172.

Weinke, A., 2015. "Die (gescheiterten) Verfahren gegen Mitarbeiter des Reichssicherheitshauptamtes nach 1945." *Recht und Politik* 51(2): 107–115.

Weinke, A., 2018. "Eichmann, Adolf." In Groenewold, K., Ignor, A. & Koch, A. (eds.) *Lexikon der Politischen Strafprozesse*. Available at: https://www.lexikon-der-politischen-strafprozesse.de/glossar/eichmann-adolf/ [Accessed April 12, 2020].

Weinke, A., 2019. *Law, History, and Justice. Debating German State Crimes in the Long Twentieth Century*. New York: Berghahn Books

Courts as a Site to Tell the "Truth"
The Case of Former Prison Commander Alexandru Vişinescu

Kristine Avram

Introduction

In September 2014, the Romanian Supreme Court of Justice indicted Alexandru Vişinescu for crimes against humanity. The then 88-year-old was from 1956 to 1963 commander of the Râmnicu Sărat Penitentiary, an infamous detention facility for political prisoners in the east of the country. The 10-month trial, dubbed by some the "Romanian Nuremberg," culminated in a guilty verdict for inhumane treatment and Vişinescu was sentenced to 20 years in prison. The Court resolved that the former commander applied a detention regime that resulted in the death of at least 14 political prisoners and entailed the premise for establishing a regime of extermination at the penitentiary. As Vişinescu was the first individual condemned for crimes committed during Romania's "obsessive decade"[1] (Rusu 2017, 1267), the case attracted widespread media attention in and outside the country. While some argued that his conviction is "too little, too late" (*Adevărul* 2016), others praised it as a "landmark case" (*BBC* 2015) and a "significant moment" (*The Guardian* 2016) in Romania's effort to address its communist past and promote the truth about past repression.

Similarly, scholars and practitioners in the fields of transitional justice or human rights commonly suggest that trials are tools to seek and determine the truth about past human rights violations.[2] The (criminal) trial, in other

1 The novelist Marin Preda (1970) first coined the term in the literary sphere, which later "gained wide usage in Romanian public discourse in designating the traumas of the 1950s inflicted by communist authorities in their bid to transform Romanian society into a socialist regime" (Rusu 2017, 1267).

2 The International Center for Transitional Justice (ICTJ), for instance, states on its website that truth-seeking initiatives such as criminal trials "can play a powerful role in documenting and acknowledging human rights violations". The Center argues that "knowing the truth about the past is more than just an important step toward justice, it is a recognized human right to which all victims and survivors of armed conflict and repression are entitled". Similarly, the European

words, is "an epistemic engine, a tool for ferreting out the truth from what will often initially be a confusing array of clues and indicators" (Laudan 2006, 2). This truth-seeking function is usually linked to a trial's "end product," i.e. the judgment, which portrays an official final account of the adjudicated events and actions of the defendant (Garbett 2013, 198). Judgments, in this regard, can be read as constituting a text that narrates a story about the past. However, the judicial narrative "does not expose the reality;" rather it "is a claim of knowledge, and a claim to absolute authority" (Almog 2001, 488) and thus serves as a device to the epistemic competence of trials. Accordingly, truth- and story-telling are intertwined in criminal proceedings with the version of past events put forward in judgments being an "authoritative claim of truth" (Brants & Klep 2013, 38). Increasingly, the participation of victims and survivors[3] (as witnesses or civil parties) is considered to contribute to the truth-telling function of courts by helping to establish a more accurate or nuanced truth of the adjudicated events (Garbett 2013; Ciorcarci & Heindel 2015).

Against this background, the present chapter interrogates the truth-telling or epistemic function of the trial against Alexandru Vişinescu, in particular its final judgment, from the perspective of the survivors' families who participated in the trial, i.e. the civil parties.[4] More specifically, the chapter asks what narrative or "truth" the court and the survivors' families have established about the events at the Râmnicu Sărat Penitentiary (hereafter R.S. Penitentiary), how these truths are interlinked, and what perception the survivors' families have of the trial and its truth-telling function. In general,

Court of Human Rights underlines the right of victims and their families to know the truth about the circumstances of events that involved a massive violation of such fundamental rights as the right to life. In general, the "right to truth/to know" has been recognized by international law more recently (Naftali 2017, 70–71). Knowing the truth, in turn, is said to bring closure, facilitate healing, and restore dignity from the perspective of victims (and survivors) and their families (ibid., 72).

3 For some time, there has been a discussion about using the term "survivor" instead of "victim" in the context of (massive) human rights violations. At the core of these debates is the goal of not taking agency from the injured persons by calling them victims, which is a term that is commonly equated with passivity. Thus, the term/concept of "survivor" is now at the fore in many contexts. In this chapter, I mostly speak of survivors, especially since my interviewees are relatives of political prisoners who survived the Râmnicu Sărat Penitentiary. The legal texts and literature to which I refer use the term victim to some extent. In these cases, I reproduce the wording of the respective author and selectively add the term survivor.

4 According to Article 84 of the Romanian Criminal Procedure Code, a civil party is a victim or the heirs of a victim who initiates a civil action within criminal proceedings. In criminal proceedings, the victim or civil party has inter alia the following rights: to be informed of its rights; to propose production of evidence by the judicial bodies; to raise objections and to make submissions; to consult the case file, under the law; to be heard; to ask questions of the defendant, witnesses and experts; and to raise objections and make final arguments (Arts. 81, 93).

different notions of "truth" exist. For instance, Aldana (2006) differentiates between three different types of truth that victims seek through trials or truth commissions about past atrocities: first, "forensic truth" or "hard facts," i.e. information about who, how, when, where, and why; second, "emotional truth," i.e. knowledge regarding the physical and psychological impact of the human rights abuses on victims and their relatives; and third, " a less individualized and more general truth, such as causal explanations of the chain of command, institutional structures, and economic problems that resulted in rights violations" (ibid., 109). Here, I understand the judgment as portraying a forensic, or rather legal truth about what happened at R.S. Penitentiary during Vişinescu's command. Importantly, rather than merely discovering "the truth," trials express concerns about procedural fairness, privileged relationships, power disparities between the state and citizens, and so on (Griffin 2013). Thus, trials are limited in their quest for truth and their narrative output by procedural and evidentiary rules, selectivity and the formalism of legal process.

In total, the chapter consists of six sections. First, I briefly outline Romania's communist past and criminal justice efforts to address crimes committed during that era. Second, I introduce the case of Vişinescu, and then present the judicial narrative as it appears in the final judgment given on February 10, 2016. In the fourth section, I expose the narrative accounts displayed in the semi-structured interviews I conducted in 2017 with two civil parties to the trial against Vişinescu.[5] The chapter shows that the court and the survivors' families share the same vision of what happened at the R.S. Penitentiary during Vişinescu's command and why. This similarity, I argue, does not stem from the courts' provision of (new) information and authoritative explanations related to Vişinescu's actions, but from the co-construction of the legal truth by the judge and the civil parties. Hence, in the fifth section, I highlight the contribution of the survivors' families in more detail and summarize their perception of the trial. Finally, I reflect on (domestic) courts as sites to seek and tell the truth from the perspective of victims, survivors and their families. The case of former prison commander Vişinescu shows that if there is a long period between the crimes and their prosecution, rather than helping survivors and victims' families to know or obtain the truth about past human rights violations, criminal trials can serve as a platform to tell, disseminate, and authenticate private stories of suffering, which ultimately co-construct official stories of repression.

5 The data was collected at the Centre for Conflict Studies, Philipps University Marburg. The project and field research in Romania are funded by the Fritz Thyssen Foundation.

Constrained justice for crimes committed during communism

After the Second World War, a communist-led regime took power with Gheorghe Gheorghiu-Dej becoming the first General Secretary of the Communist Party. His rule (1948–1965) was marked by "neo-Stalinism," forced collectivization and industrialization, as well as the prosecution and detention of "enemies of the people" (Goldman 1997, 264). Between 1948 and 1964, up to 600,000 political prisoners "were geographically placed, morally-ideologically 'reeducated' and eventually physically annihilated" (Rusu 2015, 30) in more than 120 prisons and detention centers all over the country (Boldur-Lățescu 2004, 67). In 1964, a general amnesty issued by Gheorghiu-Dej released the surviving political prisoners, marking "the transition from the phase of violent repression through physical incarceration and corporal annihilation, towards the phase of social control through mass surveillance, less brutal but more subtle and effective" (Rusu 2015, 3). After Gheorghiu-Dej's death in 1965, Nicolae Ceaușescu succeeded as Party leader and head of state, and consolidated, and later intensified, the dictatorship (Goldman 1997). His rule ended with the events of December 1989. Romania was the only country to exit communism by a violent revolution, with more than 1,100 people killed and 3,300 wounded. However, the country did not experience a resolute break with the past nor a replacement of its elite (Stan 2012, 131).

While the events of December 1989 were adjudicated in a significant number of criminal proceedings,[6] only a handful related to crimes committed during the communist regime. The first was the trial of Nicolae and Elena Ceaușescu on Christmas Eve 1989. An *ad hoc* military tribunal handed down the death sentence on charges of genocide, undermining state power and the national economy after less than two hours of deliberation (Stan 2013, 43). Due to its significant procedural and substantial flaws (e.g. no hard evidence was presented to substantiate the claims, the defendants had no right/time to appeal the death sentence), the trial can be considered a "show trial" *par excellence*. Aside from this trial, until recently, only four other cases referred

6 Proceedings in the 1990s and 2000s have almost exclusively related to crimes committed during the Revolution, emphasizing the "importance of this event as a founding moment of the new political order" (Grosescu & Ursachi 2015, 72). Overall, several hundred people were prosecuted, involving members of the central and local Party apparatus, the *Militia* and *Securitate* officers, and later also Army officers. However, a majority of the convicted benefited from delays in executing the sentences or presidential pardons limiting their jail time tremendously, and some were released for age and health reasons before carrying out their sentences (Stan 2013; Grosescu & Ursachi 2009; 2015).

to crimes committed during the communist regime, with only two of them resulting in convictions (Grosescu & Ursachi 2009). During the "Bus Trial" in 1997, eight *Securitate* (secret police agency) and *Militia* (civilian police) officers were found guilty of executing in 1981 two young persons after they kidnapped a bus with passengers and asked for passports and 10,000 dollars to leave the country. While the trial represents the first conviction of a *Securitate* officer for past abuses, all of the convicted were released early from prison due to a general amnesty from 1988, which cut their time in half, and for health reasons (Grosescu & Ursachi 2009). In 2002, two *Militia* officers were convicted for instigating the murder of political dissident Gheorghe Ursu, who was placed under arrest in a prison in Bucharest in September 1985 and died in detention a few weeks later as a result of torture. Following almost three decades of struggle by Ursu's family and two hunger strikes by his son Andrei, in August 2016, two former *Securitate* officers as well as the former Minister of the Interior and the former head of the *Securitate* were indicted for planning and covering up the murder. In October 2019, both *Securitate* officers were acquitted by the Bucharest Court of Appeal.[7]

Although the reasons for the few trials related to the communist era were manifold,[8] legal constraints impeded the prosecution of crimes committed during the 1950s and 1960s in particular (Grosescu 2017). Thus, torture and inhuman treatment of prisoners were long considered ordinary crimes (e.g. murder, abuse in office) submitted to statutory limitation. In particular, the socialist Criminal Code of 1968, in force long after the country's transition to a democracy, provided for a 15-year statute of limitations for homicide and an eight-year one for torture. Thus, after the communist regime in 1990, "it was no longer possible to investigate murders committed before 1975 and acts of torture committed before 1981" (Grosescu 2017, 510). Only in 2012 did Romania adopt amendments to the Criminal Code, introducing "crimes against humanity" and letting international crimes become punishable regardless the date of their commission. In February 2014, the new Penal

7 The former Minister of Interior and the former head of the Securitate died within the trial's first year. Ursu's family stated that they want to appeal the court's decision.

8 Grosescu & Ursachi (2009) list, inter alia, constraints related to the criminal law system, the lack of political will by the ruling class to deal with the past, and a relatively weak civil society as reasons for the small number of trials pertaining to communist crimes. In general, trials concerning both the communist era and the events of December 1989 "reflected a profound politicization of the judicial process and its instrumentalization by various political parties" (Grosescu 2019, 3). Thus, in Romania, dealing with the past was and still is highly related to domestic politics, i.e. to the electoral cycles and the various political forces in power. Regarding the political interference in dealing with the past, see Grosescu & Ursachi (2015), Grosescu (2019) or Rusu (2017).

Code entered into force[9] and "opened previously blocked avenues of justice" (Grosescu 2017, 524), thus allowing the indictment of Alexandru Vişinescu and later of another prison commander for crimes against humanity.[10]

The case of Alexandru Vișinescu

In 2006, the Institute for the Investigation of Communist Crimes and the Memory of the Romanian Exile (IICCMER) was established by the Romanian government to file criminal complaints against alleged perpetrators of human rights violations committed before 1989 (Grosescu 2017). Eventually, in July 2013, IICCMER filed a formal criminal complaint to the Prosecutor's Office attached to the Military Court of Bucharest against five former (deputy) commanders of prisons or labor camps – one of them being Vişinescu. Born in 1925, Vişinescu completed his mandatory military service by working in the *Securitate* and *Militia* forces. Later, Vişinescu was trained by the *Securitate* to become a political officer in prisons and labor camps. After graduating, he was appointed political officer at the Jilava (1950–1953), Mislea (1954–1956) and finally R.S. Penitentiary, where he was the commander until its abolition (1956–1963). Following Râmnicu Sărat, Vişinescu was prison officer at Ploieşti and Jilava Penitentiary. When proceedings started in 2013, Vişinescu was

9 After Romania's exit from communism, the socialist-era Criminal Code of 1968 was amended or supplemented 54 times (of which 23 times by means of Government Emergency Ordinances) to bring it into compliance with new constitutional regulations and the requirements of Romania's European integration process. The large number of modifications led to the inconsistent interpretation and application of the criminal law, which highlighted the need for a new penal code. On February 1, 2014, the new Penal Code (Law No. 286/2009) finally came into force, together with a new Penal Procedure Code (Law No. 135/2010), thereby abrogating the 1968 Penal Code. The strong continuity of the former nomenclature and a lack of political interest as well as of legislative strategy are among the reasons for the delay in drafting and implementing the law. Nonetheless, even after entering into force, the new Penal Code poses several challenges for legal professionals. For further information, see Trandafir (2014) and Pasca & Gál (2014).

10 Besides, in 2018, prosecutors indicted Ion Iliescu, the former president of Romania (1989–1996; 2000–2004) for crimes against humanity, contending that he shares responsibility for more than 800 deaths during the events of December 1989. Prosecutors said that Iliescu as well as former Prime Minister Petre Roman, and former Deputy Prime Minister Gelu Voican Voiculescu, who gained control of the military and the media during the uprising, had failed to prevent "numerous situations" in which people were needlessly killed. While the case against Petre Roman was dropped for lack of evidence, the trial against Iliescu, Voiculescu and former air force commander Iosif Rus started in November 2019 at the High Court of Cassation and Justice in Bucharest. (Radio Free Europe 2018; Gascón Barberá 2019).

lieutenant colonel put on reserve status, and living off a monthly pension of 3,200 RON in an apartment in central Bucharest.[11]

In August 2013, the Supreme Court of Justice seized the case from the Military Court of Bucharest, and indicted Vişinescu for crimes against humanity in June 2014. The trial began in September that year, with the Court granting civil party status in the lawsuit to a wife, a daughter, and a sister of former political prisoners. The hearings were public and at first attracted widespread media attention. After 10 months of trial, the Bucharest Appellate Court determined that the accused, as commander of the R.S. Penitentiary from July 1, 1956 to April 13, 1963, submitted the collective of "counter-revolutionary" detainees imprisoned in the given penitentiary to inhumane and degrading treatment, physical and psychological torture, and extermination. Because the Romanian Constitution grants defendants the right to be judged under the law more favorable to her/him with regard to the sanctioning treatment, the judge, Carmen Veronica Găină, changed the accusation from crimes against humanity to inhumane treatment (Grosescu 2017), and sentenced Vişinescu to 20 years in prison.[12] In addition, he was stripped of his military decorations and, together with the Romanian state (through the Ministry of Public Finance), the Ministry of Internal Affairs and the National Administration of Penitentiaries, ordered to pay €300,000 in compensation to the civil parties, i.e. the three members of the victims'/survivors' families.[13] In February 2016, the Supreme Court of Justice upheld the sentence,[14] which he served at Jilava Penitentiary Hospital until his death in November 2018.

Judicial narrative of a zealous yet criminal agent of the state

Criminal trials produce a particular version of past serious human rights violations in which the adjudicated events are portrayed as being caused by individual human agency, and the actions as being explicable in terms of the

11 The military pension of 3,200 RON is equivalent to USD 813, which is almost three times as high as the average monthly pension. As of January 2018, the average pension increased by 18.2% to RON 1,132 (USD 282). The gross minimum wage is 1,900 RON (USD 483) as of January 2018.

12 The 1968 Penal Code is more favorable since during this period the special maximum sentence was 20 years, the lowest out of all the maximum punishments provided by law in the successive penal laws. In other words, the 1968 Penal Code prescribes a lesser penalty for inhuman treatment than the 2014 Penal Code for crimes against humanity. While Vişinescu's actions could qualify as both, the judge applied the more favorable law to him and sentenced him for inhuman treatment.

13 Archive of the Bucharest Appellate Court, Verdict No. 122/F (April 20, 2015).

14 Archive of Romanian Supreme Court of Justice, Decision No. 51/A (February 10, 2016).

individual's characters (Scarry 1987). Yet narratives are not explicitly laid out in a document such as a judgment; they require interpretation and, ultimately, are a product of inquiry. Here, the object of inquiry is the 186-page-long final judgment by the Romanian Supreme Court of Justice (hereafter Decision 51/A). While the judgment of Vişinescu contains different stories and displays various narrative structures, I primarily focus on the general narrative or "truth" it conveys about the events at the R.S. Penitentiary during Vişinescu's command, in particular in the part on the "factual situation and evidence" (Decision 51/A: 19–131). The analysis and presentation of the judicial narrative is oriented along the five rhetorical elements introduced by Kenneth Burke (1969), i.e. *act, scene, agent, agency, purpose.*[15] In sum, the overall plot is that of an abnormal ("cruel", "brutal") individual who acted unlawfully and in a discretionary fashion in his position as an agent of the state.

Looking at how the storytelling unfolds, the judgment starts by sketching the background to the act (*scene*), i.e. first by delineating the historical function of the R.S. Penitentiary (*I. Penitenciarul Râmnicu-Sărat,* Decision 51/A: 19–21) and second by presenting the categories and profiles of the detained (political) prisoners (*II. Deținuții și condamnările acestora,* Decision 51/A: 21–30). Built at the end of the 19th century, the R.S. Penitentiary served first as a detention facility for ordinary criminals, but after 1938 at times also for legionary[16] and military prisoners. From 1948 on, the penitentiary functioned as a "mixed prison" for ordinary and political prisoners, of which a great number were imprisoned between 1955 and 1963. Regarding the detainee's profile, the R.S. Penitentiary was a "special" penitentiary populated with "the most dangerous enemies of the regime" (Decision 51/A, 37).[17]

15 Overall, Burke's five key terms of dramatism "may be thought of as the five key elements of a narrative" (Smejkalová 2011, 103). These elements are: act (what happened); scene (the background of the act, the situation in which it occurred); agent (the kind of person who performed the act); agency (the means or instruments used by the agent to perform the act); and purpose (Burke 1969, xv).

16 In 1927, Corneliu Zelea Codreanu founded the Legion of the Archangel Michael, which later became the Iron Guard. This Legionary movement drew on ultra-nationalism, anti-Semitism and anti-communism, and was actively involved in Romanian politics in the interwar period. With the proclamation of the National Legionary State in Romania in September 1940, in which Parliament was dissolved, the Constitution suspended and the Legionary movement the only recognized political movement, anti-Jewish legislation and attacks against the Jewish population intensified, which was accompanied by an extensive theft of Jewish property by the Legionnaires. In January 1941, the Legionnaires staged a rebellion against Ion Antonescu and engaged in a violent conflict with the army. During the rebellion, the Legionnaires killed 125 Jews in Bucharest (the Bucharest pogrom) and destroyed 1,274 commercial and residential buildings. After Antonescu suppressed the rebellion, the Legionary movement was abolished and many of its members were imprisoned. See Poliec (2019).

17 According to the judgment, mirroring communist rhetoric of that time, political prisoners transferred to R.S. were selected from the ranks of the "class enemy" and were considered the

After reconstructing the context in which human rights violations took place, the defendant appears on the scene (*III. Inculpatul,* Decision 51/A, 30–35) and the focus of "storytelling" shifts to the *agent*. Vişinescu's background and career within the Ministry of Internal Affairs (MAI) are examined with a focus on the reason for his prompt appointment as commander at the R.S. Penitentiary. Vişinescu started to work at the Penitentiary as an operative group leader in January 1955, and in April 1956 was assigned the function of the deputy commander. Shortly after, Vişinescu was appointed commander of the R.S. Penitentiary on July 1, 1956 – only months before the Hungarian Uprising in the fall of 1956, after which the situation for political prisoners all over Romania significantly worsened (Decision 51/A, 37). He performed this function until the penitentiary's dissolution on May 13, 1963. The judgment accentuates at various points that his appointment to, and long exercise of, the role of the prison commander took place despite his "low level of education", "poor cultural and political preparation" (ibid., 37), or his serious "disciplinary misconduct" (ibid., 34). Hence, his "special qualities", i.e. his "brutality" and "discretionary behaviour" towards "counter-revolutionary detainees" (ibid., 33) against whom he had already developed "class hatred", recommended this "mediocre individual" (ibid., 37) for the position.

Accordingly, the two main characters in the scene, the defendant and the collectivity of political prisoners, have an adverse relationship, essentially based on state policy (*IV. Raportul de adversitate,* Decision 51/A, 35–39). The leadership of the MAI appears as the "mastermind" behind this setting. Thus, selecting and transferring "the class enemy" on the one hand, and appointing an adequate commander to "suppress" (ibid., 132) or "destroy" (ibid., 142) them on the other hand, is the result of a process at the leadership level of the MAI led by "complementary criteria" (ibid., 35). The judgment presents the existence of this adverse relationship as the premise to Vişinescu's in/actions (*scene*).

The following section is the largest within the sentence and extensively recounts the detention conditions established and maintained by Vişinescu (*V. Condițiile de detenție,* Decision 51/A, 39–127). Here, the focus is on the

most notorious, dangerous "counter-revolutionary" prisoners (Decision 51/A, 35). For the period of the defendant's activity at the prison, the Court identified seven categories of political prisoners (ibid., 21–30): members of the National Peasants Party; high-ranking dignitaries; members of different denominations of the clergy; former ministers, senior officials, officers in reserve and cadres of the Ministry of Internal Affairs; different professional groups like doctors, engineers, lawyers, writers, journalists, teachers, traders, workers and farmers either sentenced or preventively (arbitrarily) arrested for the "disturbance of the social order"; farmers convicted for "public provocation"; members of the governments between 1940 and 1944; and one high-ranking official of the intelligence service in that period convicted for "war crimes against peace and humanity".

commander's in/actions (*act*), i.e. the direct and indirect methods characteristic of the detention regime applied to political prisoners during his command. The elements were isolation, inhumane and degrading treatment, starvation, deficient medical care, disciplinary punishment, and physical violence (beating). The conditions resulted in the "slow but efficient death" (ibid., 126) of at least 14 political prisoners – six of which were the direct consequence of Vişinescu's in/actions – or in the long-term traumatization of these (ibid., 142). Thus, the in/direct methods represent the premises for triggering and installing a regime of extermination developed by Vişinescu aiming at, and ultimately resulting in, the physical liquidation of the "class enemy" (ibid., 126–127). The account of events is repeated several times throughout the judgment.

After having laid out the act, its agent Vişinescu and his in/actions are situated once again within the legal framework and the political system and ideological context of that time (Decision 51/A, 127–132). Here, the premise for his in/actions, i.e. the adversarial relationship, as well as the *purpose* of these, i.e. the direct intent of eliminating the "class enemy," are emphasized. The judgment highlights that Vişinescu committed the in/actions by violating or disregarding the law or obligations imposed by his role as commander, or as a result of a "abusive" and "discretionary" exercise (ibid., 3, 6, 80, 10) of his attributions by abusing his power (*means*). Overall, Vişinescu is characterized as an agent of the state whose appearance is ambivalent: on the one hand, he appears as a brainwashed promoter of a state-sponsored program, an "instrument," "used by state authorities of that time to fulfil the political objective of destroying 'class enemies' specifically placed in his custody" (ibid., 142). On the other hand, he is presented as an autonomous commander and torturer, i.e. "an artisan and zealous performer of an original program of the persecution of 'counter-revolutionaries' detainees" (ibid.). Importantly, the "brutality of that program and of the defendant himself, as his promoter, but also as an individual" (ibid.) is frequently stressed. Hence, "brutality" is one of the main themes running through the judgment.

In short, the judicial narrative reveals the story about a "zealous" yet criminal agent of the state that established a novel and brutal regime of extermination that submitted the collective of "counter-revolutionary" detainees imprisoned in the given penitentiary and found under his power to illiberal treatments (inhumane and degrading), torture (physical and psychological) and extermination (ibid., 130). In other words, Vişinescu appears as an abnormal individual, i.e. an individual displaying "brutal, authoritarian and discretionary behaviour" (ibid., 144–145) who responded inadequately (unlawfully, discretionarily) to a normal situation (detention of prisoners in the former political system).

Narrative accounts of the survivors' families participating in the trial

Moving to the survivors' families' perspective, I present the narrative accounts of the civil parties to the trial with regard to what happened at the R.S. Penitentiary during Vişinescu's command and why. Here, the narrative analysis draws on semi-structured interviews I conducted in 2017 with two of the three civil parties constituted in the trial against Vişinescu.[18] In particular, I conducted an interview with N., the widow of a former general who was imprisoned at R.S. Penitentiary from 1958 to 1964 on November 14, 2017 in Bucharest. In addition, I conducted interviews with A.M., whose father and (maternal) grandfather were political prisoners at R.S. Penitentiary on November 23 and December 12, 2017 in Bucharest. Her sister M., who appeared as a witness in the trail and participated in several hearings, and mother, who was herself a political prisoner during Romania's "obsessive decade," also participated in the interviews. Names and other sensitive information of the interviewees have been anonymized to treat the information provided by the research participants carefully.

Overall, the narrative accounts display a great similarity with the judicial narrative – in terms of both the general story and certain elements (*agent*, i.e. Vişinescu, and *purpose* of his in/actions) – revealing two interlinked arguments. First, R.S. Penitentiary was (one of) the worst political prisons of that time, detaining the "most important" prisoners (*scene*). In particular, my interviewees consider that communist state organs and agents selected "the most dangerous, the most important" prisoners, the "leaders," and the "moral elite" to be imprisoned there. N. notes that her husband emphasized having suffered especially at R.S. Penitentiary, comparing the place with hell. "These are his words: 'If hell exists, hell was there. I was in hell.'" She further explains that her husband left the prison as a "living corpse," taking this as clear evidence of an extermination program. Similarly, A.M. stresses the existence of a state-sponsored extermination program:

> RS was a prison of the elite and of extermination. The purpose was to kill them and it was clear, and it also came from the documents, and the Communists recognized it. And after he [Vişinescu] killed M. [prominent political prisoner], it served its purpose.

18 The third civil party was a sister of a political prisoner who died at R.S. Penitentiary.

Second, state organs not only selected the prisoners but also its commander. According to my interviewees, communist authorities selected Vişinescu particularly for his "brutal," "cruel" or "sadistic" character and/or behavior (*agent*). For N. these personal features not only explain his appointment but also his promotion to a management position after the dissolution of the prison. She explains:

> He did such a good job at R.S. ... torturing people there as the mind of a normal human cannot conceive that after the closure of the penitentiary, he was advanced to a management position at the country level! So, he has tortured very much and was appreciated for that.

This promotion is also central in the Court's reasoning and highlights the political dimension of Vişinescu's actions. However, N. explains his actions mostly through his personal traits; in her account, intentional reasons dominate the immediate causes such as the historical context. By contrast, in the account of A.M. and her sister M., the political dimension and larger historical and ideological context of his actions is salient, arguing that "these were not murders made privately by him in the bathroom" but that "he was given the role" by communist authorities who indoctrinated him ideologically. Here, A.M. elaborates:

> They have bestialized those with a rudimentary intellect. Vişinescu is a very primitive guy. And when you take such men and wash their brains, and put it in their heads head, that they [political prisoners] are the enemies, the bourgeoisie, the fascists, that they must be destroyed, we must defend the socialist order, the working class, and you are here, in the front line fighting with the bourgeoisie, you have to be ruthless. Actually, it's a bigger crime than the physical one that Vişinescu has executed.

In as much as communist state authorities set the context for his action, the two sisters do not locate (criminal) responsibility only in the individual person of Vişinescu:

> We said we can only agree with Mr. Vişinescu when he said: "But why did you call only me? Why do not come those who are in power." That is what I said. Vişinescu was not alone, because if there was no system to allow him [to act] that way, we would not have spoken.

Similarly, N. extends the question of responsibility for the violence experienced by political prisoners to a wider group of people:

> Many should give an account for the horrors that happened there and not only there. Not only in Râmnicu Sarat, but at Aiud, Jilava, Poarta Alba; at all these places. All who participated in the hell, in which they [political prisoners] were tortured, should give an account. And not now, but in January 1990.

Overall, the characterization of the defendant as being a brutal agent of the state, who promoted and executed a state-sponsored extermination program, as well as of his relation to the political prisoners as being adverse resembles the judicial narrative. Yet the accounts of my interviewees differ in the characterization of the political prisoners: while they figure as the passive objects of Vişinescu's actions in the judgment, they are active subjects from the survivors' families' perspective. For the two sisters, their mother, and widow N. the heroic personality dimension of their relatives is at the forefront, comparing them with martyrs for the good cause. A.M. and M. present their father and grandfather as strong, active, funny, sincere, and loyal persons. Instead of being victims, they were heroes and role models in the Penitentiary and beyond. As A.M. puts it: "They were all respected and had leadership [in the prison]. They were people who, if they opened their mouth, everyone listened to." In this regard, A.M. deplores that her heroes turned victims during the trial. However, with Vişinescu's conviction, his actions are officially acknowledged as a crime, which, according to A.M., puts an end to public confusion:

> Now there is an official and very clear distinction between good and evil. Those are the people who were heroes of Romania, who suffered unjustly, and precisely because they were special people, and on the other side the killer is called a criminal, an offender.

Her sister M. adds: "Crimes must be called crimes … and who does such things, no matter how late and how old one is, one has to answer".

Another divergence is the language used for Vişinescu's actions. While his behavior was termed "abusive" and "discretionary" in the judgment and he was sentenced for inhumane treatment, my interviewees referred to it as "crime" or "horror" and "atrocity." Accordingly, the legal framework is of no or of much lesser importance to the setting of Vişinescu's actions, which is also the element in which the plot displayed in the narrative accounts of the survivors' families differs. While the judgment portrays an abnormal (brutal) state agent acting unlawfully and discretionarily in the former political regime, the civil parties' accounts espouse the narrative of an abnormal (brutal) state agent acting "sadistically" or "cruelly" in an abnormal (repressive) political regime.

Civil parties' contribution to, and perception of, the trial

Aside from the survivors' families' understanding of what happened at the prison and why, I was interested in their general perspective on the trial and its truth-telling capacity. Regarding the legal process and its outcome, my interviewees were satisfied with the course and "impressed" with the judge, who seemed "concerned about finding the truth" as she "with great patience, listened to all parties." It was not about making a "superficial" decision, as A.M., who only got involved in the trial as a civil party to avoid her mother being called to testify in court as a witness, initially feared. When she and her sister realized that "they [the prosecution, judge] really wanted to know" and that the trial was "something serious" and not a "circus," they wanted to "help".

According to the Romanian Code of Criminal Procedure, civil parties can contribute to a criminal trial as a source and provider of information and evidence by e.g. giving a statement, calling witnesses, ask questions, or handing in documents (Arts. 81, 93, 97). Overall, A.M., M. and N. handed in various documents they recovered from the National Council for the Study of the Securitate Archives (CNSAS), like internal reports about the conditions at the R.S. Penitentiary (Decision 51/A, 11), as well as memorialist literature of former political prisoners who were either their relatives or friends of the family. For instance, N. handed in her husband's autobiographic work *Robinson Island*, which is cited in long fragments to exemplify the regime of isolation carried out at the prison during Vişinescu's command (ibid., 48). In addition, A.M. handed in autobiographic works by two political prisoners who were known to the family and died before the proceedings. These works were cited inter alia as testimonies of inhuman and degrading treatment (ibid., 171). Notably, the judgment as well as the appeal decision quotes abundantly from this memorialist detention literature and from letters of former detainees or of in/direct witnesses. Thus, the voices of victims and survivors play a central role throughout the judgment, and in particular in discussing and judging the defendant's actions.

Apart from documents and memorialist literature, A.M. further presented the Court with case law of the European Court of Human Rights, consisting of the judgment in the case of *Polednova v. Czech Republic* and summaries of the judgments in the cases *Streletz, Kessler and Krenz v. Germany* and *K.-H.W. v.*

Germany (Decision 51/A, 11). These cases "were highly instrumental in shaping and supporting the judges' legal reasoning" (Grosescu 2017, 19) that "even a soldier cannot conform, completely blindly, to orders that flagrantly violate internationally recognized human rights, in particular the right to life" (Decision 51/A, 131), and that the prosecution of Vişinescu's action is not a violation of the principle of non-retroactivity of law insofar as the laws of that time are applied and interpreted according to a democratic, rule-of-law reading (ibid., 132). Overall, the role and contribution of the civil parties in the trial against Vişinescu as sources and providers of information was substantive in the legal process, and their participation an essential aspect of the legal outcome, i.e. the judgment.[19] Accordingly, their contribution was essential in establishing the legal truth about the events at R.S. Penitentiary during Vişinescu's command. In short, the participation of A.M. and N. had a "judicial effect" (De Hemptinne 2010).[20]

Asked if she learned something new during the trial, N. replied in the negative. For her, the courtroom was not a space from where she would gain new insights or obtain the truth, but a platform to distribute her husband's experience to a wider audience. Regarding her motivation to participate in the trial, N. states that she "wanted to tell the truth about the horrors that happened in the prisons" in general, and the "truth about the sufferings" of her husband in particular. Overall, she wanted people to know and to restore the memory of her husband. In her own words: "I did it for my husband's memory and for the world to know." Similarly, A.M. and her sister M. did not gain new information or knowledge. Yet they admitted having learned about the European case law, which they later handed in, from a befriended lawyer. Hence, N. and A.M. used the court as a platform to disseminate the experience, or truth, of their relatives. As such, the judgment is based on this experience/truth.[21]

19 For "exposing the detention conditions at R.S. Penitentiary," the court relied on different forms of evidence, including testimonies of political prisoners who survived the imprisonment (mostly extracted from memorialist literature), audiovisual recordings of testimonies of deceased political prisoners, testimonies of former prison staff, declarations of the civil parties and witnesses heard during criminal proceedings, and documents from the personal files of the political prisoners (for instance, medical records or medical-related information) (Decision 51/A, 39). In establishing the legal truth about what happened at R.S. and why, the court also takes other case law and the legal framework of that time (for instance, the legally established obligations for the role of a prison commander) into consideration. While N. has contributed to the first pillar, A.M. has contributed to both.

20 Apart from the judicial effect, De Hemptinne (2010) distinguishes a reparative and a symbolic effect of victim/survivor participation. Thus, granting victims the possibility to participate in trials can help them recover from the harm experienced and render the proceedings more accessible and transparent (ibid., 167–168).

21 With regard to the judgment, A.M. praised its quality. For her, it is a tremendous, accurate piece of work of history, a "document, well done, like a doctoral thesis, very serious. … A very valuable work".

Apart from having the opportunity or platform to tell the truth about their relatives' suffering, the trial had other positive effects for the survivors' families. For instance, acknowledging Vişinescu's actions as a crime was mentioned several times by M. as an important aspect of the trial and the resulting judgment in order to end public confusion and to restore the memory of the persons imprisoned. Besides, both sisters experienced positive reactions of interest and solidarity in the private (e.g. neighbors) or professional (e.g. colleagues) spheres. They also reported conversations they overheard in public. M. for example states:

> Seriously, people were talking about it, like the taxi driver, or the postman, was talking: "Did you see, oh my god, what a monster, what a bastard, what he could do, I did not know ..."

Accordingly, the trial raised awareness about Romania's "obsessive decade" and provided a space for the communication of tabooed or formerly private experiences of violence (Figari Layús 2018) as well as for restoring the memory of those imprisoned there. Speaking at trial can have a restorative effect on victims/survivors and their families when they "come to know that one's suffering is not solely a private experience best forgotten but instead an indictment of a social cataclysm" (Aldana 2006, 113).

In sum, naming Vişinescu's action a crime and sharing the stories of their (grand)father or husband was the most important motivation and outcome of the civil parties' participation in the trial. In this regard, human rights prosecutions like the one of Vişinescu are not only important for the voices of victims, survivors and their relatives to be heard but for their story, i.e. their version of the past, to be disseminated through the court trial to a wider audience, and ultimately to be authenticated.

Conclusions

The trial of former prison commander Alexandru Vişinescu was the first of its kind and highly mediated. The narrative disseminated through the judgment is one of a "zealous" yet criminal agent of the state who established a novel and, in particular, brutal regime of extermination at R.S. Penitentiary. The civil parties' accounts display a similar vision with regard to what happened at the prison under Vişinescu's command and why. In sum, the R.S. Penitentiary was (one of) the most severe prisons of Romania's "obsessive decade" that incarcerated the most important political opponents. Hence, the prison was essentially a site for the struggle with the "class enemy" to which Vişinescu was appointed for his special qualities, i.e. the "class hatred" he developed against the counter-revolutionary detainees in his custody as well as his "brutal" character and "discretionary" behavior. The convergence of the narratives put forward by the judge and the civil parties comes as no surprise, insofar as the judgment draws on testimonies and statements of A.M., N., or M., and in particular on the documents they handed in – ranging from internal reports retrieved from CNSAS to memorialist literature by their relatives or European case law. Hence, in the trial against Vişinescu, the survivors' families contributed to the establishment of the (legal) truth rather than "simply 'found' the truth from its legal judgment" (Garbett 2013, 198). The legal truth conveyed in the judgment, thus, is the result of a dynamic knowledge-production process at trial, in which the civil parties provided content and argument in salient portions of the text.

Notably, from the perspective of my interviewees, the trial did not provide (new) answers or remarkable insights. Rather, the courtroom represented a platform from which they could tell their truth, i.e. the experience of their relatives imprisoned at R.S. Instead of being a "circus," as was feared by A.M. at the beginning of the proceedings, the courtroom turned out to be a platform from which to share and disseminate the survivors' experience to a wider public. Importantly, A.M., her sister M. and N. had all been active in restoring or promoting the memory of their relatives prior to the proceedings. For instance, A.M. and her sister M. maintain a blog to inform and educate the public, and N. instigated the airing of an episode on her husband's experience of repression as part of the TV show *The Memorial of Pain* (*Memorialul Durerii*).[22] Accordingly, the civil parties had told the story about what happened at R.S. and why in private (e.g. family) and public (e.g. television) spaces long before the trial started. Hence, they used the court as one of many arenas to tell the story of their relatives and to achieve their personal (memory) agendas.

Consequently, I argue that criminal trials for past human rights violations can serve not only as a platform from which survivors and their families can tell and share experiences and stories of suffering, but also as a vehicle to disseminate these private stories to a wider public, to officially acknowledge

22 Between 1991 and 2008, 120 episodes were aired concentrating mainly on anti-communist activities during the 1940s and 1950s. In 2008, the series was re-broadcast and new episodes were added, including the "Black Series" in 2013 consisting of interviews with perpetrators and torturers. Overall, "The Memorial of Pain" was widely disseminated and is "by far the most influential movie production to dwell on communism" (Stan 2013, 231).

them, and, ultimately, to authenticate them as (legal) truth. The case of former prison commander Alexander Vişinescu thus broadens the view on trials as an epistemic engine, i.e. a site to tell and know the truth from the perspective of victims, survivors and their families. When human rights violations were committed a long time ago, as in the trial against Vişinescu, courts are rather sites to tell and co-construct the legal truth. Here, private stories of suffering not only become acknowledged but also (part of) an official account of past state repression in the public sphere. In other words, criminal proceedings can help to circulate private narratives publicly and transport these into the social and political spheres. Whether and how the story about what happened at R.S., and why, is received by Romanian society is, however, yet another question.

References

Adevărul, 2016. *Condamnarea torționarului comunist Vişinescu: un pas mic pentru Justiție, un pas şi mai mic pentru România postdecembristă* (Punishing communist torturer Vişinescu: a small step for justice, an even smaller step for post-December Romania). Available at: https://m.adevarul.ro/news/eveniment/condamnarea-tortionarului-comunist-visinescu-pas-micpentru-justitie-pas-mai-mic-romania-post-decembrista-remember-raportultismaneanu-1_56bb98265ab6550cb8a96fad/index.html [Accessed March 28, 2020].

Aldana, R., 2006. "A Victim-Centered Reflection on Truth Commissions and Prosecutions as a Response to Mass Atrocities." *Journal of Human Rights* 5: 105–126.

Almog, S., 2001. "As I read, I weep – In Praise of Judicial Narrative." *Oklahoma City University Law Review* 26(2): 471–501.

BBC, 2015. "Romania jails Communist-era prison chief in landmark case." Available at: http://www.bbc.com/news/world-europe-33649800 [Accessed March 28, 2020].

Boldur-Lăţescu, G., 2004. *The Communist Genocide in Romania*. New York: Nova Publisher.

Brants, C. & Klep, K., 2013. "Transitional Justice: History-Telling, Collective Memory, and the Victim-Witness." *International Journal of Conflict and Violence* 7(1): 36–49.

Burke, K., 1969. *A Grammar of Motives*. Berkeley, CA: University of California Press.

Ciorciari, J. D. & Heindel, A., 2015. "Victim Testimony in International and Hybrid Criminal Courts: Narrative Opportunities, Challenges, and Fair Trial Demands." *Virginia Journal of International Law* 56(1): 1–74.

De Hemptinne, J., 2010. "Challenges Raised by Survivors' Participation in the Proceedings of the Special Tribunal for Lebanon." *Journal of International Criminal Justice* 8(1): 165–179.

Figari Layús, R., 2018. *The Reparative Effects of Human Rights Trials: Lessons from Argentina*. London: Routledge.

Garbett, C., 2013. "The truth and the trial: victim participation, restorative justice, and the International Criminal Court." *Contemporary Justice Review: Issues in Criminal, Social, and Restorative Justice* 16(2): 193–213.

Gascón Barberá, M., 2019. *Romania Starts Long-Awaited Trial Over 1989 Revolution Deaths*. Available at: https://balkaninsight.com/2019/11/29/romania-starts-long-awaited-trial-over-1989-revolution-deaths/ [Accessed March 28, 2020].

Goldman, M. F., 1997. *Revolution and Change in Central and Eastern Europe – Political, Economic, and Social Challenges*. Armonk, NY: M. E. Sharpe.

Griffin, L. K., 2013. "Narrative, Truth, and Trial." *The Georgetown Law Journal* 101: 281–335.

Grosescu, R., 2017. "Judging Communist Crimes in Romania: Transnational and Global Influences." *International Journal of Transitional Justice* 11(3): 505–524.

Grosescu, R., 2019. The Trials of the Romanian Revolution. *Cultures of History Forum*. Available at: https://www.cultures-of-history.uni-jena.de/politics/romania/the-trials-of-the-romanian-revolution/ [Accessed March 28, 2020].

Grosescu, R. & Ursachi, R., 2009. *Justiția penală de tranziție de la Nurnberg la postcomunismul românesc*. Iaşi: Polirom.

Grosescu, R. & Ursachi, R., 2015. "Transitional Trials as History Writing. The Case of the Romanian December 1989 Events." In Fijalkowski, A. & Grosescu, R. (eds.) *Transitional Criminal Justice in Post-Dictatorial and Post-Conflict Societies*. Cambridge/Antwerp: Intersentia, 69–100.

Laudan, L., 2006. *Truth, Error, and Criminal Law: An Essay in Legal Epistemology*. Cambridge Studies in Philosophy and Law. Cambridge: Cambridge University Press.

Naftali, P., 2017. "The 'Right to Truth' in International Law: The 'Last Utopia'?" In Belavusau, U. & Gliszczyńska-Grabias, A. (eds.) *Law and Memory: Towards Legal Governance of History*. Cambridge: Cambridge University Press, 70–88.

Pasca, V. & Gál, I. (eds.) 2014. "Evolution of the Penal Legislation in Romania and Hungary in the Post-Communist Era." *Journal of Eastern European Criminal Law* 1. Available at: https://drept.uvt.ro/administrare/files/1481058845-journal-of-eastern-european-criminal-law-no-1-2014-1.pdf [Accessed March 28, 2020].

Poliec, M. I., 2019. *The Holocaust in the Romanian Borderlands: The Arc of Civilian Complicity*. Abingdon/New York: Routledge.

Radio Free Europe, 2018. *Romanian Prosecutors Indict Former President For 1989 Uprising Deaths*. Available at: https://www.rferl.org/a/romanian-prosecutors-indict-ex-leader-for-1989-uprising-deaths/29174615.html [Accessed March 28, 2020].

Rusu, M. S., 2015. "Battling Over Romanian Red Past. The Memory of Communism Between Elitist Cultural Trauma and Popular Collective Nostalgia." *The Romanian Journal of Society and Politics*: 24–48.

Rusu, M. S., 2017. "Transitional Politics of Memory: Political Strategies of Managing the Past in Post-communist Romania." *Europe-Asia Studies* 69(8): 1257–1279.

Scarry, E., 1987. *The Body in Pain: The Making and Unmaking of the World*. Oxford: Oxford University Press.

Smejkavlová, T., 2011. "Story-Telling in Judicial Discourse." *Comparative Legilinguistics* 5: 95–109.

Stan, L., 2012. "Reckoning with the Communist Past in Romania: A Scorecard." *Europe-Asia Studies* 65: 127–146.

Stan, L., 2013. *Transitional Justice in Post-Communist Romania: The Politics of Memory*. Cambridge: Cambridge University Press.

The Guardian, 2016. "Romanian court makes history with ruling over communist-era crimes." Available at: https://www.theguardian.com/world/2016/feb/10/romanian-prison-governors-conviction-for-crimes-against-humanity-upheld [Accessed March 28, 2020].

Trandafir, A.-R., 2014. "Criminology and Crime in Romania – Focus on the New Criminal Code." In Getoš Kalac, A.-M., Albrecht, H.-J. & Kilchling, M. (eds.) *Mapping the Criminological Landscape of the Balkans*, 315–328.

Seeking Justice for the Crimes of the Franco Dictatorship

The Politics of Victimhood in the "Argentine Legal Complaint"

Ulrike Capdepón

This contribution is dedicated to Chato Galante, survivor of Francoist torture and repression, who died on March 28, 2020 in Madrid due to a coronavirus infection.

More than 10 years ago, in April 2010, two exiled relatives of Spanish citizens murdered during the Civil War of 1936–1939 filed a complaint on the other side of the Atlantic, in the Federal Court of the Argentine capital of Buenos Aires, in order to initiate an investigation of the crimes of the Franco dictatorship (1939–1975). This contribution looks at the ongoing Argentine Complaint (*querella argentina* in Spanish) and its development over the last 10 years. The aim is to explore the effects on the dynamics of memory debates in Spain produced by a transnational lawsuit that, as a result of Spain's Amnesty Law, has sought justice abroad for the repressions of the Civil War and the Franco regime. The chapter will more particularly focus on the effects of the growing diversity and increasing visibility of Spanish victims' groups, examining the dynamics and difficulties in the politics of victimhood generated by the Complaint. In this, it seeks to critically analyze the ways in which the interpretative frame of human rights and transitional justice have been incorporated and appropriated by the complainants and by Spanish victims' associations. The underlying idea here is that the international circulation of categories such as "victim," "recognition" and of the human rights and transitional justice discourses themselves fundamentally affects the construction of victimhood in contemporary Spanish debates over memory processes and coming to terms with the Francoist past.

Drawing on fieldwork research in Madrid between 2015 and 2017,[1] during which I conducted qualitative interviews with memory activists, victims, and human rights lawyers, this contribution first analyzes how transnational attempts to investigate Francoist crimes before an Argentine court, invited for the first time to exercise universal jurisdiction, has successively shifted focus onto different categories of victims of the Franco regime, and more especially onto those of the late Franco dictatorship of the 1960s and 1970s and of the early period of Spain's transition to democracy. In so doing, the chapter sheds a critical light on the process of *social* and *political construction* of victimhood, which changes visibilities and creates inequalities and new hierarchies among victims, as well as exclusions as between different types of victims, so leading to conflict and possible victim competition. The goal is to examine the consequences for the social construction of victimhood and the implications that claims of victimhood have for struggles over memory and justice. The central research questions therefore are: firstly, what influence has the lawsuit brought in a Buenos Aires court, a suit framed in international human rights discourse, had on local practices of memory, notably the further differentiation of victims' associations dealing with the Francoist past? And secondly, what effects have the increasing judicialization, transnationalization and framing of the Francoist repression in the language of human rights had on the local "politics of victimhood" and the competition among victims?

Following Brett and Druliolle (2018), I use the notion of "politics of victimhood" to refer to how victimhood is "defined, negotiated and contested" over time, in a process that is "socially and politically" constructed (ibid., 2). The underlying idea here is that the deployment of human rights categories and of human rights discourse more generally has ambiguous effects. On the one hand, as a strategy of empowerment, articulating claims to rights, promoting visibility and fostering the social and public acceptance of new demands as a form of reparation, it can promote social change. However, it can on the other hand also lead to the social reproduction of victimization and vulnerabilization, since victimhood often connotes powerlessness, suffering, passivity or trivialization of the human rights violations suffered (Arrington 2016; Huyse 2003). The question that is finally raised is to what extent the framing in a victim-centered human rights discourse generates competitive

1 This chapter is part of the author's broader research on the topic and draws on already published but fundamentally extended work (see Capdepón 2015; 2017; 2019). I would like to thank the German Academic Exchange Service (DAAD) for supporting this work as part of a postdoctoral fellowship between 2014 and 2017.

victimhood in terms of changing visibilities that creates new hierarchies, exclusions and conflicts among the different victims' groups involved.

The importance to transitional justice and human rights of the recognition of victims and acknowledgement of their victimhood has seen significant scholarly attention in recent years (e.g. Bonacker, Oettler & Safferling 2013; Bonacker 2013). The recognition of the central importance of victims' organizations for transitional justice processes in general and criminal proceedings in particular has prompted a shift to a more victim-centered approach, resulting in an ever-growing body of literature on victim-related issues, such as reparations, restorative justice and outreach or education (Karstedt 2010; McEvroy & McConnachie 2013). Victimhood then is a "central category for transitional justice and as such it should be critically analyzed" as a social construction "shaped by a range of actors, criteria and practices" (Brett & Druliolle 2018, 2).

As regards the global circulation of memory and human rights discourses, it is important to stress that transitional justice paradigms invoking the international legal and moral obligations provided by the framework of international and humanitarian law offer victims a powerful tool for gaining acknowledgement locally (Ferrándiz 2010; 2014; Oettler 2017; Bonacker 2013), notably in winning reparation and justice in the courts. With changing perceptions of "the victim," this identity is being continuously re-constructed, in part as a result of the growing positive recognition that this legal figure enjoys in international resolutions and its translation and appropriation into local space. At the same time, the necessarily selective process of acknowledgement through criminal prosecutions and reparation and the associated shifts in public perceptions run the risk of fueling conflict, as the scholarship on victim competition has documented (Huyse 2003, 64).

The politics of victimhood and the judicialization of the debate around memory in Spain

When in October 1998 the former Chilean dictator Pinochet was detained on an international extradition warrant (see Hau's chapter in this volume), not only did this trigger global debate on the practice of universal jurisdiction but the Spanish legal initiatives to end impunity in Chile and Argentina[2] also

2 The "justice cascade" triggered by transnational legal processes was driven by an advocacy network of activist human rights lawyers and victims' associations. The most prominent Argentine cases that the Spanish *Audiencia Nacional* has investigated under the guidance of judge Baltasar Garzón since 1996 are the trials against former navy officers Adolfo Scilingo, who was the only

created a powerful boomerang effect that has in turn had a decisive impact on the discursive confrontation with the country's Francoist past (Capdepón 2015, 210–232; Encarnación 2014, 132–156). While the Spanish legal system played a crucial role in efforts to bring state human rights abuse to account, triggering domestic prosecutions in Chile and Argentina, in Spain itself the legal and administrative treatment of military personnel and officials associated with the the repression of the Franco dictatorship was governed by impunity. As the Spanish transition process was based on the above-mentioned Amnesty Law of 1977, no criminal prosecutions have been brought against those responsible for crimes of the Franco regime. The "pacted" transition process negotiated in Spain was marked by an official discourse of reconciliation and a "pact of oblivion" with regard to the repression, so that today, still, there have been no criminal prosecutions of those responsible for crimes attributable to the Franco dictatorship.

Reacting to the local pressure of Spanish victims groups and historical memory associations, who denounced the discrepancy in the treatment of dictatorships at home and abroad, in October 2008 the Spanish judge Baltasar Garzón made another important ruling. Echoing the innovative legal arguments he introduced in the Pinochet case and the cases against the Argentine Junta a decade earlier, he for the first time claimed jurisdiction for Spain's National Court to investigate evidence of mass killings and enforced disappearances during the Civil War and the postwar repression, framing Francoist violence in human rights discourses. Responding to the demands of local victims' associations, this investigation for the first time used international criminal law in an attempt to overcome the Spanish Amnesty Law and consequently impunity in Spain. Furthermore, the Historical Memory Law of 2007 was seen as inadequate by many memory associations, as it maintained the impunity of the perpetrators.

The Argentine Complaint, then, was filed as a reaction to Garzón's suspension in 2010 and his ensuing removal from the bench after he opened the first investigations into Francoist repression. Following the failure of Garzón's initiative, local victims' groups made increasing reference to supranational bodies, framing their cases in transitional justice and human rights terms. However, having failed to gain redress in the Spanish courts, the victims

one effectively sentenced in Madrid to 1,084 years in prison for his participation in the repressive practice of throwing "disappeared" prisoners alive from airplanes into the sea – the so-called "death flights" (Spanish: *vuelos de la muerte*) – and the ESMA (Escuela de Mecánica de la Armada) torturer Miguel Ángel Cavallo, who was detained in Mexico in 2001 on a Spanish arrest warrant and extradited to Spain (Roht-Arriaza 2003, 194–200). For the domestic trials in Argentina, see the contribution of Figari Layús in this volume.

of the Franco dictatorship also saw the European Court of Human Rights dismiss their demands (RIS 2012; Escudero et al. 2013, 54).

The Argentine Complaint that then followed represents the first time a court in that country agreed to apply the principle of universal jurisdiction enshrined in the Argentine Constitution. By means of this, the complainants sought to sidestep the impunity legislated in Spain. It was Inés García Holgado – niece of a member of the UGT (*Unión General de Trabajadores*) trade union and granddaughter of a republican member of the local parliament in Salamanca, both disappeared victims of the Civil War – and the then 91-year-old Darío Rivas – son of the republican mayor of the Galician town of Castro de Rei, who was assassinated in October 1936 and dumped in a mass grave – who, together with the ARMH (*Asociación para la Recuperación de la Memoria Histórica*, the Association for the Recovery of Historical Memory), one of the first such associations to emerge in Spain in the years after 2000, and several Argentine human rights organizations, that presented the Argentine Complaint, whose title explicitly refers to "charges of genocide and/or crimes against humanity committed between 1936 and 1977." Following its acceptance, it is being dealt with by the National Criminal and Correctional Federal Court No. 1 of Buenos Aires. In an interesting twist and reversal of roles it was Argentine judge Maria Romilda Servini de Cubría who opened the first international criminal investigation into the human rights abuses of the Franco regime. Since then, the Argentine Complaint has gained in importance as a crucial international criminal process. For the complainants, the investigations opened abroad represent the last opportunity to prosecute Francoist agents for crimes including the *desaparecidos* of the Civil War, but also, increasingly, less-publicized repressive acts that occurred in the later years of the Franco regime, such as cases of "stolen children" and of torture. In a process that anthropologist Ferrándiz describes as "legal download" (Ferrándiz 2010), the victims' groups emerging from the local memory movement began to increasingly frame the experience of political repression during the Civil War and the repression under the Franco regime as well as the transition process in legal discourse, adopting terms such as "impunity," "enforced disappearance," the "imprescriptibility of crimes against humanity" and "universal jurisdiction" in their local claims. They thus demand "truth, justice, and reparation," the three basic transitional justice principles, for the victims of Francoist repression. Initially supported by human rights lawyers Carlos Slepoy, who deceased in 2017, and Ana Messuti – both residents of the Spanish capital of Madrid following their exile under Argentina's last dictatorship – the initiative was intended to prompt a legal investigation of and discursive confrontation with the Franco dictatorship through the invocation of universal jurisdiction in Argentine courts, hopefully prompting and accelerating investigations and prosecutions in Spain.

As the number of complaints filed in Buenos Aires continued to increase, Spanish civil society associations established in May 2013 the *Coordinadora Estatal de Apoyo a la Querella contra Crímenes del Franquismo* (CeAQUA, National Coordination Network in Support of Legal Actions Against the Crimes of Francoism). Some 400 individual complaints have been laid and there are many more pending accusations, generating a widespread transnational public support movement with local representation in different regions of Spain as well as Argentina and other countries. From the start, the CeAQUA network was made up of victims' collectives, human rights lawyers and activists. The activists provided legal support to the complainants when filing complaints or testifying via videoconference at Argentine consulates. In this way, the Argentine Complaint has created a transnational "mnemonic space" (Hepworth 2020, 17) in which complainants, often for the first time, have access to the justice system as an institution that receives their demands, at least taking them into account. In consequence, the investigations undertaken by the Argentine courts have triggered new dynamics in the formation of memory discourses in Spain: in particular, evidence has been gathered in the way of mass grave exhumations, the creation of DNA databases, the gathering of testimony on torture, the naming of perpetrators and the presentation of extradition requests. The Complaint has received explicit support from many different victims' associations over the past 10 years – though victims' groups have bundled their efforts on the one hand but demonstrated their different interests under the Complaint on the other. CeAQUA as an umbrella organization brings together diverse groups of victims. First, there are the descendants of the "disappeared" of the Civil War, then called the *paseados* – those taken for a walk – an euphemism for the execution of civilians, many being killed during the period of the so-called "hot repression" at the start of the Civil War, and generally buried in clandestine mass graves. Furthermore, there are also the plaintiffs sentenced to long prison sentences or to forced labor, at drumhead trials conducted without any procedural guarantees. Another group that joined the Complaint were the political prisoners' associations, these being chiefly concerned with the later years of the Franco regime, representing as they do the surviving victims of torture, violence and political imprisonment under the Franco dictatorship. Another victim group are the families of "stolen children," a phenomenon documented not only during the Civil War and postwar period but also throughout the Franco dictatorship and even beyond, into the early 1980s, after the return to democracy. Partly due to the lawsuit in Argentina, which explicitly includes child abduction as a human rights crime, Spain has seen the emergence since 2010 of a broad media debate on the practice of child trafficking that was institutionalized in hospitals during the Franco dictatorship, women being deprived of their newborn babies immediately after giving birth in hospital and told that their babies were dead (Druliolle 2018). In addition to these main groups, many other type of victims found a place in the lawsuit (Messuti 2013). Although the victims' groups have different objectives and interests of their own, the number of associations linked to CeAQUA has grown steadily, leading to an increasingly differentiated and articulated landscape of victim initiatives.

A first international arrest warrant was issued by the Argentine court in September 2013, against four former Spanish officials, including members of the police, one being Antonio González Pacheco (alias *Billy El Niño* – "Billy the Kid"), an officer in the *Guardia Civil*, another Jesús Muñecas Aguilar, an agent of the *Brigada Político Social*, the secret police. Both stood accused of torture during the later years of the Franco dictatorship and were called to appear before Spain's *Audiencia Nacional* in December 2013. Although they were sought by Interpol, Spanish government officials, prosecuting authorities and judges refused to back the request for extradition, referring to the Spanish Amnesty Law of 1977, and this was therefore rejected in the court's decision of April 24, 2014. In May 2014, after several failed attempts, the Argentine judge Maria Cubría de Servini was finally able to visit Spain to obtain oral testimony from victims (in their capacity as complainants) in various parts of the country (*El País* 2014). In October 2014, notwithstanding the Spanish court's earlier decision, Servini issued arrest warrants against 20 accused former Spanish officials, ex-ministers, and former members of the police forces, as well as a gynecologist suspected of child trafficking, with a view to their extradition to Argentina, reviving the effort to pursue cases of human rights abuses outside Spain's borders (Capdepón 2019, 516). Two of the most notorious suspects were José Utrera Molina, the Minister of Housing during the last years of the Franco regime, who would die in April 2017, accused of signing the death sentence of Salvador Puig Antich, an anarchist executed in 1974, shortly before Franco's death, and Rodolfo Martín Villa, who held different high profile government positions under the Franco-regime and notably as Minister of Trade Union Relations between 1975 and 1976 as well as Minister of the Interior between 1976 and 1979. Villa is accused of ordering the "Vitoria massacre" of 1976, in which the police suppressed a general strike, killing five demonstrators and leaving many injured victims who were trying to hide in a church (Eser 2016). In June 2019, four decades after the violent events, victims and surviviors united with the basque association *Sanfermines 1978: gogoan!* travelled to Buenos Aires to testify against Villa for ordering a police attack on protesters in 1978 during the *Sanfermines* festivities in Pamplona. A student was shot in the forehead and killed, while over 150 people were injured. Rodolfo Martín Villa is investigated for at least 12 homicides in the context of crimes against humanity committed during the Spanish transition and is expected to testify via video-conference before Argentine Judge Servini in September 2020.

In focusing on these events, the Argentine Complaint highlighted the continuation of Franco's repressive apparatus into the years of transition. By requesting the extradition of these individuals, Judge Servini put the spotlight on these victim's distinctive demands and their particular experience of repression during the later years of the dictatorship, which until then had received hardly any public attention. With the appropriation of human rights and transitional justice concepts by the victims' associations that made their appearance on the public stage as new "memory entrepreneurs" (Jelin 2003), the investigations abroad injected a new dynamic into the Spanish debate around collective memory.

A growing number of associations representing victims and relatives afterwards joined the first complainants, endowing the Argentine Complaint with new impetus. The increased visibility of different episodes of Francoist repression in fact reflected the role of new actors within the local memory movement. Besides the associations of relatives of the "disappeared" and of the exiled, for instance, an association of former political prisoners and several associations of relatives of "stolen children" played a crucial role in founding and supporting CeAQUA (Druliolle 2015).

With their appropriation of legal concepts, local activists and victims' groups sought recognition on a local level, increasingly framing the political repression of the Civil War and the late Franco regime in human rights terms (Ferrándiz 2010). The human rights discourse invoked by victims' groups became increasingly salient with the Argentine Complaint and found further reinforcement in the reports of international organizations (e.g. Amnesty International, the United Nations),[3] creating and supporting historical counter-narratives about the Civil War, the Franco dictatorship and the transition process. The transnationally circulating human rights discourses and the traumatic memory of the victims and their individual stories of repression stand in sharp contrast to the dominant historical framings, notably regarding the supposedly less violent late Franco regime and the period of democratization, thereby destabilizing the long hegemonic narrative of the peaceful transition process as a politically successful model (Montoto 2014,

3 I have analyzed the discursive influence of reports offered by international human rights organizations like Amnesty International and the Equipo Nizkor or UN resolutions and communiqués elsewhere (Capdepón 2015, 275–284).

129). The narratives of Franco's victims, silenced for decades, now occupied center stage in a legal setting, bringing media attention and public visibility. Survivors and relatives were thus able to voice their memories of repression, and for the first time denounce before a judge the violence committed during the dictatorship as a crime against humanity.

The disappearances of the Spanish Civil War: the importance of the Mendieta case

While ever since its beginnings in 2000, the "movement for the recovery of historical memory" has been mainly focused on the search, identification and dignified burial of those "disappeared" in the Civil War, the case brought in Buenos Aires has seen a diversification of the category of "victim" of Francoist crimes (Montoto 2017, 13). When the Argentine Complaint was initiated by relatives of some of the disappeared of the Civil War and the repression that followed it – themselves exiled in Argentina – Argentine judge Servini asked the Spanish authorities to exhume the remains that still lay in unmarked mass graves. So it was that she requested that they take charge of the "Mendieta case."

In that case, an 88-year-old woman travelled from Madrid to Buenos Aires alongside 13 other complainants, to make her appearance before Judge Servini in November 2013, asking to recover the remains of her father, the trade unionist Timoteo Mendieta, arrested and killed in November 1939, shortly after Franco's victory in the Civil War, his body being dumped in a mass grave in the Guadalajara cemetery. After her attempts to locate and identify the remains through Spanish channels had failed, she sought legal support elsewhere in her quest to rebury her father's body. In an interview of 2016 she explained the necessity of recovering her father's remains as a symbolic act of personal reparation and collective recognition:

> My greatest wish is to have a niche in the cemetery to bury my father, and if I don't die before … that I be buried with him, at his side. That is my wish, that my father and I should be together. I am very excited. I will do it [the exhumation] with great pleasure … because finally we will have been able to do more than them. We had to change this country first to be able to find him and get him out of the mass grave, and this isn't just about my father but also all the unburied people that still lie in secret graves who should have been exhumed a long time ago. (*Público* 2016)[4]

4 Interview with Ascención Mendieta, published in *Público*, June 21, 2016.

The case became the first foreign-court-ordered exhumation in Spain (Capdepón 2019, 517). Although, as many remarked, the case was largely ignored by the Spanish media, the remains were successfully located in response to Judge Servini's request. After ascertaining that the first grave did not contain the remains of Mendieta's father, the opening of a second grave by the ARMH in June 2017 met with success, and Timoteo Mendieta's remains were reburied in Madrid's La Alumdena cemetery, with a solemn public ceremony, setting an important precedent. His daughter Ascención Mendieta died only two years later in October 2019, having achieved her goal of giving her father's remains a dignified burial. Mendieta's struggle also facilitated the recovery of the remains of 50 other victims of the Franco regime during the investigations at the Guadalajara cemetery.

The politics of victimhood: new visibilities, hierarchies and victim competition

The creation of CeAQUA saw an active and heterogeneous memory movement set in motion, united by a common objective: to obtain transnational justice and the prosecution of crimes committed during the Franco dictatorship. The growing visibility of further forms of repression related to the supposedly less violent late Franco regime, until then little known and discussed in the Spanish public sphere, has been reflected in the establishment of new victims' associations fighting ongoing struggles for recognition.

Fundamentally important for the social construction of victimhood is the length of the period under investigation under the Argentine Complaint. The impact of successive legal decisions and varying human rights criteria appealed to has produced shifts in public attention and given a new salience to different acts of repression, leading to a prioritization and hierarchization of the different victims' groups. While Garzón's order of 2008 was limited to the repression of the Civil War and the immediate postwar period of 1939–1952, and concerned mainly those victims executed and disappeared who lay still in unmarked graves, the Argentine Complaint broke new ground in encompassing the whole period from the beginning of the Civil War in 1936 to 1977, when the first democratic elections were held following the formal end of the Franco dictatorship. In doing so, it cast a particular light on the victims of the late Franco regime, to whom hardly any attention had hitherto been paid, creating new visibilities by broadening the idea of who qualified as a "victim of Francoism" – *víctima del franquismo*[5] – a term coined in that very context (Montoto 2017, 9).

Until then, victims of the late Franco regime had generally preferred to describe themselves as "resistance fighters" or as the "repressed" (*represaliados*), maintaining a critical distance from the discourse of victimhood now brought to the fore by the transnationalization and judicialization prompted by the Argentine Complaint. The Complaint led to much discussion in Spain of torture, political repression and imprisonment during the last years of the Franco regime. A growing number of associations representing both victims and relatives have thus since joined the first complainants, magnifying the significance of the Complaint. The increasing visibility of Francoist repression under the later years of the dictatorship certainly highlights the role of new actors within the local historical memory movement. The first generation of associations built by relatives of the "disappeared" of the Civil War, such as ARMH and the *Foro por la memoria* (Memory Forum) and concerned with the exhumation of clandestine mass graves, was joined in the Complaint by an association of former political prisoners, La Comuna, created only in 2010. That same year saw the establishment of Goldatu, an association of Basque victims of repression, alongside the regional instances of CeAQUA in Catalonia and the Basque Country. What is more, the associations of relatives of the "stolen babies" played an important role in the creation of CeAQUA.

The Argentine Complaint was first initiated in April 2010 by relatives of the "disappeared" whose bodies still lay in mass graves. Forensic technique and professional scientific discourse being central in that context (Montoto 2017, 19), early perceptions were strongly shaped by the impact on the public sphere of the exhumation of skeletal remains associated with the earliest cohort of the historical memory movement and by the highly effective and mobilizing transnational legal category of "enforced disappearance" adopted from the experience of the South American dictatorships (Ferrándiz 2010; Capdepón 2015). The Mendieta case discussed above offers a striking instance of the local impact of the transnational legal complaint in terms of victim recognition and collective memory.

Second came the associations of former political activists who had resisted the regime and been jailed in the late Franco period, direct victims of the late Franco dictatorship. Central to their demands is the possibility of indicting still living former military personnel, police officers, public officials and

5 Indeed, shortly after the first legal complaints were filed, the Foro por la Memoria in April 2012, held the first congress of "Victims of Francoism" in Madrid. See: http://www.congresovictimas-franquismo.org/ [accessed March 3, 2019].

politicians of the Franco regime. Their importance to the process under the Complaint and to the activities of the CeAQUA, their direct testimony regarding torture, and their capacity to mobilize and gain public awareness brought them increasing public attention as instances of a highly visible and active form of victimhood. Their visibility has been boosted by landmark charges brought against infamous torturers such as *Billy el Niño* and by human rights campaigns, among them a number by Amnesty International, that include their testimony about the tortures they suffered. The fact that victims of the repression of the late Franco regime and the violence of the transition, whose experiences date to the 1960s and 1970s, are able to present their cases before the Argentine courts has brought them greater visibility and media attention, as the perpetrators in many cases are still alive and can be charged and prosecuted, unlike the earlier cases directly associated with the Civil War. As one of the complainant activists reports:

> Initially, we cooperated strategically with the ARMH, but we were focused from the start on bringing before the courts the torture we suffered, in order to prosecute and punish those torturers we knew were still moving among us free and unpunished. This, to us, is a more pressing political issue than the exhumation of mass graves. Those who are searching for human remains and have disappeared relatives, cases that date back to the Civil War, and are not as directly effected as us. We are authentic survivors.[6]

This claim to the status of *authentic* survivor installs a hierarchy of victimhood that privileges the claims of survivors above those of relatives, who did not suffer in the same way or nor were they directly engaged in resistance.

Thirdly, there are the associations of relatives of "stolen babies" who have carved out a significant place of their own in the Spanish civil society-based memory movement, though without gaining the same recognition as the previous two groups. Their more precarious position within the Argentine Complaint derives from a lack of agreement regarding their status as "victims of Francoism," both among themselves and in the eyes of the public. This relates to issues of political strategy within the different grouping and legal opportunities (Druliolle 2018, 91) over which the stolen baby associations are themselves divided. Its strategic position within the CeAQUA, its comparability with human rights associations in other countries such as Argentina's Mothers and Grandmothers of the Plaza de Mayo, the possibility of indicting

6 Personal interview with a CeAQUA activist and *La Comuna* member, December 22, 2015 in Madrid, Spain.

the gynecologists or nuns and others involved for child trafficking, and the invocation of the international crime of child abduction gave this group a distinctive profile among the various victims associations united within the CeAQUA network. However, the fact that this crime was not confined to the Franco dictatorship, there being cases into the 1980s, made for a fragile unity within and between the relevant "stolen babies" associations, and raised questions about their status among the other types of victims' associations. A representative of the association *Todos los niños son también mis niños* stated:

> You need to consider that there were an estimated 300,000 cases of stolen babies, many more in numerical terms than there were cases of disappearance in the Civil War, which number 114,000, which of course is still a lot. ... The mothers who have lost a baby immediately upon giving birth are the ones who suffered the most, since they have been in many cases traumatized for the rest of their lives.[7]

Another kind of victim competition has been created here, even if it is not necessarily the intention, by introducing a hierarchy of suffering and drawing numerical comparisons. The relationship between the various groups and their different concerns is thus not always free of conflict; with increasing public attention, a strong competition has emerged among the victim groups organized under the umbrella of the CeAQUA network, plentifully evidenced in the fieldwork and the interviews I conducted between 2014 and 2017. The difficulty of overcoming disagreements between the different victims' associations led to conflicts over the political strategy to be adopted by the movement as a whole.

Conclusions

The emergence of new actors, combined with the adoption of a legal discourse that had been successful a decade before in strengthen the validity of the anti-impunity struggles of the human rights movement in the Southern Cone, has advanced the cause of the Spanish civil society memory associations, expressed in growing demands for the inception of criminal proceedings at home. Grounded in an appeal to universal jurisdiction, the Argentine Complaint laid in 2010 has thus been crucial to the creation of a transnational

7 Personal interview with a member of CeAQUA and the *Todos los niños son también mis niños* Association, March 24, 2016, New York City, USA.

judicial and mnemonic space (Hepworth 2020) while also promoting the emergence of new local actors and prompting victims' associations to unite their efforts, so giving new impetus to the memory movement. It has achieved a great deal too in bringing attention to the experiences of different generations and of different kinds of victimization during the Franco regime. This has seen a noteworthy increase in the public visibility and a finer-grained public perception of Francoist crimes and the demands of its victims, at both the international and the domestic level. There has also been an unprecedented intensification of pressure on Spain's political parties and judicial system to put an end to impunity for these crimes. The proceedings in Argentina have offered at least some recognition to the victims and their different demands, although none of the accused have so far been convicted. All in all, the account above shows how the creative transnational adoption of international human rights discourse, in framing the experience of Francoist repression in international human rights language and with this the strategic coinage of the notion of the *victim of Francoism*, has been a powerful mobilizing tool. The lawsuit filed in Argentina proved to be a central instrument for binding together a variety of victim and local memory initiatives, lending new dynamism to the demands for the prosecution of the crimes of the Franco dictatorship.

However, as this contribution revealed, the framing of memories of Francoist repression in human rights discourses and the associated transnationalization and judicialization of local struggles over how to deal with the dictatorship crimes has been an ambivalent process. The Argentine Complaint successively shifted the focus of debate in Spain to aspects of repression hitherto ignored and focused increasing attention on the repression that took place in the last years of dictatorship and under the transition process that continued after the formal end of the Franco regime in November 1975. On the one hand, the transnational lawsuit has granted visibility to new groups of victims, notably by shedding light on the late Franco period. On the other hand, it has created new hierarchies and exclusions. As already discussed, the difference in the kind of repression suffered in the later years of the dictatorship, whose survivors and perpetrators are still alive, has seen those cases meet with some legal acknowledgement as compared to those concerned with the repression of Civil War and the immediate postwar period. This success in visibility then led to a higher public profile for the "late" victim groups and in that sense to greater public recognition. This saw a certain competition emerge between the different victim groupings, leading to disputes between the associations involved, to the point of weakening the Complaint as a whole. As Montoto has rightly described the "vulnerabilization" and ensuing "precarization" (2017, 4) within the movement of those associations not oriented to late Francoist repression, such as those concerned with the Civil War, the immediate postwar period and the stolen babies, led to internal conflict. The privileging of the victims of the later years led to competitions, tension and conflict among victim groups. The first generation of memory associations concerned with the exhumation of mass graves seem now to get less attention, while the status of the *stolen babies'* relatives as victims of Francoism is frequently put into question, leading to decreased visibility and marginalization within the Complaint process. The final question that needs to be asked is whether there is any way of preventing this kind of sometimes unintentional but almost always debilitating and even harmful conflict from creating hierarchies of victimhood and victim competition when the definition of victim in a given social and political space is contested.

References

Arrington, C., 2016. *Accidental Activists. Victims Movements and Government Accountability in Japan and South Korea.* Ithaca, NY/London: Cornell University Press.

Bonacker, T., 2013. "Global Victimhood. On the Charisma of the Victim in Transitional Justice Processes." *World Political Science Review* 9(1): 97–129.

Bonacker, T., Oettler, A. & Safferling, C., 2013. "Valorising Victims' Ambivalences in Contemporary Trends in Transitional Justice." In Bonacker, T. & Safferling, C. (eds.) *Victims of International Crimes: An Interdisciplinary Discourse.* The Hague: Asser Press/Springer, 279–296.

Capdepón, U., 2015. *Vom Fall Pinochet zu den Verschwundenen des Spanischen Bürgerkrieges. Die Auseinandersetzung mit Diktatur und Menschenrechtsverletzungen in Spanien und Chile.* Bielefeld: Transcript. Global Studies.

Capdepón, U., 2017. "Von Nürnberg nach Madrid? Transnationale Vergangenheitspolitik und universelle Gerichtsbarkeit zur juristischen Auseinandersetzung mit der Franco-Diktatur." In Ganzemüller, J. (ed.) *Recht und Gerechtigkeit. Die strafrechtliche Aufarbeitung der Diktaturen in Europa.* Weimar/Berlin: Böhlau, 231–251.

Capdepón, U., 2019. "The Selectivity of Universal Jurisdiction: The History of Transnational Human Rights Prosecutions in Latin America and Spain." In Quataert, J. & Wildenthal, L. (eds.) *The Routledge History of Human Rights.* New York: Routledge, 507–522.

Druliolle, V., 2015. "Recovering Historical Memory: A Struggle against Silence and Forgetting? The Politics of Victimhood in Spain." *International Journal of Transitional Justice* 9(2): 316–335.

Druliolle, V., 2015. "Spain: Seeking Justice in Argentina." Justiceinfo.net, *Fondation Hirondelle.* Available at: https://www.justiceinfo.net/en/justiceinfo-comment-and-debate/opinion/430-argentina-the-right-to-intervene-in-spain.html [Accessed August 21, 2019].

Druliolle, V., 2018. "The Struggle for Recognition of the Stolen Children and the Politics of Victimhood in Spain." In Id. & Brett, R. (eds.) *The Politics of Victimhood in Post-conflict Societies.* St. Anthony's Series. Oxford: Palgrave Macmillan, 77–99.

Druliolle, V. & Brett, R. (eds.) 2018. "Introduction." In Id. & Brett, R. (eds.) *The Politics of Victimhood in Post-conflict Societies.* St. Anthony's Series. Oxford: Palgrave Macmillan, 1–22.

El País, 2014. *La juez argentina que investiga el franquismo recoge pruebas en España,* May 19.

Encarnación, O. G., 2014. *Democracy without Justice in Spain. The Politics of Forgetting.* Philadelphia: University of Pennsylvania Press.

Escudero, R., Campelo, P., Pérez González, C. & Silva, E., 2013. *Qué hacemos por la memoria histórica.* Madrid: Akal.

Eser, P., 2016. "Die querella argentina – wie spanischer Erinnerungspraxis transnationale Gerechtigkeit widerfahren kann." *Hispanorama* 147: 51–58.

Ferrándiz, F., 2010. "De las fosas comunes a los derechos humanos: El descubrimiento de las *desapariciones forzadas* en la España contemporánea." *Revista de Antropología Social* 19: 161–189.

Ferrándiz, F., 2014. *El pasado bajo tierra. Exhumaciones contemporáneas de la Guerra Civil.* Barcelona: Anthropos.

Hepworth, A., 2020. "Memory Activism across Borders. The Transformative Influence of the Argentinean-Franco Court Case and Activist Protest Movements on Spain's Recovery of Historical Memory." In Sierp, A. & Wüstenfeld, J. (eds.) *Agency in Transnational Memory Politics.* New York: Berghahn (forthcoming, unpublished manuscript).

Huyse, L., 2003. "Victims." In Bloomfield, D., Barnes, T. & Huyse, L. (eds.) *Reconciliation after Violent Conflict: A Handbook.* Stockholm: IDEA, 54–76.

Jelin, E., 2003. *State Repression and the Labors of Memory.* Minneapolis: Minnesota University Press.

Karstedt, S., 2010. "From Absence to Presence, from Silence to Voice. Victims in International and Transitional Justice since the Nuremberg Trials." *International Review of Victimology* 17: 9–30.

McEvoy, K. & McConnachie, K., 2013. "Victims and transitional justice: Voice, agency and blame." *Social and Legal Studies* 22(4): 489–513.

Messuti, A., 2013. "La querella argentina. La aplicación del principio de la justicia universal al caso de las deapariciones forzadas." In Escudero Alday, R. & Pérez González, C. (eds.) *Desapariciones Forzadas, represión política y crímenes del Franquismo.* Madrid: Trotta, 112–140.

Montoto Ugarte, M., 2014. "Una mirada a la crisis del relato mítico de la Transición: La Querella argentina contra los crímenes del Franquismo." *Kamschatka* 4: 125–145.

Montoto Ugarte, M., 2017. "Las víctimas del Franquismo en 'la Querella Argentina': Luchas por el reconocimiento y nuevas desigualdades." *Papeles del CEIC. International Jounrnal on Collective Identity Research*, No. 164: 1–24.

Oettler, A., 2017. *Transitional Justice, Recognition, and Authoritative Power*, GIGA Working Paper, Research Programme Peace and Security: Hamburg, Vol. 305: 5–18.

Público, 2016. Interview with Ascención Medieta, June 21. Available at: https://www.youtube.com/watch?time_continue=8&v=SOWKI9C7-PA&feature=emb_logo [Accessed August 21, 2019].

Rights International Spain (RIS), 2012. *Guerra y Franquismo. La decisión del TEDH en el asunto de Canales Bermejo c. España.* Available at: http://www.rightsinternationalspain.org/uploads/801publicacion/f2d650588e849dbe4480d981d8fee6ecf8b791c0.pdf [Accessed May 5, 2019].

Roht-Arriaza, N., 2003. "Of catalysts and cases: transnational prosecutions and impunity in Latin America." In Davis, M. (ed.) *The Pinochet Case. Origins, Progress and Implications.* London: Institute of Latin American Studies, 191–211.

The Struggle of Victims for Human Rights Trials in Post-Dictatorship Chile

Boris Hau

Seeking justice for the victims of the Pinochet dictatorship

The Chilean state has responded to the human rights violations committed during the dictatorship of Pinochet (1973–1990) through transitional justice policies of truth, reparation and (partial) justice. In 1990 the first democratically elected government installed a first truth commission to respond to claims by relatives of the repressive regime's political opponents, many of whom were "disappeared" or executed. Reparation laws have emerged following the recommendations in the report of that truth commission. However, the process of justice in Chile has been gradual, with relatives of the victims regularly calling for those responsible for crimes under Pinochet to be prosecuted. The struggle of these families against the impunity of the perpetrators has continued for many years now. In response to claims made on behalf of the victims, the Chilean Supreme Court in 2019 rendered judgment in 40 cases against those responsible for human rights violations under the dictatorship. This chapter analyzes the development, impact, and dynamics of such prosecutions, from the end of the dictatorship in 1990 until today, particularly showcasing the role of surviving women in pursuing justice in the courts.

When democracy returned to Chile, relatives of the victims demanded that the transitional government enact policies of truth, justice and reparation. The necessary mechanisms were implemented slowly: first, truth policies were enforced by setting up the Rettig Commission in 1991, followed by reparation programs that were based in part on the final report of the truth commission. Yet the Amnesty Decree-Law No. 2191 – a self-amnesty established in 1978 by the military dictatorship – remains in force because none of the following democratic governments have been willing or able to repeal it. That "decree law" has prevented the prosecution of those responsible for crimes committed between 1973 and 1978. For this reason, the 1990s were characterized by impunity in Chile, although there were a few cases of successful prosecution, such as the conviction of former secret police chief Manuel Contreras for assassinating former minister Orlando Letelier in Washington, DC in 1976. However, the arrest of Pinochet in October 1998 heralded a new stage in transitional justice. A justice process has been initiated that keeps evolving and has obtained guilty judgments against former agents responsible for torture, disappearance and execution of multiple individuals. After 1998, several of the relatives of the "disappeared" or executed have received justice from the courts, inasmuch as perpetrators whom all of them identified as former agents of the dictatorship were investigated and convicted. However, the implementation of these transitional justice policies has not been free of conflict. Upon the return of democracy in 1990, the ex-dictator Augusto Pinochet Ugarte managed to hold on to his power.

This chapter examines current human rights trials on crimes of the dictatorship as well as the consequences of the Pinochet case. It does so especially from the perspective of survivors and victims, while also highlighting the struggle of women for justice. The chapter likewise discusses the Chilean state's responses to these calls for justice, in addition to examining the political and social consequences of judicial accountability for crimes perpetrated under the dictatorship.

Justice, a demand not addressed by post-dictatorship governments

On March 12, 1990, just one day after the return to democracy, newly elected president Patricio Aylwin (1990–1994) gave a speech at the National Stadium, which during the dictatorship years had been turned into a former detention center for political prisoners in the Chilean capital of Santiago. He announced that his government would prioritize the search for truth regarding human rights violations committed during the Pinochet regime. Aylwin was the first democratically elected president of the government formed by the so-called *Concertación de Partidos por la Democracia* (Coalition of Parties for Democracy), a center-left coalition of political parties founded in 1988. During this period, ex-dictator Augusto Pinochet had not retired; he still headed the army, in accordance with the Amnesty Decree-Law which made it impossible to prosecute former agents of the repressive regime (Library of the National Congress of Chile 1978). Cath Collins defines these early years after the dictatorship as a "supervised transition" (2013, 84), thus referring to a democratization process from which the dictator had not yet withdrawn himself. Rather, he kept monitoring the actions of the new government as head of the army, effectively ruling out trials. However, human rights violations committed under the Pinochet regime were a matter that the *Concertación* government aimed to address. This led to the creation, on April 25, 1990, of the above-mentioned *Comisión Nacional de Verdad y Reconciliación* (National Commission on Truth and Reconciliation), also known as the Rettig Commission after its chairman, attorney Raúl Rettig. This commission issued a report revealing a list of victims killed by the Pinochet dictatorship: 1,319 executed and 979 detained-disappeared (Corporación Nacional de Reparación y Reconciliación 1996, 535), whereas all other victims, especially those of torture, were excluded from the report. When announcing this final report of the truth commission, President Aylwin apologized to the relatives of the victims. Subsequent to the Rettig Report, reparation programs were established under Law No. 19123, such as the granting of pensions to the relatives of the executed and "disappeared" (Library of the National Congress of Chile 1991). Despite the work of this first truth commission, effective justice was lacking for years thereafter. The Amnesty Decree-Law left behind by the dictatorship had prevented the criminal prosecution of its security agents responsible for human rights violations. In addition, the presence of Pinochet as head of the army shielded perpetrators of the repression, who retained their positions as army officials. Despite all this, the relatives of the victims continued to demand justice in the courts.

One of the best-known cases in Chile was that of Erika Hennings, who sought justice for her husband Alfonso Chanfreau, a leader of the clandestine MIR (*Movimiento de Izquierda Revolucionaria*, Movement of the Revolutionary Left). He was arrested on July 30, 1974 by agents of the *Dirección de Inteligencia Nacional* (National Intelligence Directorate, DINA), the dictatorship's repressive security agency, and subsequently taken to a secret detention center where he was last seen alive. In 1992, Hennings filed a criminal complaint that was investigated by Judge Gloria Olivares. Her investigation proved that former agents of the DINA were responsible for Chanfreau's kidnapping and disappearance. Nevertheless, the entire investigation was put on hold when the military justice system insisted on investigating the case itself, given that military officials on active duty had been involved. On October 30, 1992, the Supreme Court accepted the jurisdiction of the military courts, transferring the case and the entire investigation to the military justice system, which ultimately applied the Amnesty Decree-Law (Amnesty International 1992). During the first years of democracy, the Chilean Supreme Court continued to endorse the Amnesty Decree-Law, thereby sustaining the impunity of crimes perpetrated under the dictatorship. From his post as commander-in-chief of the army, Pinochet ensured that none of his soldiers would be taken to court.

The standpoint taken by the Supreme Court was nothing new to Roberto Garretón, former lawyer of the Vicariate of Solidarity. In the judiciary, he observed, "absolutely nothing had changed. In general terms, despite the restoration of democracy, the courts kept condoning impunity" (Garretón 2008, 8). Moreover, according to attorney Karinna Fernández, from the return of democracy until 1998, Chilean courts systematically applied the Amnesty Decree-Law *ipso jure*, once it had been determined "that a denounced act constituted an offense perpetrated during the years established in that decree (1973–1978). It was a period characterized by the opposition of the superior courts to the application of the legal and customary precepts of international law" (Fernández 2010, 470).

The premature closing of the judicial investigation into the circumstances of Alfonso Chanfreau's forced disappearance was a decision made by the same judges who, a few years earlier during the Pinochet regime, had systematically rejected writs of *habeas corpus* while delaying criminal complaints on behalf of the victims. In the 1990s, proceedings ordered by Judge Olivares, where military officials had to give evidence in a trial regarding someone who had been "disappeared" while detained, led Pinochet to demand that no further investigations be made of cases from the era of the dictatorship.[1]

To end the tensions with a military which was constantly threatening a new *coup d'état*, justice minister Enrique Correa, a member of Aylwin's administration, negotiated with one of Pinochet's advisors, resulting in the government's support for the *Ley de Punto Final* (Clean Slate Act). This law, aimed at ensuring Pinochet's further immunity from prosecution, stipulated that no trial could be carried out against any former military members, thus putting a final stop to any such proceedings.

Augusto Pinochet continued as commander-in-chief of the army during the subsequent government led by President Eduardo Frei Ruiz-Tagle (1994–2000), from the same coalition of center-left parties. Even though this period was characterized by legal impunity, some sparks of hope were ignited when a few members of the Chilean judiciary declined to apply the Amnesty Decree-Law. For instance, in 1995 the Supreme Court confirmed the legal judgment on the 1976 assassination (in Washington, DC) of diplomat Orlando Letelier, who had served successively as Minister of Foreign Affairs, the Interior and Defense during Salvador Allende's administration. Both men convicted for that murder – the top leader of the DINA, Manuel Contreras,

1 Pinochet had threatened to take action if one of his subordinates were to be affected, declaring: "The day they touch one of my men, the rule of law is over. I have said this once and I will not repeat it; just know that it will be like that" (*El Mercurio* 1989, quoted in Contreras 2003, 30).

as well as DINA agent Pedro Espinoza – were imprisoned at Punta Peuco, a luxury penal institution exclusively created for the detention of military personnel where they received special treatment. The fact that the Amnesty Decree-Law only prevented the prosecution of crimes committed between 1973 and 1978 made it possible to investigate cases originating outside that time frame. Such cases included the 1982 assassination of former union leader Tucapel Jiménez and the 1985 murder of three Communist party members, José Manuel Parada, Manuel Guerrero and Santiago Nattino (also known as the *Caso Degollados*, or "Slit Throats Case"). In both those instances, the Supreme Court (also in 1995) convicted the responsible agents of the dictatorship. Having occurred in the later years of the dictatorship, these were among the crimes not covered by the Amnesty Decree-Law.

The arrest and extradition request against the ex-dictator

October 16, 1998 marked the beginning of the end for the Chilean dictatorship's impunity. On that day, ex-dictator Augusto Pinochet was arrested in a clinic in London under a Spanish extradition request. That arrest would mark a milestone in the process of transitional justice in Chile. While the demands for justice had remained unanswered for years, the arrest of Pinochet brought hope that these demands would start to be adjudicated. However, the arrest of Pinochet in the UK also polarized Chilean society. On the one hand, his supporters protested in the streets for his immediate release; on the other, human rights organizations demanded that he be extradited to and tried in Spain. The latter call related to a legal action initiated two years earlier. On July 5, 1996, attorney Joan Garcés of the President Allende Foundation joined a criminal complaint against ex-dictator Pinochet that had been filed by the Spanish Union of Progressive Prosecutors. That prosecution was based on the crimes of genocide and state terrorism. It had initially been lodged in the name of the seven Spanish citizens killed in Chile under Pinochet's dictatorship. The victims with Spanish nationality named in the legal complaint were: Joan Alsina Hurtos and Antonio Llidó Mengual (both priests), Félix Figueroa Ubach, Michelle Peña Herreros (daughter of republican refugees from the Spanish Civil War), Antonio Elizondo Ormaechea, Carmelo Soria Espinosa (a UN diplomat) and Enrique López Olmedo.

More generally, that 1996 indictment claimed that the Chilean military junta had organized a systematic, massive, and severe repression against an entire sector of the population, "seeking the physical elimination of its members, the arrest, torture, murder, imprisonment or exile of thousands of citizens" (Montoya & Pereyra 2000, 61). In July 1998, Judge Manuel García Castellón reaffirmed that the National Court of Spain had jurisdiction to try the assassinations and "disappearances" recognized in the investigation against Pinochet.

Back in Chile, Pinochet resigned in March 1998 from his post as commander-in-chief of the army. Yet, despite giving up that position after holding it for 24 years, Pinochet had no intention of giving up any of his power. The day after stepping aside, he was sworn in as "senator for life." In this manner, he became a member of the Chilean Senate without democratic legitimation, in the process receiving immunity from prosecution.

It is noteworthy that, 10 months before Pinochet's arrest in London, a criminal indictment against the former dictator had already been filed in Chile. On January 12, 1998, Gladys Marín (General Secretary of the Communist Party) filed the first criminal complaint against Augusto Pinochet, charging him and the DINA with the unlawful 1976 arrest of her spouse, Jorge Muñoz. With that domestic criminal complaint, the barrier of impunity began to collapse (Marín 2009, 141). After reviewing the background information for this indictment against the former dictator, Judge Juan Guzmán declared the case admissible, thereby initiating judicial proceedings against Pinochet (Guzmán 2005, 140).

Shortly after this first domestic indictment, it was Spanish judge Baltasar Garzón who quickly drafted an order that Scotland Yard in London arrest Augusto Pinochet for crimes under investigation by the Spanish National Court (*Audiencia Nacional*). The arrest of Pinochet had worldwide repercussions. For the first time ever, a dictator was being arrested elsewhere for crimes committed under his rule while at the same time being indicted by a foreign government. The principles of "national sovereignty" and "territoriality of law" seemed to have been replaced by new ones, such as the requirement that crimes against humanity be prosecuted internationally based on the principle of universal jurisdiction. Pinochet's arrest gave attorney Eduardo Contreras a sense that "justice was coming. It was a warning to dictators that they could no longer walk freely through the streets of their countries without being prosecuted for their crimes" (Contreras 2003, 67). Pinochet's arrest in London motivated the filing of additional complaints. Even so, the Chilean government ordered his return to Santiago, arguing that he should be tried in his own country. President Eduardo Frei stated that "his government would energetically protest against the British authorities for not respecting the diplomatic immunity of Pinochet" (Montoya & Pereyra 2000, 26). The Families of the Disappeared-Detainees (*Agrupación de Familiares de Detenidos Desaparecidos*, AFDD) issued a statement that Pinochet's arrest was "a significant step toward justice and against the impunity that has been imposed in our country." At the same time, supporters of Pinochet called for their leader to be freed and organized a demonstration in front of the British Embassy (Bartholomew et al. 1998, 20). Human rights lawyer Carmen Hertz explained the relevance of his detention, pointing out that in the first years of democracy there was an "unwritten" acceptance of crimes perpetrated under the dictatorship. As a result, "the arrest of Pinochet ... dramatically highlighted the implicit pacts of impunity on which the Chilean transition was built" (Hertz 2017, 282).

On March 24, 1999, the House of Lords in London agreed once more that an extradition process could be initiated. British judge Ronald Bartle announced on October 8, 1999 that the request made by Spanish judge Garzón was consistent with British law; hence, the extradition of Pinochet to Spain could proceed. Judge Bartle determined that Spain was authorized to prosecute Pinochet for crimes in 34 cases of torture, in addition to 1,198 cases of detained-disappeared victims (Escobar et al. 2000, 38). While the process was taking its course, the Chilean government had no choice but to embark on the "political path." Thus, the Chilean Foreign Ministry requested the return of the ex-dictator for "humanitarian reasons," pressure which ultimately succeeded. After spending 503 days under house arrest in the UK, Pinochet returned to Chile. Upon his arrival at the military section of the Santiago airport, after months of being in a wheelchair in London, he stood up and walked with a cane, saluting the troops who received him enthusiastically. Among those welcoming him back was the head of the army (Loveman & Lira 2002, 294).

Legal responses to demands for domestic prosecutions

Due to the enormous international attention, human rights violations perpetrated under the dictatorship were once again a topic of public interest in Chile. While Pinochet was under house arrest in London, the relatives of the victims had initiated criminal proceedings against him in Chilean courts. As Collins explains, these "were, without exception, a product of private complaints made by relatives and survivors, and many of them were reactivating existing cases which had been dormant or dismissed within the military justice system" (2013, 99).

On March 11, 2000, voters had elected a new president, Ricardo Lagos, Chile's first socialist head of state since Salvador Allende. However, Lagos was a member of the same center-left *Concertación* coalition that had come into office in 1990. Lagos' government created a negotiations forum made up of representatives from the government, universities, churches, and the military, the so-called *Mesa de Diálogo* (Roundtable for Dialogue). The AFDD did not want to participate, arguing that it would not negotiate terms of impunity. The result of this forum for dialogue was a final declaration in which the armed forces undertook to provide information on the fate of the detained-disappeared victims. However, the data they provided was incomplete (Zalaquett 2000, 7). And it was too late, according to the criticism of Viviana Díaz, leader of the AFDD. Finally, one of the results of the Roundtable for Dialogue was a request that the judiciary appoint judges to investigate human rights cases (Garretón 2009, 80).

This new jurisprudence on behalf of the detained-disappeared started with the trial of the victim Miguel Ángel Sandoval, a militant of the MIR. An April 2003 judgment established that the victim had been abducted permanently, thereby rejecting the enforcement of amnesty or a statute of limitations. As the result of this case, former DINA agents were convicted and sent to prison. The Supreme Court supported this legal rationale in a final judgment of November 17, 2004 (Transitional Justice Observatory 2019a). Since Sandoval's case, a jurisprudence based on the argument of permanent abduction has been continuously applied. In the words of Garretón, that judgment set a precedent for cases of detained-disappeared persons, suggesting that the judges "lost their fear of doing justice" (Garretón 2009, 80).

Similar to developments in neighboring Uruguay and Argentina, on September 26, 2006, the Inter-American Court of Human Rights (*Corte Interamericana de Derechos Humanos*, IACtHR) condemned Chile for the case of the teacher Luis Almonacid, a political prisoner executed in 1973.[2] The IACtHR required the state to annul the Amnesty Decree-Law, ruling that Chilean courts should abstain from enforcing it since it was contrary to the American Convention on Human Rights. Furthermore, the IACtHR declared that "the State must ensure that Decree-Law No. 2191 does not remain an obstacle in the investigation, prosecution and, if applicable, punishment of those responsible for similar violations that have taken place in Chile" (IACtHR 2006, 65). In addition, the IACtHR demanded that human rights violations be adjudicated. The Almonacid case had originated in the struggle against impunity by Elvira Gómez, widow of the victim. She had initially filed a criminal complaint before a Chilean court which then responded by

2 This crucial role of the IACtHR sentences in the dynamics of domestic human rights trials can be compared with the changes triggered in post-dictatorship Argentina (see the chapters by Figari Layús and by Sharnak).

citing the Amnesty Decree-Law. Since that instance, however, the Chilean judiciary has abstained from applying amnesty for crimes against humanity. That new precedent was applied for the first time in December 2006, a few months after the IACtHR ruling, specifically in the case of Hugo Vásquez and Mario Superby. Since these two men had been executed for political reasons, the qualification of the crime as a "crime against humanity" was deemed acceptable. The confirmation of that decision invoked the IACtHR's ruling in the Almonacid case (Transitional Justice Observatory 2019a). This new decision has been applied to the criminal complaints filed by surviving victims in cases of torture as well as in cases of compensation paid to victims by the state. Consequently, the Supreme Court and other Chilean courts decided that, in all human rights cases, it was not possible to apply either the statute of limitation or the Amnesty Decree-Law.

From 2000 onwards, Pinochet himself had to face human rights investigations for the crimes perpetrated during his regime since new complaints were being filed in domestic courts. The first instance was known as the Caravan of Death case, referring to a military group that executed political prisoners in several Chilean cities, flying from town to town in a helicopter, in the initial months of the dictatorship (Contreras 2003, 43). On August 8, 2000, Pinochet was formally indicted for this crime. In its decision, the Supreme Court established that there were grounds to presume that the highest authorities of the dictatorship as well as of the army knew of the crimes committed by this group. Then, Judge Juan Guzmán prosecuted the ex-dictator as the "intellectual author" of these crimes. Pinochet's arrest in London had brought at least some satisfaction to many relatives of the victims. They celebrated the fact that, after years of impunity, the main person responsible for the crimes of the dictatorship was being indicted for having "disappeared" and executed detainees. However, Pinochet's return to Chile caused great uncertainty. On July 1, 2002, the Criminal Chamber of the Supreme Court declared that the ex-dictator was unable to stand trial, deeming him "mentally unfit." However, despite being acquitted in the Caravan case, Pinochet was brought to account for other crimes (*BBC* 2006). Finally, on December 10, 2006, at the age of 91, he died without having ever been convicted by Chilean courts.

According to the records of the Transitional Justice Observatory based at the Diego Portales University in Santiago, between 1995 and June 30, 2019, a total of 426 final sentences were handed down for cases involving crimes against humanity perpetrated during the dictatorship. Of these, 365 were in criminal and/or civil matters, and 61 involved civil claims only, that is, claims without an associated criminal component (Transitional Justice Observatory 2019b, 72). These 426 judgments mainly comprised cases ruled upon by the

Criminal Chamber of the Supreme Court. 163 dealt with crimes committed against detained-disappeared victims, 159 with political victims, and 22 with mixed cases ("disappeared," executed, or surviving). For the survivors, there were judgments in 18 criminal cases for torture. Despite the constant struggle to restore justice, most victims have not obtained any yet.

The justice process for the surviving victims of torture only began after complaints on behalf of executed persons had already been investigated. It was the 2004 Valech Report on Political Imprisonment and Torture, the second truth commission in Chile, that not only provided an official list of surviving victims (who had not been taken into account in the first Rettig Truth Commission report), but also disclosed a hidden issue: torture and political imprisonment had been systematically applied violations of human rights during the Pinochet dictatorship. The survivors were then encouraged to file complaints, which were in turn accepted and adjudicated. The first judgment in a survivors' case was handed down by the Supreme Court on September 24, 2009. Former members of the air force were convicted for torturing 17 young leftist militants at the Air War Academy in 1973 and 1974. Neither amnesty nor statutes of limitation were invoked, inasmuch as the crimes contained in that indictment were deemed crimes against humanity.

Another significant legal proceeding was that of Leopoldo García Lucero. A torture survivor who won a landmark case against Chile before the IACtHR, Lucero became the first living survivor of human rights violations to have his case decided by that regional court. A former political prisoner in the Chacabuco concentration camp in the Atacama Desert, he had filed his complaint against the state from London where he had been living in exile since 1975. The state was thus ordered to compensate him for having suffered torture. Subsequently, the court also found that the state had failed to comply with its obligation to open an investigation immediately (IACtHR 2013, 43). However, at the end of 2019, there had still been no verdict issued in Lucero's Chilean proceeding. This individual case is reflected in the official numbers of the second so-called Valech Commission on Political Imprisonment and Torture. For, as of 2019, only 0.58% of the 38,254 victims listed officially in the Valech I and Valech II reports have received a judgment on their complaints in these cases (Transitional Justice Observatory 2019b, 73).

Along with the criminal trials described above, demands for justice in Chile also include litigation in civil courts. A new case law has developed with respect to civil compensation from the state for survivors. Anyone who has been the victim of a crime committed by state officials can petition for monetary compensation, something which had at first been denied by the courts based on the statute of limitations. However, a new ruling in this vein has been established in civil cases by the Supreme Court, and it has been applied consistently since 2015.

According to data from the Transitional Justice Observatory, the Supreme Court has issued 61 judgments in civil suits between 2014 and June 30, 2019. On December 9, 2019, the Supreme Court issued a ruling that accepted a compensation request from Guillermo Torres, a journalist and former political prisoner at the National Stadium, who was later exiled. The state was ordered to provide CLP 100,000,000 (USD 142,857) in compensation. This new jurisprudence of the Supreme Court is based on a judgment in the case of Maria Ordenes Guerra and others, in which the IACtHR condemned the state of Chile on November 29, 2018. This case was presented prior to the new jurisprudence of 2015. Here the IACtHR required the state to refrain from applying the statute of limitations to requests for civil compensation in cases involving crimes of the dictatorship, referring to the new jurisprudence in these cases (IACtHR 2018, 26). That jurisprudence is relevant because it grants direct compensation to surviving victims as well as to the families of executed and "disappeared" victims. The compensation is specifically for the loss of their relatives or for political imprisonment that kept them from fulfilling personal life projects.

After four decades, relatives of the dictatorship's victims are continuing to seek justice. When the Chilean courts adopted the case law of the IACtHR, it paved the way for convicting the main actors of the dictatorship, such as the heads of security agencies. One such case is that of Communist militant Marcelo Concha, who was arrested and "disappeared" in 1976. Forty years after his arrest, his family finally obtained legal justice. The Supreme Court issued a final judgment on October 25, 2016, in which five former DINA agents were sentenced to 10 years and one day in prison for the crime of aggravated kidnapping. Concha's daughter, journalist María Paz Concha, felt that the final sentence against those guilty of the arrest and disappearance of her father gave some closure to a long process of demanding justice: "When the court proceeding closes with the final sentence, a personal cycle comes to an end; however, it never truly ends, because as victims, we want justice in other cases as well, for other people" (quoted in Hau 2018, 157). This also alludes to the fact that justice is still the exception in many other cases of victims of forced "disappearance." Such is the case of the detained-disappeared Carlos Berger, husband of lawyer Carmen Hertz. As of 2019, the Supreme Court has not issued a final sentence yet in this proceeding. Berger is one of the 174 people whose remains have been identified by the Human Rights Unit of the Forensic Medical Service (Servicio Médico Legal 2019). Given that, Carmen Hertz was critical of the fact that the investigation had taken far too long. Not until April 23, 2018 did Judge Hernán Crisosto issue a first appellate judgment, condemning eight retired militants to prison for having executed a group of political prisoners in Calama. The previous minister had delayed the investigation for years, something which Berger's wife deemed a "denial of justice" (Hertz 2017, 323).

According to the Transitional Justice Observatory, there were 174 offenders held in the special prison in Punta Peuco as of July 2018 (Transitional Justice Observatory 2019b, 98). It is worrying that many of them are at an advanced age and therefore eligible for so-called "biological impunity," meaning that they will most likely die without having been given a final verdict or having served their full prison sentence. The vast majority of these prisoners are former members of the armed forces or *Carabineros*, the Chilean police. And the issue of criminal liability for Chilean civilians has not been addressed by such investigations. For instance, there were farm owners or companies that handed over lists of trade unionists to those collaborating with the dictatorship (Fernández & Garcés 2019, 390). Until now, only one civilian has been convicted, namely Francisco Luzoro, in 2016. Luzoro is a truck entrepreneur who participated in the detention and "disappearance" of peasants in Paine, a town south of Santiago and the Chilean municipality with the highest relation of detained-disappeared victims to total inhabitants (Jara & Ugas 2018, 173).

Conclusions: Chile's difficult path towards policies of truth and justice and an end to impunity

Despite progress in Chilean justice, impunity persists. Although judgments have been issued for human rights violations by the dictatorship, most of the victims qualified by the truth commissions are still waiting for justice. Judicial proceedings are not moving forward as quickly as expected because only a few judges are investigating them. An additional problem is the limited penalties issued by Chilean courts. For those condemned have been given very short prison sentences, such as five years for the torture, disappearance and execution of a person. These penalties are not commensurate with the seriousness of the crimes, particularly for crimes against humanity.[3] The dictator himself, Augusto Pinochet, was essentially granted immunity. For he

3 For example, in the June 2018 case of "Hornos de Lonquén," the Supreme Court confirmed a sentence of 15 years' imprisonment for the perpetrators of the detention, torture and disappearance of 15 farmers. This case is about a group of 15 persons detained by policemen in October 1973. They

died before facing judgment, despite being under investigation for numerous crimes.

Another aspect of Chilean impunity is that there have been no institutional reforms of the armed forces or the police. In the fall of 2019, claims resurfaced of massive police violence towards people at public protests, as well as torture in police stations – both of these practices extended and institutionalized during the dictatorship. Complaints on behalf of those victimized have been made by human rights bodies, such as the National Institute of Human Rights. The system of impunity remains a legacy of the dictatorship in today's Chile. The Constitution of 1980 is still in force and the democratically elected presidents have shown no interest in transforming it into a democratically written one. In 2019, there was a political agreement to consult the citizens about changing the constitution through a plebiscite to be held the following year. That constitution endorses a neoliberal economic model that produces enormous social inequality, thereby securing a privileged standard of living for wealthy citizens while leaving the majority of the population with low-quality health and education systems.

The demands for justice in the courts of post-dictatorship Chile have not ceased and have notably been driven by women battling continuously against impunity, as illustrated in this chapter. More than 40 years have passed since the dictatorship ended, but the consequences of its human rights violations are still present in Chilean society. After decades of impunity, the demands for justice have intensified owing to constant efforts made by the relatives of victims and survivors. As a result of their pressure, Chilean courts have travelled the gradual path from impunity and amnesty to a new process that is more auspicious for restoring justice. Because of the Pinochet case, a new jurisprudence emerged in domestic trials, establishing that crimes against humanity were not subject either to a statute of limitation or to applications of the amnesty, even though that the Amnesty Decree-Law of 1978 remains valid.

Twenty years after Pinochet's arrest in London, the Chilean state has made progress in implementing policies of transitional justice. For after years of impunity, the crimes of the dictatorship have begun to be prosecuted. However, the attempt to restore justice is ongoing; many cases have still not been investigated or prosecuted. Nor have all surviving victims had their day in court.

As described in this chapter, Pinochet's arrest was a wake-up call that highlighted the consequences of the prevailing impunity. Twenty years later,

were killed and their bodies thrown into a limekiln. Their relatives had searched for them until their bodies were discovered in 1978.

the "wall of impunity" – buttressed by the amnesty decree and a judicial branch compliant with the dictatorship – is finally caving in. Even though the amnesty decree remains formally in force, Chilean courts have refrained from applying it, in compliance with the rulings of the IACtHR. All in all, the process still faces many challenges. There is the need not just to repeal the amnesty decree implemented during the dictatorship but also to get judges to investigate more quickly due to the fact that many perpetrators will soon die. The trials for the surviving victims have been few when compared with the large number of human rights violations perpetrated. While many complaints are pending, the struggle to restore justice in Chile continues.

References

Amnesty International, 1992. *Chile: La Corte Suprema de justicia continúa bloqueando las investigaciones sobre pasadas violaciones de derechos humanos: El Caso Chanfreau*. Available at: https://www.amnesty.org/es/documents/amr22/017/1992/es/ [Accessed February 18, 2018].

Bartholomew, M., Martinez, M., Rojas, H., Shields, K., Tomic, C. & Trivelli, F., 1998. *Informe sobre la detención de Pinochet en Inglaterra*. Available at: http://www.archivochile.com/Dictadura_militar/pinochet/juicios/DMjuiciopino80036.pdf [Accessed February 18, 2020].

BBC, 2006. "Pinochet: una larga vida." Available at: http://news.bbc.co.uk/hi/spanish/specials/newsid_1414000/1414000.stm [Accessed February 18, 2018].

Collins, C., 2013. "Chile a más de dos décadas de justicia de transición." *Revista de Ciencia Política* [e-journal] 51(2): 79–113. Available at: http://www.revistapolitica.uchile.cl/index.php/RP/article/view/30160/32102 [Accessed February 18, 2020].

Contreras, E., 2003. *El desaforado: crónica del juicio a Pinochet en Chile*. Santiago: El Periodista.

Corporación Nacional de Reparación y Reconciliación, 1996. *Informe de la Corporación Nacional de Reparación y Reconciliación*. Available at: http://pdh.minjusticia.gob.cl/comisiones/ [Accessed February 18, 2018].

Corte Interamericana de Derechos Humanos (IACtHR), 2006. *Caso Almonacid Arellano y otros v. Chile*. Available at: http://www.corteidh.or.cr/docs/casos/articulos/seriec_154_esp.pdf [Accessed February 18, 2020].

Corte Interamericana de Derechos Humanos (IACtHR), 2006. *Caso Omar Maldonado y otros v. Chile*. Available at: http://www.corteidh.or.cr/docs/casos/articulos/seriec_300_esp.pdf [Accessed February 18, 2018].

Corte Interamericana de Derechos Humanos (IACtHR), 2013. *Caso Leopoldo García Lucero v. Chile*. Available at: http://www.corteidh.or.cr/docs/casos/articulos/seriec_267_esp.pdf [Accessed February 18, 2020].

Corte Interamericana de Derechos Humanos (IACtHR), 2018. *Caso Órdenes Guerra y otros v. Chile*. Available at: http://www.corteidh.or.cr/docs/casos/articulos/seriec_372_esp.pdf [Accessed December 20, 2019].

Escobar, C., García, M. & López, D., 2000. *Crímen internacional y jurisdicción universal: el caso Pinochet*. Valencia: Tirant lo Blanch.

Fernández, K., 2010. "Breve análisis de la jurisprudencia chilena, en relación a las graves violaciones a los derechos humanos cometidos durante la dictadura militar." *Estudios constitucionales* [e-journal] 8(1): 467–488. Available at: https://dx.doi.org/10.4067/S0718-52002010000100018 [Accessed February 18, 2018].

Fernández, K. & Garcés, M., 2019. "Los casos de la Pesquera Arauco y Colonia Dignidad." In Bohoslavsky, J. P. et al. (eds.) *Complicidad económica con la dictadura chilena: Un país desigual a la fuerza*. Santiago: Lom.

Garretón, R., 2008. *Los tribunales con jurisdicción penal durante la transición a la democracia en Chile*. Available at: http://www.auschwitzinstitute.org/wp-content/uploads/2015/05/m25aNaturaleza-de-dictadura-Chile.-Rol-de-Poder-judicial.pdf [Accessed February 18, 2018].

Garretón, R., 2009. "Los tribunales con jurisdicción penal durante la transición a la democracia en Chile." In Almqvist, J. & Espósito, C. (eds.) *Justicia transicional en Iberoamérica*. Madrid: Centro de Estudios Políticos y Constitucionales.

Guzmán, J., 2005. *En el borde del mundo: memorias del juez que procesó a Pinochet*. Barcelona: Anagrama.

Hau, B., 2018. "Chile, 40 años de exigencias de verdad y justicia." *Razón Crítica* [e-journal] 4(1): 137–161. Available at: http:// dx.doi.org/10.21789/25007807.1275 [Accessed December 20, 2019].

Hertz, C., 2017. *La Historia fue otra*. Santiago: Debate.

Jara, F. & Ugás, F., 2018. "Caso Paine, episodio Collipeumo, contra Juan Francisco Luzoro Montenegro: el primer civil condenado por crímenes contra la humanidad en Chile." *Anuario de Derechos Humanos* [e-journal] (14): 167–179. Available at: http://dx.doi.org/10.5354/0718-2279.2018.49426 [Accessed December 20, 2019].

Library of the National Congress of Chile, 1978. *Decreto Ley 2.191*. Available at: http://bcn.cl/1v3xd [Accessed February 18, 2018].

Library of the National Congress of Chile, 1991. *Ley 19.123*. Available at: http://bcn.cl/1vuwr [Accessed February 18, 2020].

Loveman, B. & Lira, E., 2002. *El espejismo de la reconciliación política: Chile 1990–2002*. Santiago: Lom.

Marín, G., 2009. *Jamás olvido, jamás perdón*. Santiago: Fundación Gladys Marín.

Montoya, R. & Pereyra, D., 2000. *El caso Pinochet y la impunidad en América Latina*. Buenos Aires: Pandemia.

Servicio Médico Legal, 2019. *Informe anual de la Unidad de DD.HH*. Available at: http://www.sml.gob.cl/wp-content/uploads/2019/12/INFORME-GESTION-DDHH.pdf [Accessed December 20, 2019].

Transitional Justice Observatory of Diego Portales University, 2019a. *Principales hitos Jurisprudenciales en causas DDHH en Chile 1990–2019*. Available at: http://www.derechoshumanos.udp.cl [Accessed December 18, 2019].

Transitional Justice Observatory of Diego Portales University, 2019b. *La Memoria en los tiempos del cólera: verdad, justicia, reparaciones y garantías de no repetición por los crímenes de la dictadura chilena. Informe Anual sobre Derechos Humanos en Chile 2019 del Centro de Derechos Humanos de la Universidad Diego Portales*. Available at: http://www.derechoshumanos.udp.cl/derechoshumanos/images/InformeAnual/2019/01_Memoria_en_tiempos_de_colera.pdf [Accessed December 20, 2019].

Zalaquett, J., 2000. *La mesa de diálogo sobre derechos humanos y el proceso de transición política en Chile*. Available at: http://www.indh.cl/wp-content/uploads/2010/10/Mesa_de-Dialogo_CEP2000.pdf [Accessed February 18, 2018].

The State Against the State

The Impact of Governmental Contradictions on Human Rights Trials and Victims in Argentina

Rosario Figari Layús

This chapter analyzes the role of three different governments – that is, political administrations – in the criminal trials conducted in Argentina since 2005 in an endeavor to bring to justice those responsible for human rights violations and crimes against humanity in the period between 1974 and 1983. It will look at how different governmental attitudes – of support, indifference or disdain – to human rights prosecutions can help reinforce or undermine such processes, thus affecting their potential reparative effects on victims. In Argentina, after more than 20 years of impunity, the Supreme Court's abrogation in 2005 of the legislation introduced in the 1980s to protect military officers from prosecution led to new trials addressing mass violations of human rights. Such trials are currently still taking place throughout the country. The possibility of prosecution represented a significant change in state policy regarding how to deal with the crimes of the past, their perpetrators and victims. Rather than continue the policy of impunity that had been maintained for two decades, the state, as represented by its different institutions and powers (executive, legislative and judicial), began to work against it. However, human rights policies in Argentina can differ greatly from one government to another, reflecting the play of power, interests and constraints in society. From 2005 to 2020, the state has been headed by four different governments: those of Néstor Kirchner (2003–2007), Cristina Fernández de Kirchner (2007–2011, 2011–2015), Mauricio Macri (2015–2019) and Alberto Fernández (2019–present). Each of them adopted and displayed, to a greater or lesser degree, different approaches to the trials, the crimes of the dictatorship and its victims. While the trials enjoyed explicit governmental support – though with significant constraints – under the administrations of Peronists Néstor Kirchner and Cristina Fernández de Kirchner during the first nine years (2006–2015) and again under Alberto Fernández from late 2019, the right-wing government of Mauricio Macri saw a decrease in official support for the trials and a deterioration in the official treatment of victims of human rights violations. This chapter thus seeks to analyze Argentine governments' changing policies on human rights trials over the last 14 years and their consequences for human rights movements and victims. A grasp of the role of governments in the conduct of domestic human rights trials is essential to understanding some of the factors that may expand or reduce their scope and thus their potential reparative impact not only on the victims of terrible crimes but also on other sectors of society.

The results presented in this chapter are based on data gathered during interviews and on contemporary information sources such as newspapers and government and NGO reports published between 2011 and 2019. Interviews were carried out with actors in the trials, among them victims, witnesses, lawyers, judges and other members of the legal system involved in the trials, as well as academics and human rights activists. Even though this chapter evaluates some of the dynamics of these trials, it is important to bear in mind that they are still ongoing. The analysis here thus treats these findings not as a final outcome, but rather as a partial result.

The chapter is divided into four sections. The first part briefly analyzes the potential of human rights trials in terms of reparation and acknowledgement for victims of human rights violations. This is followed by a second section that deals with the role of the state and its obligations regarding the implementation of human rights and the conduct of human rights prosecutions. The third section offers a historical account of state repression and of the political and legal steps that led to the abrogation of the impunity legislation between 2003 and 2005. This includes a brief overview of the Kirchner administration and its policies toward the crimes of the dictatorship. The fourth section analyzes the dynamics and conduct of the trials during the "Kirchnerist" period of 2006–2015, highlighting not only the progress made but also the shortcomings and the most important problems cited by the actors involved. This section also gives an account of developments and problems under the administration of Mauricio Macri (2015–2019), which had little regard for the human rights problem. And finally, I briefly summarize the challenges faced by the state when seeking to provide legal redress to victims of human rights violations.

The reparative potential of human rights trials

In analyzing the role of the state and of different political administrations in the conduct of trials for human rights violations, it is important first to note the great potential of human rights prosecutions as a means of making reparation to the victims of atrocities. Penal sanctions on state perpetrators communicate publicly that the horrors of the past deserve condemnation by both the state and society. Criminal trials are thus a way for the state to express "institutional disapproval of official policies that resulted in the violation of human rights" (Malmud-Goti 1989).

In an earlier publication (2017) I analyzed reparation as the possibility of change and transformation. To be reparative, such change should in some way modify the legal, political and social conditions that help reproduce over time the damage done to the victims of repression. Impunity is one of the main social and legal conditions for the ongoing re-victimization of victims. The legal system penetrates and textures society and social relations (O'Donnell 1998, 15). The law, in its content and application, is largely a dynamic condensation of power relations that can generate changes in society. The state, through the formulation and implementation of law and also through its public discourse, seeks and indeed succeeds in influencing and even shaping public social behavior in favor of a certain social order corresponding to the power relations prevailing in each historical context (Tyler 2006). The various branches of government – executive, legislative and judicial – therefore play a crucial role in shaping public perceptions of mass atrocities and their victims and social attitudes toward them. Changes in the ways criminal justice deals with human rights violations can affect power relations within the state and also impact social interactions and victims' lives. As will be shown below, while during the Kirchnerist period many victims felt supported by the state and could see pertinent changes in their social environment (Figari Layús 2017), the anti-human-rights-movement stance of the Macri administration represented for many victims a return towards the official discourse prevailing in the decades of impunity that followed the end of the dictatorship; this government's attitude led to the withdrawal of concrete support for trials, causing frustration to survivors and human rights organizations. This partial success in Argentina is far from the universal experience, and a number of contributions to this volume (e.g. those on Kenya or the Argentine Complaint) show that prosecutions do not necessarily afford reparation to victims or societies. The extent to which retributive justice can acquire reparative dimensions depends on several factors, one being the role played by the state – and the government – at national and local levels and by its different institutions, such as the judiciary. A victim-centered perspective and the official, public acknowledgement of the role of state institutions – recognizing the wrongdoings of the state in the past and its responsibility for the violations committed against survivors, disappeared persons and their relatives – are crucial to such a process of reparation. The reparative impact of prosecutions on both victims and wider society thus depends much on the role played by the state, which can strengthen or undermine their scope and social effects.

In Argentina, even though intense and continuous struggle by civil society did lead to some degree of accountability, as exemplified by the trials of the juntas in the 1980s and a number of favorable changes in Argentine legislation during the 1990s and the 2000s,[1] the state, in the person of successive governments, generally denied its victimized citizens the right to their own justice.

The crimes of kidnapping, torture, rape and disappearance were thus reinforced and legitimated as the state imposed and maintained widespread legal impunity for perpetrators in the years following the dictatorship. As in the cases of Chile and Uruguay considered in other chapters, the Interamerican System of Human Rights played a crucial role in the fight against impunity in Argentina. Nonetheless, the state maintained its commitment to impunity for decades, an impunity that simply reproduced the unequal application of the law in favor of perpetrators, depriving victims of their rights and turning them into second-class citizens (Figari Layús 2017). Against this background, legal acknowledgement and penal sanction are able to play a role as mechanisms of control over the state and its agents, serving as means to democratization and to the recognition and inclusion of victims in the justice system.

Domestic trials can make holders of political power accountable, obliging public officials to justify their acts and policies, so helping ensure compliance with the human rights recognized by constitutions, international conventions and national laws (Gloppen, Gargarella & Skaar 2004, 1). In this sense, the legal system – by way of prosecutions, legal amnesties or pardons – can either help perpetuate human rights violations or address them and guarantee compliance with human rights and the rule of law, becoming in the latter case an instrument of social change. To make this change possible, the current state, through the new governmental regime, needs to distinguish itself from the past state that committed the systematic human rights violations. This is no easy task, since it implies the state's confrontation with official perpetrators who in many cases are still present in state institutions. The conduct of trials for systematic human rights violations, especially in countries where impunity ruled for years, is a first indicator of a current state's "will to change," its intention to break with the past. However, the mere holding of trials is not

1 One such change was the constitutional reform of 1994, which introduced Article 75, according to which international treaties take precedence over domestic laws. Furthermore, in 1995, the Argentine National Congress passed Law No. 24556, whereby it approved the ratification of the Inter-American Convention on the Forced Disappearance of Persons.

enough. Justice and reparation for mass atrocities require sustained support over time. In this context, support means making available enough staff and material resources, as well as the implementation of specific measures that guarantee the proper conduct of the trials from a victim-centered perspective. As will be shown below, such support has not been consistent over time.

State repression and the long path to justice in Argentina

For a better understanding of the potential, course and impact of the trials, it is worth outlining the features of the repression exercised by the Argentine dictatorship. On March 24, 1976, a military junta seized power in a military coup, the so-called Process of National Re-organization (*Proceso de Reorganización Nacional*; in short, *Proceso*). The regime established was crucially reliant on an apparatus of covert torture centers where military and police forces kidnapped and mostly murdered those regarded as opponents. The approximately 500 detention centers located throughout the country served as the organizational basis for the systematic disappearance of thousands of persons (CONADEP 2013; Calveiro 1998). Members of armed groups, their families and friends, as well as student representatives, labor unionists, and indeed anyone who voiced criticism of the social, political, and economic policies of the government were abducted, tortured, and ultimately made to disappear. Bodies were disposed of in different ways, among them the so-called *asaderos* (literally "rotisseries"), in which bodies were incinerated with the dual purpose of concealing both the death of the person and his or her identity; on other occasions death might be disguised as a result of an exchange of fire. Detainees were also thrown alive into the sea on the so-called "death flights" that saw bodies washed up along the Argentine and Uruguayan coasts (Verbitsky 2004). According to human rights groups, some 30,000 people were forcibly disappeared by the regime.

When civilian rule returned to Argentina in 1983, survivors, relatives of the disappeared, human rights groups and other political organizations demanded investigation of the crimes and the prosecution of those responsible. In 1984 and 1985, the leaders of the first three Argentine juntas of 1976–1983 were put on trial and sentenced to life imprisonment. However, expectation that justice would prevail more generally was dashed by the adoption of laws foreclosing any further prosecution of former military leaders for human rights crimes. The "Full Stop" (*Ley de Punto Final*) and "Due Obedience" laws (*Ley de Obediencia Debida*) were passed in 1986 and 1987 respectively, and pardons were granted by former president Carlos Menem in 1989 and

1990. Yet human rights groups continued to demand justice. Finally, the abrogation of these laws by Congress in 2003 and by the Argentine Supreme Court in 2005 again made prosecution for the violation of human rights possible. Following the Supreme Court decision in 2005, many new cases were brought to trial and prosecutions for crimes against humanity began to be brought systematically in many provinces of the country. Hundreds of survivors and other witnesses have given their testimonies, turning their memories and suffering into legally valid evidence. Unlike the junta trials of the 1980s, current prosecutions include not only key leaders, but also mid- and low-ranking perpetrators, and although prosecutions are still focused on military and police personnel, they are gradually coming to include civilians who contributed to the crimes in different ways, among them a priest, judges, and entrepreneurs. Moreover, current prosecutions also cover atrocities committed by state-sponsored security agencies prior to the *coup d'état* of 1976. This extends state responsibility beyond the period of military rule, illuminating another facet of state terrorism that was arguably overlooked by justice in the 1980s (Filippini 2009, 3).

As Figure 1 shows, between January 2006 and December 2019, 238 verdicts were issued by different federal courts in almost every province of the country and 982 former military personnel, police officers and civilians were convicted (Procuraduría de Crímenes contra la Humanidad 2019).

Figure 1. Number of verdicts issued per year between January 2006 and December 2019

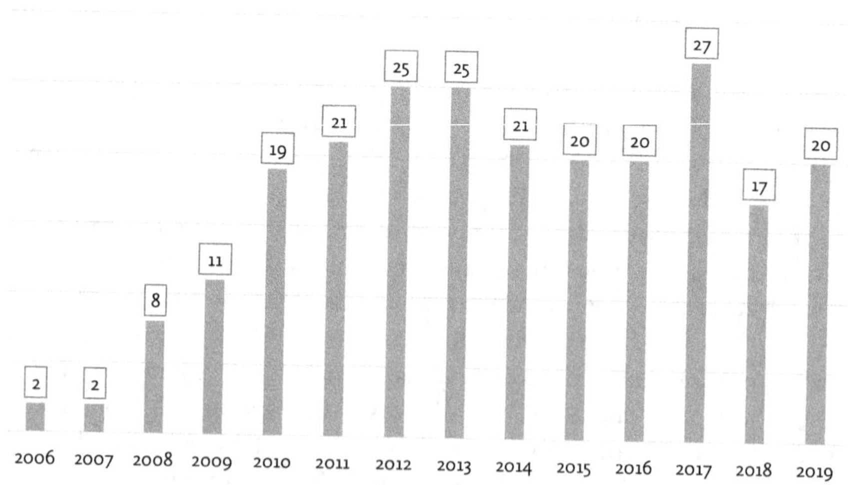

Source: Procuraduría de Crímenes contra la Humanidad 2018, 2019

Over the first three years or so, only a small number of trials were held, mostly dealing with a single accused, as opposed to large trials covering numerous perpetrators, victims, and offenses (Figari Layús 2017). This started to change gradually in 2010 when the Prosecution Coordination Unit began to introduce logistical and legal strategies to aggregate hitherto individual cases into larger trials incorporating many victims, perpetrators and offenses, the so-called "megacausas" ("mega-cases"). The large scale of these cases meant that judicial investigations and public hearings lasted much longer than they had done.

The continuity demonstrated in Figure 1 is a positive sign that the prosecution of human rights violations has not been directly affected by changes of government, having acquired the character of a state policy that goes beyond whoever is in office for the time being. However, though human rights trials cannot be abruptly halted by a new regime – especially if the new government claims to be democratic – there are different ways to undermine them. In what follows, I identify clear trends in the development of official stances towards human rights prosecutions and victims of crimes in the period between 2005 and 2019.

Advances and shortcomings in the conduct of human rights trials in Argentina

"Kirchnerismo": reparation and contradiction

Between 2006 and 2015 (when the two Kirchners held presidential office, known as *Kirchnerismo* or the Kirchnerist period) the state played a generally supportive role in the conduct of the trials, though subject to serious limitations and constraints. Responding to the intense work of human rights organizations, the government of President Néstor Kirchner (2003–2007) initiated a new and decisive justice policy focusing on the criminal prosecution of human rights violations committed during the civilian-military dictatorship. This saw the government take specific material and symbolic measures of great significance to survivors and relatives of the disappeared.

President Kirchner spoke out strongly against the dictatorship and supported the judges' declaration of the unconstitutionality of the impunity laws. The current trials are thus seen by many victims to be the outcome of a years-long struggle by the human rights movement that eventually found a positive, concrete response from the Kirchner government. As a survivor and member of a human rights organization from Buenos Aires explains:

> Kirchner embraced the struggle of the human rights organizations … as if it were his own struggle, and gave it practical effect. Otherwise, we wouldn't be at this stage of the trials. For me it was essential. (Interview 1, March 2011, Buenos Aires)

Another survivor interviewee, who participated in the trials as a complainant, explained the political role of the Kirchner government as follows:

> I think it's dialectical. The human rights organizations have been campaigning since the military dictatorship. The [human rights] organizations have always been there. What I think is that when Menem granted the pardons, the human rights organizations were there, but he didn't care. When Alfonsín passed the Due Obedience and Full Stop laws, the human rights organizations were the same ones as now … [But he] passed the impunity laws anyway. I think it's a political decision when you ask "Who do I listen to when making such an important political decision?" The human rights organizations were always there. Who do they listen to? To those who want impunity? … Or those who are fighting for truth and justice? I think there's a political decision about who to listen to. (Interview 2, March 2011, Buenos Aires)

Many interviewees understood the launch of the trials to be a *political decision*, but that does not mean that the conduct of those trials thereafter was political or "victor's justice," as many detractors of the trials contend.[2] Once started, the trials followed the normal course and typical procedural stages of any regular trial in Argentina. One of the elements that actually made this kind of decision a *political* one was the previous adoption of the impunity laws.

In fact, a number of changes began to make themselves evident under the Kirchner administration. Although the Supreme Court had still not decided on the constitutionality of the impunity laws, its composition changed substantially following the presidential election in 2003. Several judges retired or were ousted on corruption charges and some of the new judges had a more pro-human-rights background (Roht-Arriaza 2004, 116). Another measure

2 Those who oppose the trials and describe them as a form of "revenge" are mainly right-wing groups and conservative political parties that justify the military repression in the 1970s (Fran 2010; *Telam* 2015).

that Kirchner undertook after only five days in office was to purge many top-ranking officers from the military. This cemented civilian control of the military. In addition, Kirchner appointed Roberto Bendini, a relatively junior general, to the post of Army Chief-of-Staff. By Army custom, when a general is appointed to this top post, all officers above that rank who are thus by-passed for promotion are expected to retire. Thus, Kirchner's move required the retirement of almost half of the top generals (Roehrig 2009, 737). Kirchner's administration also deployed a multiplicity of symbolic measures, including the creation of a memorial wall featuring victims' names and the transformation of several former clandestine detention centers, such as the ex-ESMA, into museums and memorials for the disappeared victims (Schindel 2012). An important symbolic act marking disapproval of the crimes of the dictatorship occurred in 2004, when Kirchner ordered the removal of the pictures of General Jorge Videla and General Reynaldo Bignone, both former members of the junta, from the gallery of presidential portraits at the military college on the outskirts of Buenos Aires (Telam 2013). The act took only a few seconds, but its symbolism sent a very strong message to victims. Indeed, several interviewees mentioned this event as something they would never forget. It gave the victims confidence in the new government's intention to take human rights and the victims of the abuse of human rights seriously (Seidel 2014, 130).

For many of them, the trials helped to foster certain positive changes in their own cities. Social and institutional attitudes toward survivors and relatives of the disappeared changed. The trials represent a type of restitution since both human rights violations and legal impunity trample on citizens' rights, depriving victims of the same rights and opportunities before the law as any other citizen. In Argentina, legal impunity, albeit under formally democratic governments, made second-class citizens of survivors and relatives of the disappeared, for they were excluded from access to justice (Figari Layús 2017). Human rights trials did the opposite, recognizing such individuals as full citizens by reintegrating them into the legal system. As stated by one of the complainants, a daughter of disappeared parents from the city of Buenos Aires, when describing her feelings as she gave testimony: "It's the first time the State has listened to what I have to say. It has listened to me as a victim of genocide … The State has listened to my family history and everything, for me it was an important moment" (Interview 3, September 2012, Buenos Aires).

The trials mark an important change for victims by including and recognizing them as citizens and full participants in the state and society. They are no longer invisible. The trials grant victims their rights. By bringing those responsible for human rights violations to justice, the trials express a clear rejection of state repression. Human rights violations are no longer officially supported, and the state now officially restores the rights of victims, allowing them lay complaints for human rights violations and have these investigated rather than ignored. As a survivor from Tucumán said: "We feel supported by the State policy now in place, and the military are no longer what they were back then, they've lost power and influence, so in most cases people begin to dare to speak out" (Interview 4, September 2012, Tucumán).

As this interviewee says, the trials provided many victims with the feeling that the state supported them, while at the same time withdrawing its support from the military and the police officers suspected of crimes against humanity.

The judicial hearings represented new social and institutional spaces in which victims could talk and be heard. Yet while conditions had changed from the days of impunity, there was still much to do, as declared by a complainant from Buenos Aires: "There were people who did not testify [earlier] because they were afraid, and now they can, because conditions are different, if still not ideal" (Interview 5, October 2012, Buenos Aires). While, as the interviewees emphasized, that context was not "ideal" – and probably never would be – it represented a break from the previous context of oppression and impunity. The staging of human rights trials where previously terror and impunity had been the norm was thus a very significant index of change in the state's attitude toward victims.

Many of the victims interviewed said that they saw significant change in others' attitudes toward them, both during and after the trials. They have felt a greater sense of solidarity, respect and recognition from others since the trials started. Other victims say that since the trials have begun, they have felt that their voices are finally being heard by society and by relevant institutions (Figari Layús 2017). This has been reflected not only in public tributes paid to them but also in their being included and invited to participate in institutional spaces that had been closed to them before. Some survivors, for example, report being invited to deliver public lectures at schools, at former clandestine detention centers converted into memorials, or at universities, and also being interviewed by the press. Very little such public attention had been granted over the previous 30 years, certainly not in the provinces, far away from the capital, Buenos Aires.

The human rights trials were thus both the result and cause of changes in the political and social context in which victims lived. This was a dialectical process. As many interviewees say, the institution of domestic human rights trials and the support of the Néstor Kirchner administration changed political and social conditions; and once in progress, the trials themselves began to influence and transform the social and political context in which they were taking place. The trials thus promoted the emergence of a social context conducive to reparation, as many interviewees explained – a context very different from the one that existed before. As one survivor from Tucumán put it: "All this came as a refreshing and restorative rain in an environment that had always been very painful for us" (Interview 4, September 2012, Tucumán).

However, while the government was quite strongly involved in the initial thrust, there did not seem to be sufficient support for the efficient conduct of the trials. The administrations of Néstor Kirchner (2003–2007) and Cristina Fernández (2007–2011, 2011–2015) deployed a number of specialist institutions and programs to support the trials, notably the National Plan for Support and Assistance to Complainants and Witnesses, Victims of State Terrorism (*Plan Nacional de Acompañamiento y Asistencia a los Querellantes y Testigos, Víctimas del Terrorismo de Estado*), to offer psychological support to victims and witnesses over the course of the trials and in particular when called upon to testify, and a plan for the protection of witnesses and victims taking part in the trials. Both formed part of the *Verdad y Justicia* (Truth and Justice) program within the Ministry of Justice. In 2008, the government of Cristina Fernández set up a Prosecution Coordination Unit for the prosecution of human rights violations (*Unidad Fiscal de Coordinación y Seguimiento de las Causas por Violaciones a los Derechos Humanos cometidas durante el terrorismo de Estado*) alongside the Truth and Justice program, tasked with carrying out investigations and issuing guidelines for all public prosecutors throughout the country working on these trials. Victims and human rights organizations, however, criticized the fact that the introduction of these measures was not accompanied by the provision of sufficient public prosecutors and other personnel. This meant that, during the early years especially, many prosecutors had to work on the human rights trials in addition to their usual caseload. Many victims believed that judicial investigations were hampered by lack of resources.

Furthermore, the "slowness" of the hearings is repeatedly mentioned as the chief shortcoming by several interviewees. Inadequate provision of material and human resources meant a shortage of judges and lawyers, as well as a lack of courtroom space. Even when creative attempts were made to rectify the situation – one criminal trial, for instance, was conducted in a soccer stadium, another in a theater, for lack of courtrooms – there did not seem to be the political and legal will to find a long-term solution to the problem. The failure to support the trials by funding additional staff and new spaces was ultimately the result of a political decision. In this sense, the Kirchner and Fernández administrations manifested significant contradictions in instituting a justice policy that in practice did not provide the infrastructure necessary for the trials.

The issue of witness protection was especially troublesome during the Kirchner administration, especially after the disappearance of Jorge Julio López, one of the key witnesses and joint complainants in the trial of a former police commander in the province of Buenos Aires in 2006. After López identified the accused as one of the men who had tortured him in 1976, he was "disappeared" days before the verdict. The lack of progress in this case saw harsh criticisms made of the governments of Néstor Kirchner and Cristina Fernández. Fourteen years after López's disappearance, indeed, the investigation has not progressed significantly.

Given these very significant problems, one could say that the Kirchnerist period saw the state's justice policy go round in circles. While it was characterized by a strong initial impetus, reflected in symbolic and practical measures such as the creation of programs and institutions, it then seemed to lose momentum, with serious difficulty experienced in sustaining these measures over time, due to the lack of resources allocated. This policy ambiguity had an adverse impact on the progress of the trials, leading to the disappointment of some victims.

"Macrismo": official disdain for human rights

While trials continued to take place under the Macri administration, the government's stance toward them was completely different, offering a clear example of the difference between the state and the government. Following the installation of the right-wing government of Mauricio Macri in December 2015, the continuation of existing difficulties and new and worrying developments in the field of human rights policy adversely affected the conduct of the trials and led to victims feeling that they did not have the same support as before. With the new government, the victim-centered approach previously adopted by the state began to change. Ever since his days as mayor of Buenos Aires, Macri's attitude to the human rights policies promoted by the governments of Néstor Kirchner and Cristina Fernández had been one of reservation and disparagement. When running for the presidency in 2014, for example, he referred to state-sponsored human rights policies as a "*curro*" (a colloquial, derogatory term used in Argentina for a robbery or fraud) and described current prosecutions of military personnel as "revanchist" (Pertot, 2014), outraging national and international organizations and revealing what his position would be if he was elected president.

Although Macri's administration (2015–2019) did not halt the trials, it adopted measures that affected them. Among these were a reduction in the already insufficient budget for investigations, which increased delays in the conduct of public hearings, and the appointment to government positions of individuals supportive of the military, accompanied by repeated gestures and expressions of disinterest and even disdain for human rights organizations and their concern for human rights violations committed during the dictatorship (Verbitsky 2017; Calloni 2016; Ginzberg 2016a).

Budget cuts were among the most worrying measures, a sign of the new government's attitude toward the prosecutions. The situation worsened notably in 2016, when massive layoffs of state employees hit those involved in working in one way or another on the trials: dedicated archival researchers in a number of ministries, the Ulloa Centre for the psychological support of victims, the Truth and Justice Program and the Human Rights Secretariat (CELS 2016, 28).[3] Already by the end of January 2016, only a month after Macri took office, there had been 489 dismissals in areas of work connected with human rights (*Página 12* 2016). The recruitment of controversial individuals linked to the military to key government positions related to human rights was also a cause for concern to victims and organizations working in the field. A notable example was the appointment as director of the National Witness Protection Program of former military officer Francisco Lagos, himself the son of retired colonel Luis Hilario Lagos, who had taught at the School of the Americas in the years of the dictatorship (Ginzberg 2016b). Enrique Fukman, a survivor and complainant in the trials, said of this that: "Appointing an individual who was a member of the Army to be the head of Witness Protection policies is an in-security measure for all of us" (quoted in Dandan 2016).

Although during his presidential campaign Macri had expressed his commitment to strengthening the rule of law, strictly respecting the separation of powers and other constitutional principles and guarantees, among them the independence of the judiciary and full freedom of expression, he betrayed his electoral promises as soon as he took office in unilaterally filling two vacancies on Argentina's Supreme Court by presidential decree. The decision sparked popular outrage, with over 20,000 people demonstrating outside the Argentine Congress against Macri's economic package and the appointment of the Supreme Court judges. This was just the first of a series of attempts to gain influence over the judiciary. Indeed, the new government's attitude did not leave the judiciary unaffected. In May 2017, Argentine society and human

3 An example is the dismissal of 15 of the 33 employees working in the Human Rights Office of the Ministry of Security. With this, the team responsible for analyzing the archives of the dictatorship and assisting the federal courts with evidence, known as the *Grupo Especial de Relevamiento Documental* (Documentary Investigations Special Group), was dismantled (Ginzberg 2016b).

rights organizations were shocked by a Supreme Court ruling that reduced the sentence of Luis Muiña, a former soldier who had been sentenced in 2011 to 13 years' imprisonment for the kidnapping and torture of five people under the dictatorship. Three of the five judges – including the two appointed by Macri – ruled that the time Muiña had served in prison before conviction should count double toward his final sentence, meaning that he could be released eight years early. The Supreme Court ruling was based on a repealed law from the 1990s that had not previously been applied to human rights convictions but only to ordinary criminal cases. The so-called "two-for-one law" allowed every day spent in prison before a final sentence to count for two days when more than two years had been served. Allowed to stand, this ruling in the Muiña case would have established a precedent allowing the law be applied to other human rights cases and also appeals against sentence in the future, benefiting some 350 convicted former military officers serving sentences for crimes against humanity.

The decision was a clear expression of a synchronization between the judicial system and the political interests of the new government. However, tens of thousands of Argentines protested against the judgment in Buenos Aires under the slogan "Judges: Never again. No free genocidists." In a statement to the press, Estela de Carlotto, head of the human rights organization *Abuelas de Plaza de Mayo*, called the Supreme Court's decision "abominable." "This government is trying to make forgetfulness normal," she added (*The Guardian* 2017). As a result of the mass protest, the Congress passed a law clarifying that the "two-for-one formula" was not be applied to crimes against humanity, genocide or war crimes.

The new political climate was also reflected in other changes in the judicial treatment of the accused and their conditions of detention. During Macri's administration, there was an increase the numbers of former soldiers granted house arrest as a substitute for imprisonment, which Argentine law allows to prisoners over 70. Furthermore, many who were serving their sentences in prison were relocated to Unit 34 of the Campo de Mayo Prison, known as a "VIP Prison," whose reopening at the end of 2016 was robustly criticized by the Prosecutor for Crimes against Humanity. This prison in the town of Campo de Mayo, which offers yoga and singing classes for its inmates, had been closed in 2013 after the escape of two ex-soldiers. According to the Prosecutor, the security problems at Campo de Mayo had still not been resolved. The issue here is not the improvement in conditions of detention, but rather that such conditions were granted only to a privileged group convicted of crimes against humanity and not to thousands of ordinary prisoners who lived in inhumane conditions.

Interestingly, the relative positions of national and local governments with respect to the trials was now the reverse of that in the time of *Kirchnerismo*. The role played by the few local governments supportive of the trials could help counter – although only to a certain extent – the disregard in which the national government held human rights prosecutions. Such local support, however, could not conceal the fact that the public political rhetoric and policy of the Macri administration manifested indifference, disrespect and disdain for victims and the human rights movement. In August 2017, Macri scandalized the human rights community when he appeared to doubt the long-accepted historical understanding that 30,000 people were made to disappear under the dictatorship. Asked in a foreign TV interview how many people had been murdered, he testily replied: "I have no idea. That's a debate I'm not going to enter, whether they were 9,000 or 30,000" (*The Guardian* 2017). In fact, several officials of his government, sympathizers with the military regime, had long raised doubts over the number of disappeared, but Macri's words marked the first time that such denialist rhetoric gained admittance to mainstream political discourse. The 9,000 cited by Macri refers to a list of names compiled in the first years of democracy by the National Commission on the Disappearance of Persons (*Comisión Nacional sobre la Desaparición de Personas*, CONADEP). Long touted by denialists as the only valid count, this list was never intended to be final. Work still continues today on the identification of human remains in secret, unmarked mass graves. Furthermore, the CONADEP list did not include non-disappeared victims whose bodies were returned to their families or the undoubtedly vast number of unreported victims. The actual number of disappeared, however, was not really the issue, but rather Macri's open provocation of the human rights movement. The Macri administration's public discourse on the dictatorship reveals an important ideological turn in relation to the interpretation of the past put forward by *Kirchnerismo*. The dictatorship was no longer characterized as state terrorism or genocide, as it had been during the Kirchnerist period, but as a "dirty war," a narrative already established during the dictatorship in order to put victims and perpetrators on the same level. Macri's use of the term "dirty war" also chimed with denialist thinking, which holds that there was no genocide, only an internal battle between the dictatorship and "terrorists."[4] Furthermore, while Macri said that he had no time available to meet with human rights organizations (*El País* 2016), members of his government seemed to have

4 Partly to stop such creeping denialism, Argentina's Supreme Court ruled in 2009 that the dictatorship's killings between 1976 and 1983 constituted "crimes against humanity within the framework of [a] genocide."

time to meet pro-military activists such as Cecilia Pando and the Center for Legal Studies on Terrorism and its Victims – CELTYV (*Centro de Estudios Legales sobre el Terrorismo y sus Víctimas*), a group pressuring to reopen trials against former guerrillas even though the Supreme Court has conclusively ruled that guerrilla actions constituted ordinary crimes that have long fallen under the statute of limitations. For these, who then had the ear of Macri's government, former soldiers in prison were "political prisoners" who should be amnestied (*The Guardian* 2017). These opinions appeared to have received a sympathetic hearing from Macri's administration. Validating the "dirty war" understanding of the dictatorship, Secretary for Human Rights Claudio Avruj declared after meeting CELTYV representative Victoria Villarruel that: "What they seek is very valid, the recognition of civilians killed by terrorist groups" (*La Nación* 2016). Human rights activist Estela de Carlotto would ask: "What are they seeking with this new language they've invented for human rights? … Why do they meet with representatives of groups who claim that convicted murderers are political prisoners? They're not political prisoners, they are genocidal killers, abominable assassins who refuse to confess who they gave our grandchildren to" (*Página 12* 2017). The Macri administration's political (and economic) sympathy for the former military government and its contempt for the human rights movement was difficult to hide.

Along with these kinds of public declarations, the introduction of measures intended to restrict the free expression of contemporary social movements and increase the role of the military in matters of domestic security issues was worrisome. In July 2018, President Macri announced that the armed forces would take on tasks related to domestic and border security "to protect national sovereignty and the integrity of [Argentina's] territory." This expansion of the responsibilities of the armed forces was effected by decree, a move immediately criticized by human rights organizations. Macri said he wanted to lift the ban on military involvement in fighting crime, terrorist threats and other domestic security issues. However, human rights activists argued that President Macri's decree could authorize military espionage, repression and violence. According to CELS: "Involving the Armed Forces in security issues threatens civil government and human rights … we have to reject this reform and defend the strict separation between defense and security" (*Buenos Aires Times* 2018). Human rights organizations and thousands of protesters marched in Buenos Aires from the famous Plaza de Mayo to the Defense Ministry, rejecting the decree and calling for it to be withdrawn. Many demonstrators accused the government of secretly intending to militarize the nation's streets in the face of growing social unrest. Former defense minister Agustín Rossi (2013–2015) argued that the separation of national defense from internal security had been state policy since 1983 and should remain unchanged (ibid.). In fact, such reforms of the Defense Law were likely to give the armed forces the power to intervene in social conflicts, thus reinforcing the role of Gendarmerie, another questionable security force operating within the national borders.

In general terms, the support provided to the victims under *Kirchnerismo* seemed to evaporate under the Macri administration. The situation, however, appears to have changed again with the Peronist/Kirchnerist victory in the presidential election of 2019. Like Néstor Kirchner, the new president Alberto Fernández is more sympathetic to the human rights movement and its demands. He owed his victory not only to his human rights views but also to the fact that Macri's government had seen inflation, poverty and unemployment soar, while social protest and political opposition were criminalized. However, in assessing these changes it is important to bear in mind that prosecutions are ongoing and the Fernández government is only in its early days.

Concluding reflections

This chapter has shown how the position of the state and of the governments that represent it at the national and local level can impact human rights trials with significant consequences for victims. The position adopted – ranging from explicit support reflected in material, political, financial or symbolic measures on the one hand to a disdain and disregard that find expression in budgetary cuts and even sympathy and solidarity with human rights abusers on the other – affects the trials' potential as means of official reparation to the victims of human rights violations. In this respect, it should be noted that the mere conduct of trials is not enough to if they are to properly fulfill their reparative function as an acknowledgement of the state's own responsibility for the perpetration of serious crimes. While trials need to be supported in terms of process (through the provision, amongst other things, of material and symbolic resources), the state has also to adopt corresponding human rights policies. The adoption of measures that call victims into question and enable practices similar to those pursued by the repressive state of the past hinders the conduct of the trials, impeding the restoration of basic human rights that they were intended to bring about. The undermining of inclusive human rights policies, together with denialism and the demonization of human rights movements became more and more evident under the Macri administration, jeopardizing the rule of law and respect for international human rights standards. Victims and human rights organizations will hope that the new government of Alberto Fernández will revive Kirchnerist policy but at the same time avoid earlier shortcomings, so that human rights policy is more consistent, inclusive and sustainable. The longer-term outcome remains to be seen. It should be stressed, however, that human rights policies should not be subject to the changing political orientations and policy priorities of governments, but rather reflect the national and international standards and norms that should properly govern state policies.

References

Buenos Aires Times, 2018. "Macri sparks controversy with move to expand role of Armed Forces," July 28. Available at: http://www.batimes.com.ar/news/argentina/macri-sparks-controversy-with-move-to-expand-role-of-armed-forces.phtml [Accessed November 11, 2018].

Calloni, S., 2016. "Macri ubica en 6 mil 348 la cifra de desaparecidos en la dictadura." *La Jornada*, November 9.

Calveiro, P., 1998. *Poder y Desaparición. Los campos de concentración en Argentina*. Buenos Aires: Colihue.

CELS, 2016. *Derechos humanos en la Argentina. Informe 2016*. Buenos Aires: Siglo Ventiuno Editores.

Comisión Nacional sobre la Desaparición de Personas (CONADEP), 2013. *Nunca más. Informe de la Comisión Nacional sobre Desaparición Forzada*. Buenos Aires: Eudeba – Editorial Universitaria de Buenos Aires.

Dandan, A., 2016. "Un funcionario que no transmite seguridad." *Página 12*, April 3.

Fran, E., 2010. "Los juicios por delitos de lesa humanidad no buscan justicia, sino venganza," *Agencia Federal de Noticias*, December 14. Available at: https://www.derf.com.ar/los-juicios-delitos-lesa-humanidad-no-buscan-justicia-sino-venganza-n385664 [Accessed August 11, 2020].

El País. 2016. "Macri recibe a las organizaciones de derechos humanos y sus críticas," February 24. Available at: https://elpais.com/internacional/2016/02/24/argentina/1456276558_658260.html [Accessed July 11, 2020].

Figari Layús, R., 2017. *The Reparative Effects of Human Rights Trials: Lessons from Argentina*. Transitional Justice Series. London: Routledge.

Filippini, L., 2009. *ICTJ Briefing Criminal Prosecutions for Human Rights Violations in Argentina*. Buenos Aires: International Center for Transitional Justice.

Ginzberg, V., 2016a. "Macri mostró desprecio y desinterés." *Página 12*, August 11.

Ginzberg, V. 2016b. "Del hecho al dicho." *Página 12*, August 15.

Gloppen, S., Gargarella, R. & Skaar, E. S., 2004. "Introduction: The accountability function of the courts in New Democracies." In id., *Democratization and the Judiciary*. London: Frank Cass Publishers, 1–6.

La Nación, 2016. "El secretario de Derechos Humanos recibió a familiares de víctimas del terrorismo," January 14. Available at: https://www.lanacion.com.ar/1862254-el-secretario-de-derechos-humanos-recibio-a-familiares-de-victimas-del-terrorismo [Accessed July 11, 2020].

Malmud-Goti, J., 1989. "Trying Violators of Human Rights: The Dilemma of Democratic Governments." In The Justice and Society Program of the Aspen Institute, *State Crimes: Punishment or Pardon*. Queenstown: Justice and Society Program of the Aspen Institute.

O'Donnell, G., 1998. "Polyarchies and the (Un)Rule of Law in Latin America." Paper presented at the Meeting of the Latin American Studies Association. Chicago: Kellogg Institute and Department of Government University of Notre Dame.

Página 12, 2016. "Fueron dictadas 20 sentencias por crímenes de lesa humanidad en 2016," December 30.
Página 12, 2017. "Pretenden borrar la memoria," March 26. Available at: https://www.pagina12.com.ar/27994-pretenden-borrar-la-memoria [Accessed July 11, 2020].
Pertot, W., 2014. "Otra de Macri y los derechos humanos." *Página 12*, December 24.
Procuraduría de Crímenes contra la Humanidad, 2018. *Informe Estadístico sobre el Estado de las Causas por Delitos de Lesa Humanidad en Argentina*. Buenos Aires: Ministerio Público Fiscal.
Procuraduría de Crímenes contra la Humanidad, 2019. "Estado actual del proceso de juzgamiento: son 238 las sentencias dictadas, pero sólo un tercio se encuentra firme." Available at: https://www.fiscales.gob.ar/lesa-humanidad/estado-actual-del-proceso-de-juzgamiento-son-238-las-sentencias-dictadas-pero-solo-un-tercio-se-encuentra-firme/ [Accessed January 11, 2020].
Roehrig, T., 2009. "Executive Leadership and the Continuing Quest for Justice in Argentina." *Human Rights Quarterly* 31(3): 721–747.
Roht-Arriaza, N., 2004. "Argentina: Truth and Consequences." In id., *The Pinochet Effect. Transnational Justice in the Age of Human Rights*. Philadelphia: University of Pennsylvania Press, 97–117.
Schindel, E., 2012. "'Now the Neighbors Lose Their Fear': Restoring the Social Network around Former Sites of Terror in Argentina." *International Journal for Transitional Justice* 6(3): 467–485.
Seidel, K., 2014. *The Power of Absence. An Ethnography of Justice, Memories of Genocide, and Political Activism of a New Generation in Post-Transitional Argentina*. PhD Thesis. NUI Maynooth, Faculty of Social Sciences.
Telam, 2013. "El 24 de marzo de 2004, el día que Kirchner hizo bajar el cuadro del Colegio Militar," May 17.
Telam, 2015. "Carrió cuestionó los juicios de lesa humanidad y dijo que ser presidenta impulsaría 'la revisión de las cosas juzgadas,'" April 11.
The Guardian, 2017. "Fury in Argentina over ruling that could see human rights abusers walk free," May 4. Available at: https://www.theguardian.com/world/2017/may/04/argentina-supreme-court-human-rights [Accessed July 11, 2020].
Verbitsky, H., 2004. *El vuelo: una forma cristiana de muerte, confesiones de un oficial de la armada*. Buenos Aires: Editorial Sudamericana.
Verbitsky, H., 2017. "Macri envía a la CIDH a un defensor de represores, banqueros y servicios ¿Son o se hacen?" *Página 12*, February 5.

List of interviews

Interview 1: Female survivor and member of a human rights organization from Buenos Aires. Interview conducted in March 2011, Buenos Aires.
Interview 2: Female survivor and complainant in the trials in Buenos Aires. Interview conducted in March 2011. Buenos Aires.
Interview 3: Complainant in the trials in Buenos Aires and daughter of disappeared parents. Interview conducted in September 2012, Buenos Aires.
Interview 4: Male survivor and witness in the trials in the province of Tucumán. Interview conducted in September 2012, Tucumán.
Interview 5: Female complainant and relative of a disappeared person in Buenos Aires. Interview conducted in October 2012, Buenos Aires.

Operation Condor Trials Abroad
The Innovation and Domestic Constraints of Transnational Prosecution

Debbie Sharnak

Amnesty International's annual global report noted that in 2016 Uruguay made "little progress ... in the few criminal prosecutions of crimes under international law and human violations committed during the period of civil-military government (1973–1985)." Indeed, this was true at a domestic level. While Uruguay is a regional leader for its progressive policies in areas such as drug policy and LGBTQ rights, the country has struggled to provide accountability for crimes committed during the nation's dictatorship in the face of legal and then de facto amnesty since its transition back to democratic rule in 1985.

In light of this domestic intransigence, Uruguayans seeking justice have pursued innovative legal tactics at both the regional and international level. The Operation Condor trial in neighboring Argentina marked a high point in this strategy. In this case, an Argentine court became the first to try transnational crimes committed under the banner of a military operation by the same name. During the wave of military dictatorships across the Southern Cone during the 1960s and 1970s, six states coordinated efforts to kidnap, torture, and execute political opponents in one another's territory. Working together to counter what they saw as a region-wide threat, the military regimes of Brazil, Chile, Argentina, Uruguay, Paraguay and Bolivia organized to eliminate people who these governments considered subversive, left-wing opponents (Dinges 2004; McSherry 2005). The case is notable for several reasons. First, it allowed claims to be entered in a national court not only by Argentines but also foreign nationals, including Uruguayans, Chileans, and Paraguayans. Second, and perhaps even more incredibly, the process completed the trials of 17 individuals, one being the Uruguayan colonel, Manuel Cordero. Indeed, for the first time, a national court tried and ultimately convicted an Uruguayan foreign national for transnational human rights violations.

This chapter explores the transnational dynamics that led to this pioneering trial and its subsequent reverberations in Uruguay. After outlining a brief history of legal impunity within the country, it argues that the trial was undertaken, at least in part, because Uruguay proved unwilling to prosecute many of these crimes domestically. With 109 victims' relatives and lawyers filing cases on behalf of the disappeared victims in the Operation Condor portion of the trial, the largest number – 48 – actually came from Uruguay (Lessa 2019a, 427).[1] Many of these claimants used another nation's federal court system to seek justice because it was the only available avenue. However, they also hoped that after the trial, the successful prosecution of an Uruguayan national abroad would perhaps provide an incentive for Uruguay to take up more cases at the domestic level (*T13* 2016). What this chapter claims, however, is that in the years since the conviction, the opposite has actually occurred – more delays, stonewalling, and attacks on human rights defenders transpired and perhaps even intensified.

As such, this chapter will investigate the domestic implications of these transnational prosecutorial efforts for Uruguay. By analyzing archival documents from the US and Latin America, reports on the trial, and conducting interviews in Uruguay, it contends that even when accountability has been successfully pursued at an international or transnational level, domestic successes are in large part dependent on the political will of judges in local and federal courts, an element still seemingly missing from the Uruguayan political scene. Lastly, this chapter will briefly explore the continued failure to pursue retributive justice since the Condor trial sentence from the perspective of an "unleashing" theory – a phenomenon that legal scholar Cass Sunstein describes as the effects of norm subversion (2017). In this article, Sunstein explains that often the pressures of social norms lead people to hide their true beliefs; yet, once norms are weakened through social action or the revision of laws, it is then possible to uncover preexisting preferences and spur action – either positive or negative. Although Sunstein explores this concept from a domestic US perspective, this chapter puts the theory into an Uruguayan context, where the continued intransigence of domestic courts, even in light of international progress on justice issues, has resulted in a backlash against human rights defenders. This has meant the further closing of doors and elimination of opportunities for pursuing legal justice in the aftermath of the trial – the opposite of what many Uruguayans and international observers had hoped with the convictions in the groundbreaking Operation Condor

1 As Lessa (2019, 427) outlines, the charges related to 65 victims in the Automotores Orletti trial and 109 for Operation Condor, while two appeared in both lawsuits. The number of 48 Uruguayans comes from the Condor victims specifically. The other nationalities included 22 Chileans, 16 Argentines, 13 Paraguayans, nine Bolivians, and one Peruvian.

trial. In this sense, even as norms for international justice strengthen abroad, Uruguay's current political and judicial climate means that domestic trials are unlikely.

History of impunity and Uruguay's amnesty law

After enjoying strong democratic traditions for most of the 20th century, Uruguay descended into increasingly repressive rule until the elected president, Juan María Bordaberry, closed Parliament and handed governing authority to the military in 1973. Indeed, Uruguay's civil-military rule lasted from 1973 to 1985, a 12-year period characterized by widespread political imprisonment and torture. In a country of only three million people, this terror reached nearly one in 50 people, resulting in the highest rate of political incarceration in the world (Amnesty International 1979). Both within Uruguay and in neighboring countries, hundreds more were "disappeared" as part of Operation Condor – kidnapped by state agents and never heard from again. Around the Southern Cone, the military operated clandestine torture centers to question and torture suspected members of revolutionary groups (Lessa 2019). Even with a great number of Uruguayans suffering under this system, many of those fortunate enough to remain outside of the regime's prisons nonetheless endured extensive government monitoring of political activities to determine who might fall under the regime's broad definition of a leftist subversive (Rial 1992). Fear thus became a pervasive feature of military rule. More than 10% of the population fled these conditions, a number which equated to between 300,000 and 400,000 citizens of this small nation being in exile. As journalist Lawrence Weschler noted, "the sheer scope of this emigration, detention, and incarceration … only begins to suggest the extent of the military's absolute rule of Uruguayan daily life during the military dictatorship" (Weschler 1998, 88).

After years of intense and fraught negotiations to bring the government back to democratic rule, elected officials finally took office again in March 1985. Soon after, an amnesty law was passed for those who had been political prisoners under the military government, but no reciprocal amnesty was offered to members of the military. Instead, human rights groups pushed for trials so as to seek accountability for the crimes committed during the previous 12 years. The military fought back against these efforts and tensions reached a high point on the night of December 22, 1986, just hours before the first members of the military to be tried were supposed to appear in court. At this point, a full 21 months after the elected government had taken power, Parliament caved in to pressure and passed an amnesty bill, the *Ley de Caducidad de la Pretensión Punitiva del Estado* (Law of Expiry of the Punitive Power of the State) which protected the military and police against potential prosecution for crimes and human rights violations that had occurred during the period of the military dictatorship from 1973–1985 (Sharnak 2017). The only exceptions were for cases that had already reached the indictment stage at the time of the law's passage (although there were none) and crimes that had been committed for economic gain (Lessa 2013, 137).

Civil society groups, led by the newly formed *Comisión Nacional Pro-Referéndum* (National Pro-Referendum Commission, CNPR), immediately tried to overturn the law through a popular referendum. While the CNPR succeeded in obtaining the requisite number of signatures to force a vote, the constitutional process took almost three years and ultimately failed in 1989 when 57% of the population voted to keep the amnesty law intact (Delgado 1989).

For many years, this result seemed to stem the push for judicially based retributive justice and it was only through a legal loophole that cases eventually proceeded at all (Burt et al. 2013; Fried 2016, 58–59). Over a decade later, the first significant case to reach the courts creatively challenged the amnesty law that only covered members of the military. This 2002 case put the former Minister of Foreign Affairs, Juan Carlos Blanco, on trial since he was a civilian member of the civil-military government. Blanco was tried and convicted for the disappearance of Elena Quinteros – a teacher who was involved in the Student-Worker Resistance and a member of the *Partido por la Victoria del Pueblo*.[2] During the early years of dictatorship, she had been periodically arrested for her activism and eventually fired from her teaching post by the military dictatorship. Her final arrest occurred in 1976 when the military sent her to one of the clandestine centers where citizens were subject to incredibly harsh conditions and frequently tortured.[3] Despite an attempt to flee to the Venezuelan embassy, she was dragged away by the military and disappeared in *Batallón* 13. The case caused a major diplomatic incident and resulted in Venezuela cutting ties with the Uruguayan regime. Blanco's successful prosecution provided a symbolic victory for civil society groups by employing an innovative legal maneuver to achieve justice that

2 The case concluded in 2010 and Blanco was sentenced to 20 years in prison. An international tribunal in Rome trying the crimes of Operation Condor also sentenced him in absentia to life imprisonment in 2017.

3 Many of these torture centers were located in basements and buildings around military headquarters, including the place in Uruguay where Quinteros was taken: Batallón 13 or Infierno Grande del 300 Carlos (López Mazz 2009, 37).

charged the Minister on the basis of his civilian status without challenging the fundamental tenets of the *Ley de Caducidad* (Skaar 2013, 49). However, the amnesty law still remained in place.

When Tabaré Vázquez, the first elected president from the leftist *Frente Amplio* (Broad Front) party, took office in 2005, a handful of other emblematic cases began to make their way through the courts after continued pressure by civil society groups. While not overturning the *Ley de Caducidad*, Vázquez allowed approximately 25 cases to move forward under Article 4 of the Amnesty Law, which gave the executive discretion to allow certain investigations of state crimes to proceed. At the time of the law's passage in 1986, this tenet of the law justified inaction for the most severe crimes. However, by 2005, it was used for just the opposite. In another creative legal tactic spearheaded by members of civil society and eventually embraced by the Vázquez government, cases could proceed, for example, if crimes were committed before the official June 1973 coup, or if crimes had taken place abroad as part of Operation Condor. These improvisations ultimately paved the way for a handful of prosecutions that ranged from lower-level officials to former presidents such as Bordaberry and Gregorio Álvarez (Burt et al. 2013; Skaar 2013; Lessa 2013). The success of these trials, however, was still dependent on innovative strategic maneuvering and was not a full acknowledgement of the amnesty law's incompatibility with international law. With this momentum, civil society groups attempted to overturn the *Ley de Caducidad* by popular referendum again, a measure which also failed in 2009.[4] This second referendum lost by a smaller margin than 20 years prior, but it failed nonetheless (Lessa 2013, 152–153). This was yet another setback in the victims' long fight for justice and democratically confirmed the amnesty law's continuation.

The law was officially annulled in 2011 when Parliament overturned it after an Inter-American Court of Human Rights (IACtHR) case censured the nation. In *Gelman v. Uruguay*, the IACtHR officially declared that the *Ley de Caducidad* was incompatible with international law and ordered Uruguay to guarantee that the amnesty law did not present further obstacles to the identification and punishment of parties responsible for crimes

4 Referendums have a long and storied history in Uruguay as part of the nation's strong democratic roots, where many public issues have been submitted to votes. The 1934 Constitution introduced direct democracy, in which voters could voice their opinions on issues of national importance. The referendum process was revised and expanded in both 1942 and 1967. From the return to democratic rule in 1985 until 2010, direct-democratic procedures were used 17 times in Uruguay, including the two referendums on the *Ley de Caducidad* in 1989 and 2009 (Barczak 2001). It is the only country in the world where two amnesties were popularly reaffirmed by referendums.

against humanity. In the ruling's aftermath, Parliament officially repealed the amnesty.[5] Subsequently, claims flooded the court system that sought to reopen or begin to investigate crimes committed during the country's military rule. In the end though, these efforts were stymied as well. Even the official annulment of the amnesty law did not clear the path for domestic justice.

The first major setback in the period after the *Ley de Caducidad* was overturned occurred in February 2013 when Mariana Mota, a judge who was one of the strongest champions of human rights trials in the country, was transferred from her criminal post to a civilian jurisdiction without any explanation (Galindez 2013).[6] Mota's judicial record demonstrated her tenacity in fighting impunity on the bench as she convicted former civil president Juan María Bordaberry (Lutz and Reiger 2009). In 2013, Mota alone had more than 50 cases under investigation on her docket after the flood of suits began to reach the courts in the aftermath of the amnesty repeal in October 2011. Her transfer, however, was announced without notice or explanation, a practice that Uruguay had utilized in the past to skirt human rights trials. The transfer was handed down just as trials were slated to begin (Lessa & Payne 2012, 146). Mota herself admits that although the court has never given a reason, nor is it required to do so, her transfer was most likely due to political pressure to halt the cases (Mota Interview 2018). In the aftermath of her move, very few of the cases on Mota's docket were investigated by her replacement, Beatriz Larrieu. As a result, the judicial process for these cases slowed considerably, and subsequently there have been minimal efforts to have cases proceed through the national courts.

Days after Mota's transfer, the Uruguayan Supreme Court further limited potential cases with a decision about a statute of limitations. Defying a body of international law, the Court ruled that the dictatorship's human rights abuses were not to be considered crimes against humanity, for which there is no set time period in which they need to be tried. Instead, the Court interpreted

5 Under international law, amnesties are impermissible if they: (1) prevent prosecution of individuals who may be criminally responsible for genocide, war crimes, crimes against humanity, or gross violations of human rights; (2) interfere with victims' right to an effective remedy; or (3) restrict victims' or societies' right to know the truth about violations of human rights and humanitarian law. The Court's decision cited both the American Convention and a large body of precedents which found that there was a non-compatibility of amnesties with serious human rights violations (*Gelman v. Uruguay* 2011, 69).

6 The practice of transferring judges without explanation is allowed under Uruguayan law and had been utilized in the past to thwart attempts to bring members of the military to justice. For example, in 1997, Alberto Reyes was transferred from a criminal to a civil court after ordering an investigation into the disappeared. Similar pressures were placed on three other judges in the following eight years in at least four other cases (Lessa & Payne 2012).

the military's abuses, mainly political imprisonment, torture, and disappearances, as common crimes (Sentencia 186/2013; Ámbito 2013). Thus, the pending cases fell outside the time allotted to bring complaints before the court and had to be dropped. As Amnesty International explained, the ruling effectively meant that the key provisions of the amnesty law were brought "back to life" and that many gross human rights violations committed under the dictatorship would go unpunished (2014). It was a clear signal from the upper court that any cases that advanced at the lower levels of the judicial system would continue to be opposed by the highest court in the country.

Therefore, throughout the first 30 years of the country's return to democratic governance, impunity had proven intransigent in Uruguay. Despite significant but limited emblematic cases, the country's pursuit of retributive justice was generally characterized by this lack of accountability. The advances that were made were achieved not through a straightforward challenge to the impunity regime, but by creative maneuvering that worked around conservative judges that were resistant to changes of international human rights norms. The setbacks in the post-repeal era served to compel another turn towards a pioneering approach, this time at a transnational level.

Innovative legal maneuvering: the Operation Condor trial

At the same time that these delays were occurring in Uruguay in 2013, the historic Operation Condor trial began in neighboring Argentina, demonstrating a severe disconnect between the possibilities of retributive justice in the two countries. While scholars such as Kathryn Sikkink (2011) have called Argentina a "global protagonist," in part for its trial in 1985 of the juntas, the Operation Condor trial also broke new ground for trying the complex web of transnational human rights violations and coordination between the Southern Cone military governments in the 1970s and 1980s (Dinges 2004, 4). As analyzed in the Figari Layús chapter, Argentina has also systematically conducted domestic human rights trials since 2006, adding to the sense of possibility across the Rio de la Plata, as opposed to Uruguay's intransigence.

While Operation Condor's formal military coalition reached across the Southern Cone in this period, its center of operations was located in one of Argentina's 300 secret detention centers, Automotores Orletti in Buenos Aires.[7] Here, a majority of those detained were foreigners, apprehended in

7 Orletti was only one of several centers for Condor operations during the 1970s; however, it is arguably one of the better-known ones.

Argentina and either disappeared in Argentina or returned to their home country often to a similar fate (Lessa 2015, 499). The building itself was fairly innocuous; it was a former automobile repair shop with a large metal door in front. Inside, however, the activities were far more sinister. As journalist John Dinges describes in his book, *The Condor Years*, prisoners were kept on the first floor of the building in cells surrounded by pieces of old cars. Meanwhile, savage torture took place on the second floor where the civilian and military officials also had their offices. Notably, it was not just Argentines questioning foreign nationals there, but foreign military officers from around the region operated and aided in the torture at the detention center (Dinges 2004, 206). As the operational center for the Condor Alliance and the country in which the majority of Condor's documented crimes took place, Buenos Aires was a natural place to proceed with the trial.

Indeed, the case originally sought to try 27 individuals and took into account claims about the disappearance and murder of over 100 individuals from around the region.[8] Due to the deaths of some defendants, the court completed trials for 17 individuals. Two were acquitted and 15 were found guilty. Of those who were found guilty and received sentences, 14 were Argentines and one was Uruguayan, Manuel Cordero Piacentini.[9] Cordero was one of the most infamous torturers of the Uruguayan regime. His trial was a notable advance for victims who had been forced to encounter him on the streets in the years since the transition back to democratic rule (Fried Amilivia 2016). In the years since the fall of the military regime, evidence had emerged that Cordero had been deeply involved in the working of Operation Condor. As early as 1974, for example, he had been in contact with Argentine intelligence officials about a joint mission to disappear members of guerrilla groups in Argentina and Uruguay (López 2016, 192; Movimiento de Liberación Nacional-Tupamaros 2011). This evidence ultimately made Cordero a prime target for prosecutors to pursue in the transnational trial.

In addition to an Uruguayan defendant, the majority of the victims who made claims in the trial also came from abroad. Indeed, the largest number originated in Uruguay, with a total of 48. Part of the reason stems from the fact that many Uruguayans had fled the 1973 coup in their country for refuge in neighboring Argentina, where the military did not officially take over until 1976. However, such large numbers of Uruguayans also made claims in the foreign court due to lack of domestic judicial accountability. After the numerous setbacks and persistence of both *de jure* and *de facto* amnesty in

8 The roots of the case actually go back even further to 1999 (Lessa 2019a).

9 Sentences ranged from eight to 25 years.

the country, the trial in neighboring Argentina provided an opportunity to pursue retributive justice through the courts – an avenue which was largely closed at home. This strategy also relied on an innovative legal maneuver, demonstrating the continued domestic frustration that resulted in such a high number of claims.

During the course of the trial, from 2013 to 2015, judges heard testimony from over 500 witnesses and experts (*Democracy Now* 2003). Researcher Francesca Lessa, who observed parts of the trial, writes of witness after witness from around the region taking the stand to tell their heart-wrenching stories of questioning, repeated torture, and endemic fear where foreign military officers operating in Argentina did not even attempt to conceal their identity (Lessa 2015, 504). Documents from archives in Paraguay, Brazil, and even the US-based National Security Archive also contributed thousands of pages of evidence and offered testimony that documented the origins and evolution of the coordinated repression against individuals (Dandan 2015; National Security Archive 2015).

A verdict was finally handed down in May 2016. The Court delivered its decision in the largest courtroom in Buenos Aires. Dozens of survivors and relatives of the victims had traveled from across the region to hear the result and packed into the space. In the end, the judges in the Argentine Federal Court found 15 of the defendants guilty. The convicted men received prison sentences that ranged from eight to 25 years. Cordero received one of the harshest penalties of 25 years (Associated Press 2016).

All around the Southern Cone, victims' groups celebrated the verdict. There was even an Uruguayan flag hung in the hall on the day that the judges handed down the sentence. From within the courtroom, victims proclaimed "*presente*" (present) in response to the decision, a call noted during rallies over the past decades to signal the continued memory of their disappeared loved ones (BBC 2016). In Montevideo, another group of victims and families gathered at the Argentine embassy, responding to the verdict with cheers, applause, and tears (*T13* 2016; *El Confidencia* 2016).

After decades of setbacks in Uruguay, the verdict was seen as a sign of hope that "it was possible to do justice, even in spite of challenges." Groups that had been working in Uruguay also believed that the decision in a foreign court, which permitted claims from Uruguayans against an Uruguayan national, might even provide "an incentive" within Uruguay to reopen possibilities for domestic trials (*T13* 2016). In the 1990s, foreign prosecution of Argentine individuals "hurt the pride of local judges" and encouraged them to investigate the crimes in domestic courts. Uruguayans hoped that the same might occur in their country (Lessa 2015, 506). This hope, however, ultimately proved misplaced.

Continued stonewalling in Uruguay

Several years after the verdict of the Operation Condor trial, there has been very little progress on measures to provide retributive justice at a domestic level in Uruguay, as a result of continued stonewalling and judicial intransigence. In the immediate aftermath of the trial, though, there was hope and some initial momentum that helps explain the dynamics of accountability obstruction within Uruguayan society.

The first positive steps seemed to come even before the trial was over. In November 2014, Tabaré Vázquez was reelected to a second term as the president. Uruguayan presidents cannot serve consecutive terms, and his first administration had lasted from 2005–2010, a period where many of the initial trials of members of the military had taken place. While progress had slowed considerably under José Mujica's government, many activists were optimistic about judicial possibilities with Vázquez's return to government, especially since he would now take the oath without the official constraints of the amnesty law. On assuming office again in March 2015, he launched a Working Group on Truth and Justice (Decreto del Grupo de Trabajo 2015;[10] ICTJ 2015; *UYPress* 2015). This prominent body was tasked with gathering information on past crimes, as well as advancing the possibilities of both trial and reparations.[11] Comprised of well-known and well-regarded figures across the country, the move was seen as an important political step and commitment by the Vázquez government to advance the cause of accountability "without the distraction generated by attending to other matters" (*Buenos Aires Herald* 2015).

This pressure from above was combined with momentum from below, one of the prime drivers of accountability in the past (Burt et al. 2013; Skaar 2013). In October 2017, human rights groups and unions such as Crysol, SERPAJ, Madres y Familiares de Uruguayos Detenidos Desaparecidos (Mothers and Families of Detained and Disappeared Uruguayans), PIT-CNT, FEUU, and Observatoria Luz Ibarburu launched a campaign on social media and in the streets to highlight judicial delays and to prompt movement from the national courts to proceed with trials in the aftermath of the Operation

10 The author thanks Felipe Mechilini for providing the *decreto* and *nombramiento* establishing the Working Group.

11 Reparations previously advanced most significantly under Vazquez's first term in office (2005–2010). Parliament passed two laws during this period. The first restored pension rights to individuals who were prohibited from working during the period of the military dictatorship for political reasons and the second set up a special commission to pay reparations to victims, including political prisoners, minors born in detention, those who were disappeared or exiled, and torture victims (Lessa 2013, 150).

Condor decision. Under the hashtags #26Oct and #nohayderecho, the campaign was accompanied by a march in Montevideo and the opening of the 165th Regular Session of the Inter-American Commission on Human Rights, which coincidentally was taking place in Montevideo for the first time (OAS 2017; Lessa & Burt 2017). Powerful testimonies by victims about their experiences of torture and political imprisonment were broadcast across Twitter and Facebook. This new media campaign showed men and women sitting in or around the former detention centers, a powerful visual message about the physical location of the crimes and the enduring pain they caused (Damián 2017; Pertuy 2017a, 2017b, 2017c). Alongside gaining international attention for the Commission proceedings and garnering executive support, the civil society groups hoped to parallel its pressure from the ground up with a top-down commitment by Vázquez.

This pressure, however, was not enough. Ultimately, continued judicial intransigence prevailed over these other efforts – perhaps best demonstrated by yet another setback in the courts. In late 2017, the Supreme Court issued a ruling that displayed its unwillingness to advance the cause of retributive justice. In this trial, a woman from the city of Tacuarembó, known as "A.A." in court documents, issued a claim against the military, accusing it of illegally detaining and torturing her in 1972 as part of the military's larger political project. The Supreme Court, however, responded with a ruling that the violations committed did not constitute crimes against humanity and therefore were subject to statutes of limitations whose expiry dates had already passed. As a result, the case did not proceed to a decision (*La Diaria* 2017). While the *Ley de Caducidad* had been overturned, this case demonstrated the continued *de facto* amnesty that operated within Uruguay from conservative justices who were set on stonewalling attempts to proceed with trials in domestic courtrooms. Pressure from above and below were not enough to overcome the lack of judicial political will. If Argentina had used innovative legal maneuvers to move forward with the Operation Condor trials, the opposite seemed to be occurring in Uruguay (Huneeus 2010).

Recent evaluations of Vázquez's Working Group on Truth and Justice confirm a slowed push towards justice. Three years after its creation, the Working Group had made little progress in its goal of proceeding with trials. Amnesty International's 2017/18 report on the country noted that the body had "not achieved concrete results" (Amnesty International 2018). Even the head of the Working Group, Felipe Michelini admitted that while the expectations were very high, he "always was pessimistic" about the possibilities for advancing trials due to the length of time that had passed since the violations had occurred and the "mafia agreement/pact among perpetrators not to talk" about what happened (Michelini Interview 2018). These shortcomings were further confirmed within Uruguay when the prominent human rights organization, Madres y Familiares de Uruguayos Detenidos-Desaparecidos, decided to leave the Working Group and withdraw its support and cooperation. In a press release, the organization expressed its frustration with the slow pace of the Working Group's attempts to advance its objectives and claimed that its stagnation had yielded no new information or advances towards retributive justice (Madres y Familiares 2018; *El País* 2018). Instead, the organization committed itself to working for justice through other means. Vázquez's government and Parliament, believing that they had done their part by setting up the Working Group and overturning the amnesty law, have displayed little, if any, additional political will to overcome the Working Group's inadequacies in the face of judicial obstinacy (Michelini Interview 2018). These shortcomings, however, have not been confined to continued intransigence within the courts; they perhaps have even emboldened and strengthened pushback in other spheres as well.

Unleashing effect

In addition to the legal setbacks, another worrisome development since the Operation Condor sentences is the overt attacks against human rights groups that are continuing to pursue claims. First, the work of the Uruguayan Forensic Archeology Group has been hampered. Since 2004, forensic anthropology processes have led to major advances in solving crimes and shedding light on human rights abuses from the dictatorship period. Their work has located the whereabouts of disappeared persons, and identified injuries and causes of death, with the sort of empirical evidence that can be used in trials (López Mazz 2016). However, both the archeological sites and the laboratory have been broken into and robbed in order to disrupt the work of the anthropologists and prevent the evidence from being used in a court of law (*La Red 21* 2017a).

The precarious state of justice work was made worse when in March 2017 a set of death threats was made against authorities and human rights defenders who have been working to advance the possibility of trials. Sent by email, the note was a direct response to the suicide of General Pedro Barneix the previous year. After learning that he was about to be arrested for killing Aldo Perrini during a torture session in 1974, Barneix took his own life (*Resumen LatinoAmericano* 2015). The anonymous death threat stated that "the suicide of General Pedro Barneix will not remain unpunished … no more suicides or unjust prosecutions will be accepted. From now on, for every suicide, we will kill three people selected at random from the following list" (WOLA 2017). The list included the Uruguayan Defense Minister, a prosecutor of the court, the Director of the National Human Rights Institute, human rights lawyers, and foreign scholars.

There was an immediate outcry. Amnesty International, the Washington Office on Latin America, and the Inter-American Commission on Human Rights all condemned the death threats, seeing the letter as a clear attempt to thwart efforts to have trials take place. A letter was sent to the Uruguayan government by 150 scholars from 15 different countries in support of those being threatened and urging the government to protect the work of these defenders of human rights (the author of this chapter was also a signatory). The government, however, did not respond publicly and provided no information about the status of investigations into the threats or who is responsible for them, even as many suspect that the emails came from former members of the military and police (Angelucci 2018; Front Line Defenders 2018).

These alarming developments, therefore, do not just point to continued intransigence by the courts, but perhaps indicate that the lack of progress has actually opened up possibilities for further backlash against human rights defenders. Legal scholar Cass Sunstein has advanced a theory about "unleashing" that can be applied to this context. In his work, Sunstein notes that under the pressure of social norms, people at times "falsify their preferences ... [and] do not feel free to say or do as they wish." However, he argues that the revision of norms, through either law or private efforts, can uncover, and unleash, preexisting preferences (Sunstein 2017).

In the case of Uruguay, the global ascendency of memory work and the justice cascade created an atmosphere where the pursuit of justice became more of working normative framework (Fried Amilivia 2016; Sikkink 2011). Despite continued setbacks, there has been a nonlinear push towards justice, perhaps causing many of those who wanted to act against the emerging norm of justice to be silent. Many domestic activists and scholars initially saw the Operation Condor sentences as another positive sign that domestic trials might proceed. Instead, the opposite has occurred. Under Sunstein's theory, the statute of limitations rulings from the courts weakened the move towards justice, creating the opportunity to unleash a new norm that sided against justice, replete with active domestic pushback. It unleashed the preference, previously hidden inasmuch as it was not acted on, to openly thwart and threaten the work of those pursuing justice. In this sense, the backlash began with the death threats and the break-ins at the premises of the forensic anthropological investigators. It became even more visible with the 2019 presidential candidacy of Guido Manino Rios, the former commander of the army who had actually been dismissed from his post by Vázquez for questioning how local courts handled trials concerning the crimes of the dictatorship. His campaign actively praised the work of the dictatorship and his party received 11.46% of the vote (Caetano 2019; Saldías 2019). Instead of there being a renewed pursuit of domestic justice in the aftermath of the Operation Condor trials as many had hoped, the norms of accountability have been further weakened from a retributive justice perspective. The government's impotent Working Group for Truth and Justice is further proof of an inability to pursue these ideas at an official level. Yet it now accompanies overt "unleashed' attacks against human rights practitioners in various spheres around the country and a resurgent praise of the period of military rule by electoral candidates.[12] Even Michelini admitted that there are both perpetrators and those on the left like former president José Mujica who believe that "the issue will end when all the actors die" and are content to wait out this period with inaction and stonewalling (Michelini Interview 2018).

Conclusion

With domestic momentum blocked or severely slowed, Uruguayans continue to pursue justice in foreign domestic courts. In May 2018, judges in Argentina rejected appeals filed by the defendants in the Operation Condor case, confirming the sentences of Cordero and others handed down two years previously (Mayer 2018). In addition to Argentina, Uruguayans have also helped support cases in Italy, such as the prosecution of Jorge Troccoli, an intelligence officer of the *Cuerpo de Fusileros Navales* (FUSNA), who had conducted torture sessions during the dictatorship. With dual Uruguayan–Italian citizenship, Troccoli had fled to the Italian town of Marina di Camerota, where his grandparents once lived, in order to evade possible charges in Uruguay, where he was under investigation. The Italian justice system rejected Uruguay's extradition request in 2008 and under international law provisions, which state an obligation to either extradite or prosecute, it proceeded to prosecute Troccoli for the charges he faced in Uruguay (Lessa 2019b; Iozzi 2016).[13] He was found guilty and sentenced to life in prison in July 2019.[14] While retributive justice stalled within Uruguay, other innovative

12 For more on this phenomenon in Latin America, see Kyle (2016).

13 The charges included cases filed on behalf of 18 Uruguayan and two Argentine-Uruguayans.

14 Although 24 people were tried, all but Troccoli were tried in absentia. He was the only one in Italy for the trial.

legal maneuvers have continued to be pursued abroad. For now, foreign domestic courtrooms appear to be the only place for Uruguayans to advance claims against aging defendants.

Mota, the judge who was transferred from her criminal post for allowing trials to proceed in 2013subsequently became the head of the country's National Institute for Human Rights (*Institución Nacional de Derechos Humanos*, INDDHH). In this position, she was able to strengthen the protection of domestic rights in improving the country's prison system and protecting traditionally vulnerable populations from discrimination, including Afro-Uruguayans, women, and people with disabilities. However, she remained pessimistic about the possibility of trials going forward in Uruguay. She noted that while transnational trials were indeed important and an innovative strategy, Uruguayans who resist retributive justice efforts did not see it as a compelling motivation to reopen the issue within national courtrooms. She explained that they claimed, "It is Argentina, nothing more." To them, there was no domestic relevance. Even as international observers and organizations condemn Uruguay's lack of progress and "backwardness [on the issue of justice] ... it really does not generate any change, it's very striking" (Mota Interview 2018).

Indeed, if anything, the last few years have demonstrated that international advance has had no effect on the domestic pursuit of justice in these cases. Despite some support from the executive and pressure from civil society groups, intransigence on the part of the judiciary has managed to stonewall any continued advance for retributive justice pursuits. Thus, the aftermath of the Condor trial has shown a contradiction between international and domestic efforts at justice. Further, it reveals that continued backlash, even in light of international progress, has unleashed further attacks from the military and its sympathizers who had previously hidden their disdain for these proceedings. Now, with the weakening of norms around domestic accountability, these actors seem more emboldened than ever. This phenomenon stands to be furthered even more with the ousting of the Frente Amplio from the presidency in the 2019 election. They were arguably the party most sympathetic to claims for accountability and vacated the executive branch after 15 years.

From a retributive justice perspective, this trend is worrisome, especially as potential defendants get older, pass away, and the possibility of pursuing claims in domestic courts diminishes. Those that pursue justice initiatives more broadly in a holistic framework have had more success in other areas such as memorialization. For example, since 2013, Montevideo has put up 34 *marcas de memoria* (memory plaques) around the city (Memoria 2013).

Plaques describing momentous events regarding the dictatorship that occurred in the location are placed around the city, surrounded by small white stone structures where people can sit and contemplate those violent events and places of resistance. Further, in November 2017, another memorial was erected at a former clandestine detention and torture center, La Tablada. In this case, artist Susan Escudero created a sculpture to acknowledge and commemorate the horrific torture that took place at the prison (*La Red 21* 2017b). More recently, in May 2018, Parliament approved a law to more systematically acknowledge former torture and detention sites around the country, which had thus far been done on an *ad hoc* and community-driven basis (*La Red 21* 2018). In this sense, as avenues for retributive justice remain closed, there exists a parallel structure to grapple with the legacy of abuses in other spheres – ones that remain perhaps inadequate for victims and those under threat – but ones that advance the memory narrative of the dictatorship that currently remains elusive in domestic courtrooms.

References

Ámbito, 2013. "Uruguay: Corte anuló ley que habilitó juicios por la dictadura." Available at: http://www.ambito.com/676901-uruguay-corte-anulo-ley-que-habilito-juicios-por-la-dictadura [Accessed July 31, 2018].

Amnesty International, 1979. *Political Imprisonment in Uruguay: AMR/52/BS1/79*. London: Amnesty International Online Archive. Available at: https://www.amnesty.org/download/Documents/204000/amr520131979en.pdf [Accessed February 27, 2012].

Amnesty International, 2014. *Uruguay: Key Human Rights Concerns. Amnesty International Submission to the Universal Periodic Review of Uruguay: 18th Session of UPR Working Group*, January–February. Available at: http://www.refworld.org/docid/5264dca84.html [Accessed November 28, 2017].

Amnesty International, 2016/17. *The State of the World's Human Rights*. London: Amnesty International Online Archive. Available at: https://www.amnesty.org/download/Documents/POL1048002017ENGLISH.PDF [Accessed April 3, 2018].

Amnesty International, 2018. *Uruguay 2017/2018*. London: Amnesty International Online Archive. Available at: https://www.amnesty.org/en/countries/americas/uruguay/report-uruguay/ [Accessed May 2, 2018].

Angelucci, N., 2018. "Con Francesca Lessa, a un año de las amenazas del Comando Barneix." *La Diaria*, January 29. Available at: https://ladiaria.com.uy/articulo/2018/1/con-francesca-lessa-a-un-ano-de-las-amenazas-del-comando-barneix/ [Accessed May 2, 2018].

Associated Press, 2016. "Operation Condor: Argentine court sentences South American ex-army officers for atrocities." Available at: https://www.telegraph.co.uk/news/2016/05/27/operation-condor-argentine-court-sentences-south-american-ex-arm/ [Accessed May 3, 2018].

Barczak, M., 2001. "Representation by Consultation? The Rise of Direct Democracy in Latin America." *Latin American Politics and Society* 43(3): 37–59.

BBC, 2016. "Operation Condor: Former Argentina junta leader jailed." Available at: http://www.bbc.com/news/world-latin-america-36403909 [Accessed May 3, 2018].

Buenos Aires Herald, 2015. "Uruguay moves to tackle dictatorship crimes," October 13.

Burt, J., Lessa, F. & Fried Amilivia, G., 2013. "Civil Society and the Resurgent Struggle against Impunity in Uruguay (1986–2012)." *International Journal of Transitional Justice* 7(1): 1–22.

Caetano, G., 2019. "The Far Right is Growing in Uruguay." *Jacobin,* November 24. Available at: https://jacobinmag.com/2019/11/uruguay-elections-frente-amplio-national-party [Accessed January 16, 2020].

El Confidencial, 2016. "Emoción y lágrimas durante la lectura de la sentencia Plan Cóndor en Uruguay," May 28. Available at: https://www.elconfidencial.com/ultima-hora-en-vivo/2016-05-28/emocion-y-lagrimas-durante-la-lectura-de-la-sentencia-plan-condor-en-uruguay_922022/#lpu6t4GXLDFjx9Q8 [Accessed December 2, 2018].

Damián, D., 2017. *#nohayderecho.* [video online] Available at: https://www.youtube.com/watch?v=Dw-mMFR5xXc [Accessed May 1, 2018].

Dandan, A., 2015. "La etapa final en el juicio al Cóndor." *Página 12,* June 9. Available at: https://www.pagina12.com.ar/diario/elpais/1-274504-2015-06-09.html [Accessed April 18, 2020].

Decreto del Grupo de Trabajo de Verdad y Justicia, 2015. May 19. Personal Files of Felipe Michelini, on file with author.

Delgado, M. 1989. *'So the people can decide': The Experience of the Referendum Against the Impunity Law in Uruguay.* Montevideo.

Democracy Now, 2013. "Operation Condor Trial Tackles Coordinated Campaign by Latin American Dictatorships to Kill Leftists," March 7. Available at: https://www.democracynow.org/2013/3/7/operation_condor_trial_tackles_coordinated_campaign [Accessed April 2, 2020].

Dinges, J., 2004. *The Condor Years: How Pinochet and His Allies Brought Terrorism to Three Continents.* New York: The New Press.

El País, 2018. "Familiares dejan grupo por 'Verdad y Justicia,'" March 1. Available at: https://www.elpais.com.uy/informacion/familiares-dejan-grupo-justicia.html [Accessed April 3, 2020].

Fried Amilivia, G., 2016. *State Terrorism and the Politics of Memory in Latin America: Transmissions across the Generations of Post-Dictatorship Uruguay, 1984–2004.* Amherst, NY: Cambria Press.

Front Line Defenders, 2018. "Failure to Properly Investigate Death Threats Against Human Rights Defenders." Available at: https://www.frontlinedefenders.org/en/case/failure-properly-investigate-death-threats-against-human-rights-defenders [Accessed April 31, 2020].

Galindez, M., 2013. "Uruguay: Human rights judge Mota transferred to civil court duties." *PulsAmérica.*

Huneeus, A., 2010. "Judging from a Guilty Conscience: The Chilean Judiciary's Human Rights Turn." *Law & Social Inquiry* 35(1): 99–135.

ICTJ, 2015. "Uruguay to probe dictatorship crimes."

Iozzi, D., 2016. "The Italian Trial on Operation Condor: Justice from Abroad," *Council on Hemispheric Affairs.* Available at: http://www.coha.org/the-italian-trial-on-operation-condor-justice-from-abroad/ [Accessed April 3, 2020].

Kyle, B., 2016. *Recycling Dictators in Latin American Elections: Legacies of Military Rule.* Boulder, CO: Lynne Rienner Publishers.

La Diaria, 2017. "SCJ declaró inconstitucional la imprescriptibilidad de delitos de lesa humanidad para un caso de torturas en Tacuarembó." Available at: https://ladiaria.com.uy/articulo/2017/10/scj-declaro-inconstitucional-la-imprescriptibilidad-de-delitos-de-lesa-humanidad-para-un-caso-de-torturas-en-tacuarembo/ [Accessed December 2, 2019].

La Red 21, 2017a. "Justicia citará a jefe del Grupo de Artillería de Defensa Antiaérea por robos en zona de excavación," October 16. Available at: http://www.lr21.com.uy/comunidad/1348270-robo-zona-excavacion-batallon-desaparecidos-dictadura [Accessed April 2, 2020].

La Red 21, 2017b. "Inauguran Memorial a las víctimas del terrorismo de Estado en La Tablada ex centro de secuestro y tortura," November 21. Available at: http://www.lr21.com.uy/comunidad/1351921-inauguracion-memorial-victimas-terrorismo-estado-la-tablada [Accessed April 2, 2020].

La Red 21, 2018. "Diputados aprobó proyecto que propone recordar sitios donde se sufrió el terrorismo del Estado," May 10. Available at: http://www.lr21.com.uy/politica/1367680-terrorismo-estado-memoria-parlamento-dictadura [Accessed April 2, 2020].

Lessa, F., 2013. *Memory and Transitional Justice in Argentina and Uruguay: Against Impunity*. New York: Palgrave Macmillan.

Lessa, F., 2015. "Justice beyond Borders: The Operation Condor Trial and Accountability for Transnational Crimes in South America." *International Journal of Transitional Justice* 9: 494–506.

Lessa, F., 2019a. "Operation Condor on Trial: Justice for Transnational Human Rights Crimes in South America." *Journal of Latin American Studies* 51(2): 409–439.

Lessa, F., 2019b. "Rome Court of Appeals Condemns 24 to Life Imprisonment for Murders during Operation Condor." *Impakter*. Available at: https://impakter.com/court-condemns-24-to-imprisonment-for-operation-condor/ [Accessed June 8, 2020].

Lessa, F. & Burt, J., 2017. "New Ruling by Uruguay's Supreme Court of Justice once again Jeopardizes the Search for Truth and Justice for Dictatorship-Era Crimes." *Washington Office on Latin America*. Available at: https://www.wola.org/analysis/new-ruling-uruguays-supreme-court-justice-jeopardizes-search-truth-justice-dictatorship-era-crimes/ [Accessed November 15, 2019].

Lessa, F. & Payne, L. (eds.) 2012. *Amnesty in the Age of Human Rights Accountability: Comparative and International Perspectives*. New York: Cambridge University Press.

López, F., 2016. *The Feathers of Condor: Transnational State Terrorism, Exiles and Civilian Anticommunism in South America*. Newcastle: Cambridge Scholars Publishing.

López Mazz, J., 2009. "The Archaeological View of Political Repression in Uruguay (1971–1985)." In Pedro Funari, et al. (eds.) *Memories from Darkness: Archaeology of Repression and Resistance in Latin America*. New York: Springer.

López Mazz, J., 2016. "Forensic excavations and burials in Uruguay, 2004–10." *Human Remains and Violence* 2(2): 56–66.

Lutz, E. & Reiger, C., 2009. *Prosecuting Heads of State*. New York: Cambridge University Press.

Madres y Familiaries, 2018. "Comunicado a la Opinión Pública." Available at: https://desaparecidos.org.uy/2018/02/comunicado-a-la-opinion-publica/ [Accessed April 2, 2020].

Mayer, A., 2018. "Plan Cóndor sin impunidad." *Página 12*, May 5. Available at: https://www.pagina12.com.ar/112597-plan-condor-sin-impunidad [Accessed April 5, 2020].

McSherry, J. P., 2005. *Predatory States: Operation Condor and Covert War in Latin America*. New York: Rowman & Littlefield Publishers, Inc.

Memoria, 2013. Proyecto "Marcas de la Memoria." Available at: http://www.memoria.org.uy/marcas_2013.html [Accessed April 5, 2020].

Michelini, F., 2018. *Author Interview*. Interviewed by Debbie Sharnak [by Skype], July 24.

Mota, M., 2018. *Author Interview*. Interviewed by Debbie Sharnak [in person], Montevideo, January 17.

Movimiento de Liberación Nacional-Tupamaros, 2011. "Tomo 1 Hechos Represivos."

National Security Archive, 2015. "Operation Condor: National Security Archive Presents Trove of Declassified Documentation in Historic Trial in Argentina." Available at: https://nsarchive2.gwu.edu/NSAEBB/NSAEBB514/ [Accessed April 30, 2020].

OAS, 2017. "IACHR Wraps up 165th Regular Session in Uruguay." Available at: http://www.oas.org/en/iachr/media_center/preleases/2017/168.asp [Accessed April 14, 2020].

Pertuy, L., 2017a. *#nohayderecho.* [video online] Available at: https://www.youtube.com/watch?v=4vpWowarK_I [Accessed April 1, 2020].

Pertuy, L., 2017b. *#nohayderecho.* [video online] Available at: https://www.youtube.com/watch?v=7S-pkqT4LTQ [Accessed April 1, 2020].

Pertuy, L., 2017c. *#nohayderecho.* [video online] Available at: https://www.youtube.com/watch?v=V7kr2ObJnZc [Accessed April 1, 2020].

Resumen LatinoAmericano, 2015. "Uruguay. Imputado por el homicidio de Aldo Perrini. Se suicidó el general Pedro Barneix." Available at: http://www.resumenlatinoamericano.org/2015/09/05/uruguay-imputado-por-el-homicidio-de-aldo-perrini-se-suicido-el-general-pedro-barneix/ [Accessed April 2, 2020].

Rial, J., 1992. "Makers and Guardians of Fear: Controlled Terror in Uruguay." In Corradi, J. E., Weiss Fagan, P. & Garretón Merino, M. A. (eds.) *Fear at the Edge: State Terror and Resistance in Latin America.* Berkeley, CA: University of California Press, 90–103.

Saldías, N., 2019. "The Newcomers Shaking Up Uruguay's Election," August 1. Available at: https://www.americasquarterly.org/content/newcomers-shaking-uruguays-election [Accessed January 16, 2020].

Suprema Corte de Justicia. Sentencia 186/2013. Available at: https://www.fder.edu.uy/sites/default/files/2017-11/sentencia%20186%20de%202013%20pdf.pdf [Accessed April 1, 2020].

Sharnak, D., 2017. *De Luz y Lucha in Uruguay: Contesting the International History of Human Rights.* PhD Thesis. University of Wisconsin-Madison.

Sikkink, K., 2011. *The Justice Cascade: How Human Rights Prosecutions Are Changing World Politics.* New York: W. W. Norton.

Skaar, E., 2013. "Wavering Courts: From Impunity to Accountability in Uruguay." *Journal of Latin American Studies* 45(3): 483–512.

Sunstein, C., 2017. "Unleashed." *SSRN.* Available at: https://ssrn.com/abstract=3025749 [Accessed April 30, 2020].

T13, 2016. "Víctimas celebran en Uruguay condena de militares por Operación Cóndor." Available at: http://www.t13.cl/noticia/mundo/victimas-celebran-uruguay-condena-militares-operacion-condor [Accessed April 5, 2020].

UY.press, 2015. "Ejecutivo creó el Grupo de Trabajo por Verdad y Justicia." Available at: http://www.uypress.net/auc.aspx?60301 [Accessed April 1, 2020].

Weschler, L., 1998. *A Miracle, A Universe: Settling Accounts with Torturers.* Chicago: University of Chicago Press.

WOLA, 2017. "International Organizations Denounce Death Threats against Human Rights Defenders in Uruguay." Available at: https://www.wola.org/2017/03/international-organizations-denounce-death-threats-human-rights-defenders-uruguay/ [Accessed April 2, 2020].

Tensions Between Criminal Trials and the Sense of Justice in Post-Conflict Peru

Iris Jave

Introduction

The recent period of violence in Peru started in 1980 when the radical organization known as Shining Path launched an armed struggle seeking to overthrow the newly restored democracy and to bring about a communist revolution.[1] During that period, which lasted until 2000, both Shining Path and the state security forces committed a wide array of atrocities against the population. According to the official truth-seeking body, the Truth and Reconciliation Commission (*Comisión de la Verdad y Reconciliación*, CVR), abuses by armed actors produced an estimated number of 70,000 victims (killed or forcibly disappeared).

Since the earliest years of the conflict, several groups of victims, comprising mainly indigenous people, sought justice and demanded the truth about their relatives' fate, albeit to no avail. Even though some trials took place during the 1980s and 1990s, they were mostly a miscarriage of justice and consolidated impunity for state crimes. Only after a political transition in 2000 did the victims and the human rights organizations find an opportunity to press for trials finding a more positive response from the state.

In this chapter I will consider the impact of those trials from a particular viewpoint. Through a couple of very significant cases, I will show that these criminal processes have the potential to grant a sense of justice for the victims not in terms of punishment of the perpetrators but in terms of recognition of the victims and a means of memorialization of recent history. In order to analyze this effect, the chapter is divided in four sections. The first section provides a contextualization of the conflict in Peru. The second section

1 The official Commission established in 2001 to investigate the human rights crimes committed during the conflict, the CVR, estimated the number of fatalities at 69,260, including dead and disappeared.

presents a brief discussion of the place of retributive justice and restorative justice in the process of dealing with a violent past, and attempts to establish a link between both types of justice. In the third part, the chapter addresses the dynamics of prosecution of human rights violations in Peru showing its advances and setbacks. Finally, the fourth section discusses how victims understand and perceive the processes of the post-conflict period.

In this assessment of the meaning of trials for victims, it is important to highlight how their participation in judicial processes has changed in recent years. More than 20 years after the end of the internal armed conflict – and 40 years after it began – evidence from the trials is very difficult to recover and the Ministry of Defense does not provide information about the military who took part in the events. However, victims insist on demanding their recognition not just as witnesses – standardly part of a legal scenario – but also citizens having a greater involvement in the process. They also insist on their recognition by other state bodies, such as those involved in the search for the disappeared and those responsible for reparations.

Our interpretation of the *senses of justice* will focus on two cases considered emblematic: the first known as "Los Cabitos" (after the military facilities where the violations took place), which involves the disappearance of 53 people in a military barracks in the Ayacucho region in 1983, and the case known as "Manta and Vilca" (the name of the two communities where the abuses were committed), relating to ongoing sexual violations of indigenous women in the region of Huancavelica in 1984. Both cases occurred in areas considered "emergency zones," due to the magnitude of the violence during the conflict, and therefore under the jurisdiction of the military.

The Peruvian armed conflict and the denial of justice

Peru's internal armed conflict started when a small and radical organization, the *Partido Comunista del Perú*, more widely known as *Sendero Luminoso* (hereafter Shining Path), launched a war to carry out a communist revolution. The first armed actions occurred on the same day (May 17, 1980) as Peruvians were voting to restore democracy after 12 years of military rule. The new civilian administration commissioned police forces to fight back against Shining Path in the Andean countryside, but by the end of 1982 the military was also engaged in the countersubversive effort. From the start Shining Path resorted to terrorist methods in the cities and exerted brutal repression over the peasant communities who disobeyed its orders and politics. The state security forces, for their part, also perpetrated numerous atrocities. This situation lasted almost 20 years under four administrations.[2] The period included a *coup d'état* staged in 1992 by Alberto Fujimori, who had been democratically elected in 1990. In April 1992, the government captured the leader of Shining Path and the whole terrorist organization was dismantled. However, the regime continued using the notion of a "terrorist threat," as a justification to exert repression against political opposition and social organizations (Burt 2006). Hence, political violence continued until the end of the decade. In 2000 Fujimori was reelected in rigged elections for an unconstitutional third term, but a huge corruption scandal forced him to resign. The subsequent political transition was presided over by the then President of Congress, Valentín Paniagua.

During the period of armed conflict, mass atrocities were committed by both Shining Path and by the state security forces.[3] Human rights abuses included arbitrary execution, forced disappearance, kidnapping and hostage taking, torture and degrading treatment, sexual violence, massacres and violence against children, amongst other crimes. An official investigation conducted in 2001–2003 by the CVR established that all the armed actors had committed crimes against humanity.

From the beginning some small groups of victims –in particular, relatives of disappeared persons in Ayacucho, the extremely poor, mostly indigenous region where the violence had begun, mobilized, demanding information about the whereabouts of their loved ones. However, they did not receive a satisfactory response from the state, and, even though some investigations and trials took place during the 1980s and 1990s, the large amount of human rights violations remained a secondary issue for the state.

As the political transition took place, and the interim government was rebuilding the democratic institutions shattered by the Fujimori regime, victims' groups and human rights organizations found an opportunity to bring this matter to the table. Their demand of justice for the victims was first addressed by the creation of a truth commission, following the example of the official investigative bodies created in Argentina, Chile, El Salvador and Guatemala in the aftermath of dictatorships or armed conflict. However, the demand for a fair and complete response to the victims also included claims for criminal justice and reparations. The CVR, which operated from 2001 to 2003,

2 Fernando Belaunde Terry (1980–1985), Alan García Pérez (1985–1990) and Alberto Fujimori Fujimori (1990–1995; 1995–2000).

3 The period included other armed actors, namely paramilitary forces, self-defense organizations supported by the military, and a revolutionary organization (*Movimiento Revolucionario Tupac Amaru*, MRTA).

documented the crimes that had been committed, assessed the actual scope and intensity of violence, and the damage suffered by the victims and society. It also made recommendations for criminal investigations and prosecutions, reparations for the victims, and for advancing the search for the disappeared persons through forensic inquiry, and institutional reforms. Seventeen years later, these recommendations have yet to be fully implemented, but they have yielded some responses by the state, mainly involving reparations and, in a very limited way, criminal prosecutions and justice.

Thus, justice, reparations, truth, memory and attempts to prevent a repetition of such events are open issues within Peru. In this chapter I refer to this set of social demands and state obligations as a transitional justice agenda. I focus on one dimension of the agenda, that is, the advances made by the criminal justice system in Peruvian society and its impact thereon. There are many different ways to consider these impacts. In this chapter I consider these impacts from a specific perspective, that is, the significance of trials for the victims in terms of their recognition and the restoration of their dignity. I argue that this sort of symbolic satisfaction gives a different *sense of justice*, which may appear even when the outcome of a judicial process is not entirely satisfactory for the victims. This approach leads us to establish a connection between retributive justice, which is the conceptual realm where trials belong, and restorative justice, which is more frequently associated with reparations, either material or symbolic.

It is important to consider that even though the human rights violations were widely neglected during the conflict, some judicial processes did take place in the 1980s and 1990s. However, the overall result of these processes was to reinforce impunity, especially in the cases of crimes committed by state agents. This was due to several factors, such as reluctance of the courts to act, and the prevalence of military over ordinary jurisdiction in all the cases involving military personnel.

The CVR pointed out that a structural problem of the Peruvian justice system is its lack of independence: norms guaranteed impunity to accused figures and insecurity that beset magistrates. In the 1980s, the lack of autonomy in the judiciary led to decisions that prevented the military, who were presumed responsible, from being tried. There were also threats against judges or prosecutors who decided to investigate crimes and human rights violations, and many judges were incapable of prosecuting those cases because of ignorance or rejection of international human rights law. Lack of economic resources and infrastructure of the judicial apparatus in carrying out its work was also an evident shortcoming. Other political obstacles added to these institutional limitations: the denial of information from and cooperation of the armed forces and the police and, above all, the continuous transfer of jurisdiction to military courts. The majority of cases during the period between 1980 and 2000 were referred to military jurisdiction, which in turn led to the systematic exoneration of the accused (CVR 2003a).

During the 1990s, judicial proceedings became more restrictive due to the greater and more intrusive interventions by the Alberto Fujimori regime after the *coup d'état* on April 5, 1992. Among the features that characterized the administration of justice were intimidating gestures such as tank deployment and military mobilization before the military were arraigned and the political control of the judicial apparatus. In addition, impunity was legalized through amnesty laws. First, in 1995, Law No. 26479 was enacted, which established a general amnesty for any person accused of, investigated for, or convicted of human rights violations; later, Law No. 26492 came to the statute books, which declared that the judiciary had no power to review the Amnesty Law. As the lawyer Yván Montoya points out, "according to our legislation, amnesty is one of the ways penal action can be dropped modalities for the extinction of criminal action, which preventing any ongoing investigation or process" (2012, 33). Thus, between 1995 and 2000 judicial processes were inhibited by the application of those norms of impunity.

This situation changed after the political transition between 2000 and 2001. The reestablishment of the rule of law and the process of democratization, as well as the investigation conducted by the CVR, allowed the judicial institutions to start some trials or to reopen cases that had been closed in the previous period. Even though the new situation is far from satisfactory, some advances have taken place and some judicial processes have made some slow progress in the last two decades. Up to September 2019, according to Peruvian human rights groups, courts had issued rulings in 86 cases related to abuses committed during the armed conflict, including 44 convictions (Human Rights Watch 2020).

Retributive and restorative justice

Before discussing the dynamics of criminal justice and its impact on Peruvian victims, it might be useful to consider the relation between retributive and restorative justice in the context of a transitional justice process.

The response to victims` demands for justice is one of the central aspects of the systematic violation of human rights (Van Zyl 2011). From a transitional justice perspective, it is particularly relevant to ensure that legal norms and judicial processes focus on the rights of victims and their families. However, prosecutions for human rights violations can also be seen as a means of producing collective history by establishing the truth of controversial or even competing facts (Wilson 2005), in addition to identifying the responsibility of individuals (Teitel 1997). This contribution to the truth would be one of the main social impacts of the trials, beyond its obvious effect in terms of criminal justice.

As Van Zyl (2011) states, legal proceedings against perpetrators of human rights violations can serve numerous ends: to prevent future crimes, to provide redress to victims, to reflect the hegemonic set of social norms, to initiate the process of reforming institutions and to generate trust in them. The trials should be seen not only as a way of achieving the victims' right to justice, but also as a public reaffirmation that the violation of certain norms and values generates sanctions (Van Zyl 2011). When this reaffirmation becomes public, it builds bridges between citizens and the institutions of the justice system.

This social and symbolic projection of legal truth, as produced in a court of law, implies a link with other dimensions or senses of justice, namely retributive justice. To see this link more clearly, it is useful to consider the many ways in which victims understand, or make use of, the proceedings or outcomes in a judicial process. The senses of justice, understood as the different ways in which justice and criminal processes are experienced, will be shaped by the concentration of several factors, including personal experiences and belonging to certain social groups (Clark 2008). The sense of justice is not related just to the investigation and punishment of crimes, but also to the way in which victims experience the judicial processes.

Thus, these different experiences and meanings derived from a judicial process are not confined to the notion of retribution. Victims can access other types of justice that are performed in the form of recognition, the bestowal of dignity, respect and also the enhancement of their status as citizens whose rights are protected or guaranteed by the state institutions. On the other hand, the overall dynamics of a trial, in which victims speak of their past grievances as individuals, as members of a community or even as representatives of a demographic range (i.e. women, poor, peasants, indigenous, Quechua-speaking people), can strengthen their self-images (individual and communal) as respected members of the body politic. These varied effects relating to the victims' ability to recover by having dignity restored to them suggest a common base between retributive justice and restorative justice.

Some elements of the definition of restorative justice allow us to consider the role of trials in the Peruvian post-conflict process in a particular light, especially regarding the experience of victims. Marshall defines restorative justice as "a process whereby parties with a stake in a specific offence resolve collectively how to deal with the aftermath of the offence and its implications for the future" (2003, 28). Clamp & Doak (2012) argue that restorative justice needs to be foregrounded at the beginning of the process, but also in its objectives and results. It must be kept in mind that, in either judicial or non-judicial processes, the recognition of the participation of the parties, and above all the victims, in all stages of the process is essential for a restorative effect to take place. However, in the case of Peru, restorative processes are not communal settings where offenders and victims are brought together to perform an act of reconciliation and forgiveness. What we have are judicial processes where the victims are involved through participation in some sense of recognition.

Clark (2008) differentiates restorative from retributive justice. On the one hand, retributive justice is designed to punish those who commit crimes and transgress the norms. Restorative justice, on the other hand, not only sees crime as a violation of a norm, but also conceives it as a violation of the rights of (a) people. Its focus includes the victims, the perpetrators and the community as a whole.

Regarding the cases under consideration in this chapter, the judicial process known as the "Los Cabitos" case refers to an instance of detention, torture, disappearance and extrajudicial execution of 53 persons, a crime denied for more than 30 years by the state. By contrast, the trial of alleged perpetrators of rape and sexual abuse against indigenous women in "Manta and Vilca" represents the first time in the country that the justice system had prosecuted gender-based violence as a crime committed during the internal armed conflict. Both cases entailed the official acknowledgement of crimes, and victims that had remained invisible for decades. In the third section I show how the victims can find not only an answer to their demands for *retributive* justice in the judicial proceedings, but also a road to experience justice in a *restorative* sense.

The judicial back and forwards toward justice

As noted, in cases of human rights violations during the armed conflict in Peru it was very difficult to access the justice system to carry out investigations and determine responsibility. Though it might have taken more than 30 years, accountability has advanced through the persistence of the relatives of victims approaching courts, barracks, Congress and the media. In doing so, survivors and relatives of disappeared persons went through a learning process in the search of truth, justice and citizenship.

In the 1980s and 1990s, there were several attempts to bring those responsible for human rights violations to justice. However, most of them failed. One of the emblematic cases of those years was that of "Accomarca," dealing with a massacre of 61 villagers (among them men, women and children) on August 14, 1985, in the peasant district of Accomarca (Ayacucho). A lieutenant of the Peruvian Army, Telmo Hurtado Hurtado, known as the *carnicero de los Andes* (the butcher of the Andes) was accused, alongside others, of having commanded the patrol units that executed the massacre. Hurtado was sentenced in 1993 by the military justice system to six years in prison for abusing his authority through his involvement in the massacre, while simultaneously being acquitted of the charges of murder, negligence and disobedience. The media narrative that accompanied those years drew a picture of a military man with mental problems who had acted of his own free will. In 1995, however, he was granted amnesty by the Peruvian government and even received four decorations, as he was promoted to the military rank of major. Finally, the case was reopened by the ordinary courts in 2007 and Hurtado was detained in the United States and extradited in 2011 to Peru, where he is now serving a sentence. When Hurtado testified before the National Criminal Court[4], he admitted that human rights violations were committed in Accomarca and argued that he did not act alone but following orders from his superiors and identified military officers higher up the command chain.

Another example of how the justice system functioned in the 1990s is represented by the "Chuschi" case, which relates to the arrest and forced disappearance of four villagers in 1991 at the hands of a combined patrol composed of police and military from the Pampa Cangallo Counter-subversive Military Base in Ayacucho. The complaint, lodged almost immediately by the NGO *Asociación Pro Derechos Humanos* (APRODEH) and the Asociación de Residentes Chuschinos in Ayacucho, was received by the Superior Prosecutor for Human Rights of the province of Huamanga. This was unusual in a context of increased resistance from the government's anti-subversive strategy. However, the plaintiffs and the advocacy groups managed to bring the case before the Congress of the Republic,[5] where an Investigative Commission on the events of Chuschi and Huancapi[6] was formed. Despite great media

4 The National Criminal Instance is an ordinary and specialized jurisdictional body with competence at the national level that has been created for the prosecution of terrorism, crimes against humanity and other human rights violations, as well as the crimes related to them. It is made up of five Colleges or Courts composed of three or four judges.

5 The case was brought to Congress in search of political support and greater visibility. The residents' association maintained relations with some congressmen and human rights organizations.

6 Huancapi is another nearby community that had suffered the killing of seven people.

exposure, the judicial process was stopped due, among other reasons, to the Amnesty Law passed by Alberto Fujimori in 1995 that grants amnesty to "military personnel, police officers and civilians who had been reported, investigated, prosecuted, tried or convicted for acts arising from or originating in the fight against terrorism since May 1980" (Art. 1 of Act No. 26479). After the return to democracy, the case was reopened in 2004 and in 2014 there was a final judgment, which blamed the immediate perpetrators but excluded the members of the high command that had been implicated by the witnesses.[7]

It should be noted that courts have made less progress in cases that were lodged earlier in the 1980s, and which specifically included extrajudicial executions, disappearances, and torture committed by the security forces. As mentioned above, this situation of almost systematic impunity changed after the political transition following the demise of Alberto Fujimori's regime in 2000, when a decision was taken to address the demands of the victims and of human rights advocates through some extraordinary measures.

To this effect, the interim government created a truth-seeking official body, the above-mentioned CVR, with the mandate to conduct an investigation into the 20 years of violence; to document the events that occurred; to identify and study the main political and social actors; to identify and analyze those responsible; and to propose recommendations for reconciliation (Decreto Supremo No. 065-2001-PCM). The CVR also investigated 74 cases from a legal perspective, i.e. seeking to identify the perpetrators, to gather evidence and to establish the type of crime committed involved; 45 of these cases were referred to the Public Prosecutor's Office (*Ministerio Público*) and two additional ones to the Judicial Power (*Poder Judicial*). The majority of the cases included members of the military, due to the fact that the main members of Shining Path were dead or had already been prosecuted and sentenced to serve jail terms (Burt 2011). However, progress is still slow.

The advocacy of civil society organizations contributed to the reopening of cases that had been closed in the 1980s and 1990s and made possible new judicial processes to prosecute those responsible for human rights violations. However, this aim was not so easy to achieve. On the one hand, the Ministry of Defense has repeatedly refused to provide information on the military personnel stationed in the emergency zones during the internal armed conflict, thus making it difficult to clarify the facts. On the other hand, it was necessary to prevent cases being transferred to the military courts, which still

7 Four military commanders of Pampa Cangallo Base were declared to have been in command during the crime of forced disappearances and as the ones responsible were sentenced to jail terms of 16 years.

claimed jurisdiction over cases involving military personnel. Nowadays, the competence of military justice has been restricted to crimes committed in the exercise of the military function (which excludes human rights violations) and the name has been changed to military police jurisdiction.

Following the CVR's investigation, there were some efforts to set up a specialized human rights system within the justice system. Within the Public Prosecutor's Office, the *Fiscalía Superior Especializada en Derechos Humanos, Desapariciones Forzosas, Ejecuciones Extrajudiciales y Exhumación de Fosas Clandestinas* (Prosecutor's Office Specialized in Human Rights, Forced Disappearances, Extrajudicial Executions and Exhumation of Clandestine Graves) was created on December 2003 and invested with national jurisdiction.[8] On November 25, 2004, the name of the *Fiscalía Superior Especializada en Delitos de Terrorismo* (Prosecutor's Office Specialized in Crimes of Terrorism) was changed to the *Fiscalía Superior Penal Nacional* (National Criminal Superior Prosecutor's Office).[9] In that way, this judicial instance assumed competences in crimes against humanity. These last measures were also taken over by the *Físcalias Provinciales Especializadas en Delitos de Terrorismo* (Provincial Prosecution Offices Specialized in Crimes of Terrorism), which were renamed *Fiscalías Penales Supraprovinciales* (Criminal Prosecution Offices) in 2003. Specialized offices were replicated in many regions or departments.

Besides these administrative changes, the judiciary took legal measures, for example rejecting the claim of officers' lawyers that it was not possible to prosecute cases of military jurisdiction under civil law. Rejecting this, the Supreme Court initiated preliminary investigations in some cases that had been previously closed by the military jurisdiction.

One of the most significant reopened cases was that of Santiago Martin Rivas, an Army captain and head of the *Grupo Colina*, a secret military task-group created during the government of Fujimori,[10] which was in effect a death-squad in charge of selective assassinations of persons allegedly affiliated to Shining Path. Rivas was tried by the military jurisdiction in 1995 and his case was dismissed.[11] Subsequently, in 2005 the Constitutional Court, the highest court of justice in the country, declared that process null and void,

8 See *Resolución de la Fiscalía de la Nación* No. 2034-2003-MP-FN, December 11, 2003.

9 See *Resolución de la Fiscalía de la Nación* No. 1645-2004-MP-FN, November 22, 2004.

10 The *Grupo Colina* was a military detachment that depended on the Army Intelligence Service and the Army Intelligence Directorate for the purpose of carrying out special intelligence operations through the exercise of violence, terror and coercion (CVR 2003c).

11 The War Instance of the Supreme Council of Military Justice issued a resolution of definitive dismissal in July 1995. Subsequently, the Review Instance of the Supreme Council of Military Justice confirmed the resolution that same year.

and the officer was tried in the ordinary courts.[12] Finally, after a long trial, Rivas was sentenced in 2010 to 25 years in prison.

In this sense, there are two cases that have acquired an exemplary value in the functioning of the criminal justice system, although it cannot be said that they are representative of overall performance. One is the trial of the leader of Shining Path, Abimael Guzmán; the other is the process undertaken against the former president Alberto Fujimori. These two trials have generated important national jurisprudence in the area of human rights articulated with international standards. In October 2006, Guzmán was put on trial by the National Criminal Instance (he had remained in prison since his capture in 1992 after being tried by military courts) and was sentenced to life imprisonment.[13] The trial set a precedent in Peruvian judicial history since the theory of mediated authorship was applied for the first time,[14] but also because it meant the opening of new forms of trial with their autonomous processes taking place in a democratic context.

The trial of Alberto Fujimori, carried out between 2008 and 2009, represents a milestone in the judicial processes in Peru, with him being found guilty of four cases of human rights violations committed during his term as President of the Republic. In 2009, the court confirmed his responsibility.[15]

In spite of these promising advances of achieving justice in the courts, it must be said that since 2010 there is no longer a specialized unit within the system of administration of justice dealing with cases of human rights violations. At that time, its mandate was widened to include cases of corruption and drug-trafficking, thus diluting the importance of human rights cases once seen as its primary task.

Many of the crimes prosecuted involved members of Shining Path rather than members of the military. During Fujimori's administration, when Shining Path's members were tried in military courts, the trials were conducted by

12 See Tribunal Constitucional, Expediente No. 4587-2004-AA/TC, November 29, 2005.

13 The Constitutional Court annulled life sentences for treason against Guzmán that had been handed down by the military courts with *jueces sin rostro* ("faceless judges"). The faceless judges were magistrates whose identity remained concealed and who were not visible to the defendants and their legal counsel during the judicial proceedings. This type of judge was introduced by the Fujimori regime (allegedly following the Italian judicial policy in the trials against the Cosa Nostra "mafia" in the early 1990s) in order to avoid the intimidation of judges by Shining Path.

14 According to the theory of mediated authorship, responsibility for the crime of terrorism was attributed to Abimael Guzmán, as he was the author who dominated and led Shining Path, regardless of other ascriptions of responsibility of those who carried out Shining Path tasks (Meini 2006).

15 See *Sala Penal Especial, Expediente* No. A.V. 19-2001, April 7, 2009.

jueces sin rostro.[16] However, since these procedures did not meet the minimum guarantees, the judicial proceedings were declared unconstitutional and the trials were carried out anew in the civil jurisdiction. The trials against the 12 leaders of Shining Path took place at a Navy base in 2006 surrounded by strong security measures and with very limited access to the media.

In contrast with the judicial proactivity to bring non-state perpetrators to account for their crimes, prosecutions of military personnel are still few and slow. Root (2012) identifies three reasons for the resistance of the military to participating in judicial proceedings: civil jurisdiction, the political defense of the armed forces, and the poor logistics of the national courts themselves.

If we add to this a growing current of *negacionismo* (denial) by the military and right-wing political sectors, it can be understood why the justice system (prosecutors and judges) prefers to inhibit or stall the processes, alleging lack of evidence. Denial as a strategy has permanently sought to reduce or exempt the armed forces from all responsibility during the internal armed conflict. In consequence, all the acts of violence are presented as being the responsibility of Shining Path and MRTA. As a result of this particular narrative, artistic, symbolic, and generally public representations of that period of violence undertaken by civil society – or even by state institutions, such as the *Lugar de la Memoria, la Tolerancia y la Inclusión Social*[17] – aiming to give a more complete and comprehensive account, including an acknowledgement of the victims, are labelled "terrorists".

Beyond retribution: understanding of justice from a victims' perspective

As we have seen, during the period prior to the political transition the possibilities of finding justice were very limited. After the CVR's truth-seeking process, this dynamic changed to a certain extent: a specialized human rights system was created and with this some progress was made. However, the greatest challenge lies in the incipient capacity of judges to handle the legal instruments needed in complex cases of human rights violations (Quinteros 2012). Although judicial action remains scarce, some progress has been attained by the redefinition of the victim's role. The victims have gained

16 See note 12 above.

17 The *Lugar de la Memoria, la Tolerancia y la Inclusión Social* (*The Place of Memory, Tolerance and Social Inclusion*) is the national museum located in Lima, in the district of Miraflores, and is dedicated to the period of the internal armed conflict from 1980 to 2000.

a different identity, enhanced by the discourse of transitional justice and memory narratives. At the same time, they have gained a certain notoriety in society, or at least in certain media and social sectors. This increasing public attention gained by the trials has provided victims with a sense of vindication, self-affirmation and opportunities for memorialization. Thus, while trials are still limited, there are some significant changes. On the one hand, impunity is being challenged. On the other hand, the victims find in the judicial process itself, and not just the sentence at the end of the trial, an experience of justice. In the following section, this phenomenon will be analyzed in the two legal cases already mentioned in the introduction: "Los Cabitos" and "Manta and Vilca".

"Los Cabitos" judicial process: an emblematic case

According to the final report of the CVR, members of the Army in Barracks No. 51 Domingo Ayarza, known as "Los Cabitos," and members of the Intelligence Unit, better known as the "Casa Rosada," located in the region of Ayacucho, ordered, allowed or committed numerous human rights violations between 1983 and 1984, which included arbitrary arrests, torture, forced disappearances and extrajudicial executions to the detriment of at least 136 people (CVR 2003a). For years after the events, relatives of the victims urged the Public Prosecutor's Office to start investigations, and also took their demands to the media and human rights organizations asking them to investigate. These complaints were collected by the Ayacucho Bar Association, which pushed the Public Prosecutor's Office to carry out the investigations in 1983. However, the response to their complaints and their demands for information from the authorities was far from satisfactory.

As mentioned above, to make things worse in 1995 the government of Alberto Fujimori issued an amnesty law that prevented prosecutors from carrying out judicial proceedings for human rights violations during the internal armed conflict (Cano et al. 2014). The law was repealed in 2000 during the transitional government.

It would not be until the publication of the final report of the CVR that the Special Prosecutor's Office for Enforced Disappearances, Extrajudicial Executions and Exhumation of Clandestine Burial Sites of Ayacucho opened an investigation into the accusations accumulated between 1983 and 1985, formalizing the complaint in December 2004.

In 2017, more than three decades after the events, the National Criminal Instance issued a sentence corresponding to one of the processes relating to "Los Cabitos." In its judgment (2017), this Instance established that in 1983 the barracks had been the headquarters of a command led by Army general Roberto Clemente Noel, in which several people were detained, suffered ill treatment and solitary confinement and were detained without their relatives being made aware of the fact. The Criminal Instance also determined that in La Hoyada, an area adjacent to the barracks controlled by the Army, an oven was built to incinerate people. In this location, mass graves containing human remains of 109 victims were found (Jave 2017).

In 2017, the National Criminal Instance convicted the retired officers Humberto Bari Orbegozo Talavera and Pedro Edgar Paz Avendaño to 30- and 23-year custodial sentences respectively, having found them responsible for the crimes of murder, aggravated abuse of authority and arbitrary detentions.[18] In addition, it disqualified them from exercising any public office and ordered their immediate arrest, since neither of the convicted persons were present at the reading of the sentence. The judiciary withheld its sentence in the case of other military personnel such as Carlos Millones Destefano and Carlos Briceño Zevallos because of their mental health, and Arturo Moreno Alcántara for being fugitive in Chile. In the same way, the court acquitted retired Colonel Roberto Saldaña Vásquez for insufficient evidence and ordered the payment of civil reparations (Poder Judicial 2017).

Although the victims appealed against the sentence, considering it incomplete, at the same time the judgment was received as a vindication of their struggle for justice after more than 30 years. Not only were those responsible for the crimes identified, but also the victims' account of the events was corroborated, which lends the sentence a double meaning. First, it makes the practice of disappearances visible in a formal judicial process, when it had been systematically denied by elements of the military; second, it strengthens the recognition of the demands of the relatives of the disappeared, which are not limited to the identification of those responsible, but include symbolic reparation, public recognition of the pain suffered and a vindication of their relatives.

It is important to mention that one of the most significant claims of the victims' relatives in this case was the assertion that there had been ovens to incinerate the victims' bodies. The recognition by the courts that the remains of a furnace were found in the area known as La Hoyada, close to the barracks,

18 In May 2018, the film *La Casa Rosada*, by director Palito Ortega Matute, which narrates the events discussed, was released and won the Ministry of Culture Prize. During the first week after its release in cinemas in Lima, some representatives of pro-military sectors accused the director of favoring terrorism. However, this accusation contributed to the success of the movie, keeping it on the billboard charts for four weeks (Fowks 2018).

incorporates the truth component of justice, but above all recognizes the dignity of the victims' relatives as citizens.

The main actor on the side of the victims was National Association of Relatives of Kidnapped, Detained and Disappeared of Peru the National Association of Relatives of Kidnapped, Detained and Disappeared of Peru (*Asociación Nacional de Familiares de Secuestrados, Detenidos y Desaparecidos del Perú*, ANFASEP), founded in 1983 as the first victims' organization in Peru. The members of ANFASEP – mostly indigenous women from Ayacucho who had been demanding truth and justice at great peril since the early 1980s – were very vocal about the significance of this trial and its outcome. The founder, president and emblematic figure of the organization, Angélica Mendoza de Ascarza, also known as "Mama Angélica," wrote on her Facebook page:

> "The court has pronounced a sentence in the #Cabitos case and the families have got some degree of justice; those responsible for the crimes were found guilty. However, we must remain vigilant and see that justice is finally consolidated and that it sets a precedent for our memory, for our struggle, for peace and justice for the families of Ayacucho and of Peru. I'd like to thank those that accompanied the families until the end of this long process" (Mamá Angélica, August 18, 2017, Facebook).[19]

One of the most important demands of the members of ANFASEP and other victims' groups has been to safeguard the area were many of the victims killed in "Los Cabitos" had been illegally buried. Their demand is to transform the area into a memorialization site and also to prevent any evidence lying there from being obliterated. The Sanctuary of the Memory *La Hoyada* is an area of some seven hectares that has been officially conceded at Ayacucho regional government level in order to create a memorial site for ANFASEP, dedicated to the hundreds of disappeared in the region. In fact, the "mothers of ANFASEP," as they are frequently referred to, had been using this area adjacent to "Los Cabitos" as a memorialization site since the beginning of the trial in 2005.

This is an emblematic case because the judge in charge of the judicial process ordered exhumations on the land in 2007. In order to obtain the recognition of public authorities, the mothers of ANFASEP have, over many years, been involved in a process of dialogue and participation with a wide array of actors. Their aim was to acquire a place of remembrance, a memorial representing and acknowledging their search and pain. Therefore, the Ministry of Justice and Human Rights has ordered the construction of a memory site

19 For more details see https://www.facebook.com/yuyarisumangelica/posts/10154670584303414.

at La Hoyada, with a transfer of 400 million soles (approx. USD 117 million) (Ministerio de Justicia y Derechos Humanos 2019). Adelina García, who lost her husband in 1983 and joined the women who founded ANFASEP, explains the importance of this memorial:

> "[S]ince the time that [the burial site] was found, and exhumations have begun on the site, we have demanded that this place becomes a sanctuary of memory ... Even earlier still, in 1986, 1987, we knew that they were murdering people in that place, that there was a furnace, but that has always been denied to us ... [W]e are Quechua speakers, many mothers [of the victims] cannot write or read ... [but] from that time on we have found the strength to demand the creation of a Sanctuary of Memory." (Adelina García, former president of ANFASEP, cited in Jave 2017, 11)

For the mothers of ANFASEP, the site is sacred because the remains of their relatives rest there. Although the creation of the Sanctuary was a direct result of the judicial process of "Los Cabitos" –which continues at higher judicial instances – for the mothers of the victims and members of ANFASEP, the preservation of the place is a response to and an acknowledgement of their 36-year struggle and their organizational capacity in seeking dialogue with the state. For them, the Sanctuary is a kind of symbolic reparation that is intertwined with the meaning that the judicial process has for them: there is a recognition that the military committed the crime of enforced disappearance, and that the Sanctuary and the oven were at the actual site where the human remains were cremated. The active participation of the mothers of ANFASEP is recognized as part of the process of advocating for and managing the Sanctuary. The symbolic recognition of ANFASEP, constitutes a reference for jurisprudence pointing towards other human rights lawsuits.

The next section deals with the trial of members of the military forces accused of having raped nine women in the villages of Manta and Vilca in the region of Huancavelica. This process gives another viewpoint of the transformation of the role of victims and their experience of accessing justice through their participation in the judicial proceedings.

"Manta and Vilca": the first judicial process addressing a gender perspective

In the early years of the 1980s, Shining Path had great influence in the Huancavelica region, located in the central highlands of the country. Faced with this situation, and in view of the increase in subversive actions, in March 1984 military bases were installed in the villages of Manta and Vilca which operated, respectively, until 1998 and 1989. In this context, numerous cases of rape and sexual violence against women were systematically committed, attributed mainly to members of the Army stationed at the military bases (CVR 2003b; Boesten 2012).

The CVR reported 24 cases of sexual violence against the women of Manta and Vilca. Of the reasons given by the military, sexual violence against girls and women was used to search for and obtain information, and to punish them for presumably belonging to Shining Path, among other reasons (CVR 2003b; Crisóstomo 2015). However, as Crisóstomo (2015) points out, the women of Manta and Vilca were already victims of sexual violence before the armed conflict began, so during the armed conflict only the aggressor changed. This allows us to understand the violence as the result of a historical process based on relations of domination, where violence against women transcends the arguments used by the Army. The CVR itself even concluded that these events formed part of a "broad context of discrimination" against women in Peru, and therefore urged the Public Prosecutor's Office to carry out the corresponding investigations to identify those responsible (CVR 2003b). The judicial process began in 2004 with the preliminary investigation against eight Army agents identified by the CVR; nevertheless, the process was delayed several times. Over time, as investigations went forward, the number of defendants involved in the matter increased. Another important factor is the psychological trauma that accompanies the social embarrassment that makes it difficult for the victims to report the facts or to give their testimonies (Salazar 2006). In this regard, in September 2017, the Judicial Control Office initiated an investigation into the magistrates of the National Criminal Instance (Otto Verapinto Velásquez, Carlos Payano Barona and Emperatriz Pérez Castillo). They were suspected of favoring the accused and of conducting a "stereotyped and prejudiced" trial to the detriment of the victims. For the same reason, the victims' attorneys demanded that the judges recuse themselves. It was claimed that the trials were conducted in contravention of international human rights standards, that there was a refusal to provide psychological support to the victims during the oral proceedings, and that the accused were allowed to be present at the hearings when the victims gave their statements – all constituting forms of intimidation (DEMUS 2017).

Subsequently, due to pressure from the victims and their lawyers, a change in the process was achieved. The court incorporated a gender perspective and the right to equality for women. A lawyer of the NGO Instituto de Defensa Legal in charge of the case, Juan José Quispe, said that: "The positive thing, according to my evaluation, were three decisions that this court made: First, that the trial was public, at the request of the victims themselves; second that they received psychological support during their statements at the trial; and third that their testimonies could be given in Quechua in the Huancavelica region, having interpreters for translations" (Instituto de Defensa Legal 2020). These are some steps on the path to achieve victims' recognition. While those responsible have not yet been sentenced, these actions constitute an acknowlegement of the rights of the victims.

The opening of this case is particularly emblematic because it is the first time that Peruvian justice has recognized the crime of sexual violence and discussed its implications in a comprehensive way. The trial remains open; however, in August 2019 13 soldiers were prosecuted for rape against nine women in the Manta and Vilca districts. The fact that the judicial control system characterized the initial judicial approach as "stereotyped and prejudiced" shows a recognition of the different effects of sexual violence and a vindication of rural and Quechua-speaking women (La Mula 2017). The case of "Manta and Vilca" could become the first experience of access to justice for female victims of sexual violence during the internal armed conflict, constituting not only an important step in criminal justice but above all a public recognition of what women have suffered and a return of their dignity after the history of sexual violence in the country.

The public acknowledgement of the crimes of the past is an element that contributes to the construction of these new senses of justice for the victims; it means that the aggressions of which they were victims become more visible. As in the case of "Los Cabitos," even though the trial process takes a long time, the public acknowledgement of the facts is experienced as a form of reparation by the victims.

Symbolic reparations are not just significant as state gestures but come also from civil society and are vectors of meaning. Among these acts, artistic interventions such as those carried out by the Trenzar collective are of key importance:[20] by using documentary theater to put the problem of sexual violence resulting from the internal armed conflict onto the political agenda, a link with structural violence against women up to the present day is created. What started as the NGO DEMUS taking up a strategy of public advocacy to accompany the judicial process has evolved into symbolic reparation and acknowledgement for the women of Manta and Vilca and, through them, for other women who have also suffered sexual violence.

20 See https://www.facebook.com/UnHombreNoViola/.

Conclusions

The analysis of the perceptions of the prosecution of human rights violations in the Peruvian case has shed light on the scope of criminal justice in post-conflict contexts, including its limitations and challenges. Although the application of criminal justice is limited in terms of the number of cases investigated and sanctioned, there are other aspects of justice that can be understood as a form of reparation. There is a sense of justice linked to the official recognition of human rights violations committed that also takes place in the judicial sphere. The "Los Cabitos" case, for example, implies the official and public recognition of a certain type of criminal conduct by state agents. The crime of enforced disappearance is documented, not only through the remains of the incinerating furnace but also through the evidence of human remains existing in La Hoyada, which stands next to what was the military barracks. The state in its recognition takes charge of the symbolic reparation for the crimes, even as the judicial process continues. The Ministry of Justice and Human Rights has ordered the start of the construction of a memory site at La Hoyada, with a transfer of 400 million soles (approx. USD 117 million) (Ministerio de Justicia y Derechos Humanos 2019). The "Manta and Vilca" case is not only a landmark case of official recognition of sexual violence against women as a crime committed by the state during the conflict, a crime that had been systematically denied for more than 30 years, but above all it recognizes the gender perspective, the psychosocial attention and the victims' right to participation in the judicial process.

Secondly, formal criminal justice mechanisms advance as long as they have institutional support, but when regimes break down or governments weaken, it seems that truth and justice no longer reinforce permanent impunity. However, there are alternative ways to look for forms of justice or to make it more visible. Victims construct a new role from their own demands, developing a capacity for agency in processes of deliberation that the state creates, for example in the discussions of symbolic reparations. This is possible because the victims themselves have gone through a learning process, which allowed them to obtain resources and to develop symbolic and social capital, strengthening their relation to state institutions in the struggle for their demands. For example, the new generation of leaders of victims' organizations in the post-CVR period has changed its relationship with the state and social institutions, and now has greater access to education, social networks and political communication resources. This is the case of ANFASEP and other organizations for relatives of victims who participate in formal spaces for decisions regarding public policies for reparations or, more recently, the search for missing persons.

Finally, it is necessary to admit that in spite of the victims' efforts, and notwithstanding the advocacy of human rights groups, the prevailing public attitude towards state crimes is "denialism" or trivialization of the facts and responsibilities. The dominant historical interpretation still in place favors the role of the military as saviors against the "terrorist threat," with the implication that paramilitary crimes, if they happened, were committed "in defense of the fatherland and of democracy." This narrative pervades public discourse in the media and prevails among political actors.

In the midst of this scenario, however, human rights violations that had not previously been incorporated into the preoccupations of criminal justice, such as sexual violence, are becoming more visible. This progress opens up opportunities for justice for the victims of this crime and makes the gender issue an important affirmation of human rights. This is particularly important in a context where Peruvian neoconservative groups are seeking to emplace discourses and policies that dilute gender equality. These issues, paradoxical and complicated as they are, show how past and present yield permanent struggles as justice remains to be achieved.

References

Boesten, J., 2012. *The State and Violence against Women in Peru: Intersecting Inequalities and Patriarchal Rule.* Oxford: Oxford University Press.

Burt, J. M., 2006. "Quien Habla Es Terrorista: The Political Use of Fear in Fujimori's Peru." *Latin American Research Review* 41(3): 32–62.

Burt, J. M., 2011. "Desafiando a la impunidad en tribunales nacionales: juicios por derechos humanos en América Latina." In Reategui, F. (ed.) *Justicia transicional: manual para América Latina.* Brasilia: Comisión de Amnistía, Ministerio de Justicia/New York: Centro Internacional para la Justicia Transicional.

Cano, G. et al., 2014. *Cuartel Los Cabitos: lugar del horror y muerte. 30 años de lucha por la justicia. El camino recorrido por las víctimas, sus familiares y APRODEH.* Lima: APRODEH. Available at: http://www.aprodeh.org.pe/documentos/publicaciones/legal/Cuartel_Cabitos_Lugar_de_horror_y_muerte.pdf [Accessed March 11, 2020].

Clamp, K. & Doak, J., 2012. "More than words: Restorative Justice Concepts in Transitional Justice Setting." *International Criminal Law Review* 12(3): 339–360.

Clark, J., 2008. "The three Rs: retributive justice, restorative justice and reconciliation." *Contemporary Justice Review* 11(4): 331–350.

Comisión de la Verdad y Reconciliación (CVR), 2003a. *Informe Final. Tomo III. Los actores políticos e institucionales.* Lima: Comisión de la Verdad y Reconciliación.

Comisión de la Verdad y Reconciliación (CVR), 2003b. *Informe Final. Tomo VI. Sección cuarta: los crímenes y violaciones de los derechos humanos.* Lima: Comisión de la Verdad y Reconciliación.

Comisión de la Verdad y Reconciliación (CVR), 2003c. *Informe Final. Tomo VII. Capítulo 2: Los casos investigados por la CVR*. Lima: Comisión de la Verdad y Reconciliación.
Crisóstomo, M., 2015. *Mujeres y fuerzas armadas en un contexto de violencia política. Los casos de Manta y Vilca en Huancavelica*. Lima: Instituto de Estudios Peruanos.
DEMUS – Estudio para la Defensa de los Derechos de la Mujer, 2017. "Sala Penal Nacional vulnera derechos de mujeres en el caso Manta y Vilca." Available at: https://www.demus.org.pe/noticias/sala-penal-nacional-vulnera-derechos-de-mujeres-en-el-caso-manta-y-vilca/ [Accessed March 11, 2020].
Fowks, J., 2018. "Dos películas andinas sacuden la cartelera peruana." *El País*, 20 May. Available at: https://elpais.com/cultura/2018/05/19/actualidad/1526686967_131239.html [Accessed March 11, 2020].
Human Rights Watch, 2020. *Peru Events 2019*. Available at: https://www.hrw.org/world-report/2020/country-chapters/peru [Accessed March 30, 2020].
Instituto de Defensa Legal, 2020. "¿Qué pasa con el juicio oral del caso Violaciones en las Bases Militares de Manta y Vilca?" March 17. Available at: https://idl.org.pe/que-pasa-con-el-juicio-oral-del-caso-violaciones-en-las-bases-militares-de-manta-y-vilca/ [Accessed March 17, 2020].
Jave, I., 2017. *El Santuario de La Memoria La Hoyada, Ayacucho. El proceso de diálogo y negociación en la construcción de un espacio de memoria*. Lima: Pontificia Universidad Católica del Perú. Available at: http://repositorio.pucp.edu.pe/index/handle/123456789/110581 [Accessed March 11, 2020].
La Mula, 2017. "Investigan a Jueces de caso Manta y Vilca. September 14th, 2017." Available at: https://contraelolvido.lamula.pe/2017/09/14/investiga-a-jueces-de-caso-manta-y-vilca/amandameza/ [Accessed April 17, 2020].
Marshall, T., 2003. "Restorative justice: An overview." In G. Johnstone (ed.) *A restorative justice reader: Texts, sources, context*. Cullompton: Willan Publishing.
Meini, I., 2006. *La autoría mediata de Abimael Guzmán por dominio de la organización*. Available at: https://es.scribd.com/document/324607736/La-Autoria-Mediata-de-Abimael-Guzman-Reynoso [Accessed March 11, 2019].
Ministerio de Justicia y Derechos Humanos, 2019. "MINJUSDH transfiere presupuesto para construcción del Santuario de la Memoria de La Hoyada en Ayacucho." October 10, 2019. Available at: https://www.gob.pe/institucion/minjus/noticias/52358-minjusdh-transfiere-presupuesto-para-construccion-del-santuario-de-la-memoria-de-la-hoyada-en-ayacucho [Accessed March 17, 2020].
Montoya, Y., 2012. "Límites y avances de la justicia penal frente a las violaciones de derechos humanos ocurridas durante el periodo del conflicto armado interno en el Perú." In Quinteros, V. (ed.) *Temas de derecho penal y violación de derechos humanos*. Lima: IDEHPUCP, PNUD, 21–62. Available at: https://idehpucp.pucp.edu.pe/wp-content/uploads/2012/04/temas_de_derecho_penal_y_violacion_de_ddhh.pdf [Accessed March 29, 2020].
Poder Judicial, 2017. "Nota de prensa. Poder Judicial condena a dos militares por asesinato de 53 personas en cuartel 'Los Cabitos' de Ayacucho." August 18, 2017. Available at: https://www.pj.gob.pe/wps/wcm/connect/cortesuprema/s_cortes_suprema_home/as_inicio/as_enlaces_destacados/as_imagen_prensa/as_notas_noticias/2017/cs_n-pj-condena-militares-cuarte-ayacucho-caso-cabitos-18082017 [Accessed March 11, 2020].
Quinteros, V., 2012. "Introducción." In id. (ed.) *Temas de derecho penal y violación de derechos humanos*. Lima: IDEHPUCP, PNUD. Available at: https://idehpucp.pucp.edu.pe/wp-content/uploads/2012/04/temas_de_derecho_penal_y_violacion_de_ddhh.pdf [Accessed March 3, 2020].
Root, R., 2012. *Transitional Justice in Peru*. London: Palgrave Macmillan.

Salazar, K., 2006. "Género, violencia sexual y derecho penal en el período posterior al conflicto en el Perú." In Magrell, L. & Filippini, L. (ed.) *El legado de la verdad: la justicia penal en la transición peruana*. Lima: Centro Internacional para la Justicia Transicional, IDEHPUCP.
Teitel, R., 1997. *Transitional Justice*. Oxford: Oxford University Press.
Van Zyl, P., 2011. "Promoviendo la justicia transicional en sociedades post conflicto." In Reategui, F. (ed.) *Justicia transicional: manual para América Latina*. Brasilia: Comisión de Amnistía, Ministerio de Justicia/New York: Centro Internacional para la Justicia Transicional.
Wilson, R., 2005. "Judging History: the Historical Record of the International Criminal Tribunal for the Former Yugoslavia". *Human Rights Quarterly* 27: 908–942.

The International Criminal Court's "Africa Problem" and Suppression of the "Justice Cascade"

Geoffrey Lugano

The International Criminal Court (ICC) was created as a result of the global community's renewed struggle against impunity for crimes of genocide, crimes against humanity and war crimes. The intention was that by enhancing complementarity and international cooperation, those most responsible for mass atrocities would not go unpunished.[1] It was held that the prosecution of international crimes would contribute to their deterrence,[2] and hence to a more just and secure world for humanity.

To fulfill these aspirations, the ICC was created as a permanent institution, as opposed to the *ad hoc* international criminal tribunals that had been specifically established for the former Yugoslavia, Rwanda, Sierra Leone and Lebanon. In addition, the ICC's formation was meant to overcome the frailties of the *ad hoc* tribunals, which were believed to be costly, selective and sluggish (Meron 2011, 142). Unlike the *ad hoc* tribunals, whose jurisdiction was limited to case-specific crimes, the ICC has wide jurisdiction across 123[3] countries in the world.

This chapter draws on Sikkink's concept of the "justice cascade" to interrogate the unintended consequences of the ICC's interventions into the diffusion of norms of accountability. More specifically, the chapter demonstrates how the ICC's "Africa problem," or exclusive focus on the continent, has contributed to suppression of the justice cascade in two inadvertent ways: destabilization of the ICC's power position as *the* institutional backstop for prosecuting heinous crimes and fragmentation of the norm of accountability. Collectively, these developments are reflections of how the ICC's selection bias promotes resistance to prosecutions amongst domestic authorities and

1 Preamble of the Rome Statute.

2 Ibid.

3 Number of ICC member states as of August 2020.

political elites, with long-term effects on the global shift to accountability for atrocity crimes.

So far, the ICC has partially lived up to the aspirations of its founders by intervening in several African situations, namely: Uganda, the Democratic Republic of the Congo (DRC),

Côte d'Ivoire, Mali, Central African Republic (CAR), Kenya, Libya and Sudan. Some of the Court's interventions have led to the indictment of some powerful state actors, such as Sudan's former president Omar al-Bashir, Libya's Muamar Al-Gaddafi, Côte d'Ivoire's Laurent Gbagbo, and Kenya's Uhuru Kenyatta and William Ruto.[4] The ICC has also focused on the top leadership of the armed opposition in the DRC, Libya, Sudan, Uganda, CAR and Mali.

Consequently, the Court's interventions have resulted in some convictions in the DRC and Mali, with acquittals for Kenya, CAR, Côte d'Ivoire and Sudan, and ongoing trials for Uganda, Côte d'Ivoire and CAR (ICC 2020). Nonetheless, several other ICC indictees are still fugitives of justice, notably figures from Libya, Sudan, Uganda, Kenya, Mali and Côte d'Ivoire (ibid.).

Outside Africa, the ICC has indicated its intentions to intervene in the Georgian conflict of 2008, although it has yet to formally charge suspects. This is in addition to the Court's preliminary investigations in Afghanistan, Iraq/United Kingdom, Palestine, the Philippines, Ukraine, Colombia, Venezuela, as well as Africa's Guinea and Nigeria (ibid.).

Given the ICC's proactive responses in Africa, it has emerged as a central actor in diffusing the norm of individual criminal accountability in a continent which has otherwise been associated with impunity for serious crimes. Even so, the ICC's "Africa problem" has attracted considerable attention and criticism from some African leaders and their respective constituencies.[5]

For example, while speaking at an African Union (AU)[6] summit in 2013, the former Ethiopian Prime Minister and AU chairman, Hailemariam Desalegn, lamented how the ICC had degenerated into an institution that was engaged in a "racial hunt," as opposed to its original intentions of the pursuit

4 Kenyatta and Ruto were senior government officials at the time of their indictments for their alleged responsibilities in Kenya's 2007/2008 post-election violence. They partly built on their difficulties with the ICC to weave a campaign narrative under which they delegitimized the ICC as neocolonial. As a result, they won Kenya's March 2013 elections, and thus became the country's president and deputy president, respectively.

5 It is however important to note that some African states, notably Botswana, contested such claims of the ICC's bias in Africa.

6 The AU was established to safeguard Africa from imperialism and promote regional solidarity and cooperation, given the continent's history of colonial domination. The Assembly of the Heads of States is the supreme organ of the Union, and it is headed by an elected chairman. See Constitutive Act of the African Union of 2000.

of justice (Daily Nation 2013). Moreover, President Kagame of Rwanda has on several occasions accused the ICC of unfairly targeting Africans under the West's instruction (Amin 2017; Edroos 2018). In a similar vein, Uganda's president, Yoweri Museveni, called for Africa's withdrawal from the ICC, as he accused the institution of oppressing Africans, contrary to its original intentions (Makana 2014).

Similarly, President Uhuru Kenyatta of Kenya expressed his concerns at the ICC's focus on Africa, despite international crimes being carried out in other continents (see Vegh Weis's chapter in this volume; PSCU 2013, 5). Kenyatta underscored the fact that all cases before the ICC were from Africa, and Africans had been the only defendants brought before the Court since its establishment (ibid.). Admittedly, empirical evidence points to conflicts in other regions with their associated atrocities, such as in Afghanistan, Nepal, Myanmar, Pakistan, India, Pakistan, Kashmir, Philippines and Israel/Palestine (Schofield 2010; Gelvin 2014; Taylor 2016; Human Rights Watch 2017). Moreover, recent conflicts in Yemen and Syria have been more intense and resulted in greater human rights violations and the commission of more atrocities than most of the African ICC situations (see for example Tisdall 2016).

The African leaders' apprehensions about the ICC's selectivity are shared by many of the continent's citizens and observers. For example, a Nigerian commentator observed how the Court's actions manifest broader aims of humiliating African leadership in order to perpetuate imperialism (Yeebo 2012, 1). Similarly, Smith (2009) reveals that over the years there has been disquiet in African states over the ICC's singular focus on the continent.

The ICC has also been accused of practicing "distant justice" in Africa as manifested in its geographical, philosophical and procedural detachment, which exacerbates its problematic encounters (Clark 2018). However, it is also widely agreed that the African people – specifically victims of international crimes – as well as those communities directly affected, support the ICC (Annan 2016).

Perhaps the mixed perceptions of the ICC's forays in Africa are best illustrated in Kenya, Sudan and South Africa. Whereas the ICC's interventions in Kenya and Sudan broke the cycles of impunity for alleged perpetrators of atrocity crimes (see Vegh Weis's chapter), the Court also attracted accusations of neocolonialism and generated a public backlash (Lynch 2014; Lugano 2017). Prompted by concerns for its regional reputation, South Africa opted to comply with the AU's collective defiance of the ICC, as illustrated by its decision not to arrest Omar al-Bashir in June 2015 (Boehme 2017).

The arguments in this chapter build on my evaluation of secondary literature on the ICC's interventions in Africa, as well as several years analyzing the Court's legacy on the continent. Some of the secondary sources that have enriched my discussions include: journal articles, books, chapters in edited volumes, media sources, reports from non-governmental organizations (NGOs) and governments, as well as the AU's and the ICC's official documents.

This introduction is followed by an analysis of the ICC's power position vis-à-vis other national and international efforts in combating impunity for international crimes. Then, it turns to the ICC's "Africa problem" and its implications for the justice cascade. The chapter then concludes with a brief summary of the previous discussions and some general remarks on the unintended consequences on the ICC's interventions in Africa for the enterprise of international criminal justice.

Setting the scene: the International Criminal Court's power position in the justice cascade

Over the years, there has been an increase in the prosecutions of alleged perpetrators of human rights violations across the world. This phenomenon has been characterized as the "justice cascade," denoting a new turn in world politics towards individual criminal liability for human rights violations (Sikkink 2011). As shown in the different chapters of this volume, the justice cascade marked a fundamental departure from previous trends where impunity for alleged perpetrators was the norm, with the Nuremberg and Tokyo trials some of the notable exceptions (ibid.).

Whereas the increasing prosecution of alleged perpetrators of serious crimes can occur in domestic, foreign and internationalized tribunals, the ICC has emerged with an advantageous position of power vis-à-vis other mechanisms in the justice cascade. This is due to the Court's near universal acceptance across the world's regions, granting it a wider jurisdictional potential than any other institution.

Besides, the ICC can potentially intervene in a given country under three different mechanisms: state referrals[7] (Art. 14); United Nations Security Council (UNSC) referrals[8] (Art. 13(b)) and the *proprio motu*[9] provision (Arts.

7 Under this provision, a member state of the ICC can invite the Court to intervene in its territory.

8 The UNSC can similarly trigger the Court's actions pursuant to Chapter VII of the UN Charter.

9 The prosecutor's own motion.

13(c), 15 and 51(1)). As a result, the ICC's jurisdictional reach is not limited to those states which are party to the Rome Statute, or domestic authorities' discretions on commencing investigations and referring cases to it.

Furthermore, the ICC has close working relations with the United Nations (UN) system. First, the UNSC has a prominent role in the Rome Statute, given its capacity to refer cases to the Court, and to defer cases for 12 months as laid out in Article 16 of the Statute. Second, the UN and the ICC entered into a "Negotiated Relationship Agreement" that acknowledged the latter's critical role in the prosecution of core crimes that also threaten international peace and security (UN 2004). Lending further credence to the ICC's position of power in the justice cascade are the Rome Statute's principles of victim-centeredness, cooperation and complementarity. Taken together, they reinforce the international community's renewed efforts to combat impunity for serious crimes.

With regard to victims, the Rome Statute provides for their protection and participation in Court processes (Art. 68), as well as an elaborate reparations regime under Articles 75 and 79. Also, the ICC established the Office of Public Counsel for Victims (OPCV), the Victims Participation and Reparations Section (VPRS) and field outreach offices. The ICC's discretion as to when to begin investigations is also premised on "the interests of victims" as expressed in Article 53 of the Statute. Generally, the ICC positions itself as a victims' court, given its provisions on victims' participation in proceedings, reparations, and legal assistance (Stover 2010, 4).

The principle of cooperation establishes a mutual relationship between the ICC and national jurisdictions in collective efforts to combat impunity. With the ICC's lack of executive power, territory and police force of its own, it relies on state authorities to make arrests and collect evidence (Kaul 2011). More succinctly, in the preamble of the Rome Statute, it is noted that the prosecution of atrocity crimes should be achieved by "taking measures at the national level and by enhancing international cooperation."

Crucially, cooperation links to the principle of complementarity that envisions the ICC as a court of last resort. In the preamble and Article 1 of the Rome Statute, it is expressly stated that the ICC "shall be complementary to national jurisdictions." Hence, the Court only intervenes where states are unwilling and/or unable to do so, as further elaborated under Article 17. Moreover, it has been rightly argued that complementarity was predicted to have a catalyzing effect on the justice cascade by prompting state actions in order to ward off the ICC's involvements, or states living up to their normative responsibilities under the Rome Statute (Meron 2011; Nouwen 2011).

It is thus clear that the ICC has emerged as a critical actor in the justice cascade given its jurisdictional reach, near-global acceptance and its principles of cooperation, complementarity and victim-centeredness. As such, Cody et al. (2015, 59) rightly observe that the ICC has greater potential for justice in relation to the commission of international crimes than any local or regional judicial mechanisms.

At the same time, the ICC's power position has been massively challenged by perceptions of a bias against Africa in its selection of cases. In turn, these accusations have created platforms that destabilize the ICC's position as *the* institutional backstop for prosecuting international crimes and fragmenting the norm of accountability

Destabilizing the International Criminal Court's power position and fragmentation of the norm of accountability

The ICC's exclusive focus on Africa exposed normative paradoxes in the international criminal justice enterprise. Notably, the Court's interventions in Africa prompted critical concerns about the rationale for an international criminal justice that gave attention to some places and people and not to others (Clark & Waddell 2008, 8). However, the ICC's inaction in other deserving situations could be attributed to a variety of causes: lack of jurisdiction (Yemen and Myanmar), deadlocks in the UNSC in referring non-ICC member states (Israel/Palestine and Syria), and caution in avoiding confrontations with some of the major world powers (UK, USA and France) that had committed atrocities in Iraq and Afghanistan (Plessis 2013; Bosco 2014).

Nonetheless, inaction in such situations fueled perceptions of the ICC's preoccupation with Africa and lack of interest in other sites of international crimes. Such interpretations were reinforced by the ICC's prolonged preliminary investigations in other regions, but prompt action in some African situations. As legitimate concerns about the ICC's envisaged universality of justice, perceptions of an anti-African bias contributed to suppression of the justice cascade by triggering: (1) ways of contesting the ICC's discretion to select cases, and (2) a chain of anti-ICC counter-reactions.

Ways of contesting the ICC's discretion to select cases

Before the ICC's establishment in 2002, the African continent had recorded many instances of atrocity crimes that were largely understood under local interpretations and remained largely unaddressed due to domestic inaction and traditions of impunity. As Baker (2004) rightly observed, impunity prevailed in Africa despite the development of international law and changes in world opinion since the end of the Cold War. It is within this context that Sudan, Uganda, Kenya, the DRC, CAR, Burundi, Côte d'Ivoire, and several other African countries experienced deadly conflicts with subsequent domestic impunity that necessitated the ICC's intervention.

Conversely, the ICC's internationalization of the conflicts raised their profile and hence the urgency of addressing them, including the search for justice and reparations for the harm suffered by victims. In the absence of the ICC's interventions, many accounts of the serious atrocities that had occurred in specific African situations would have been marginalized under dominant national discourses or the versions of history written by the victors. By intervening in the conflicts, the ICC brought to the fore many instances of crime, their alleged perpetrators and victims, as well as their correct understanding as serious crimes that were to be punished under international law.

For example, the ICC's involvement in Sudan after the 2005 UNSC referral highlighted various forms of international crimes that had occurred in the country, namely genocide, war crimes and crimes against humanity (see Savelsberg's chapter in this volume; ICC 2018a). With regard to genocide, the Office of the Prosecutor (OTP) identified the acts of causing bodily and mental harm, and targeting groups for annihilation (ibid.). For war crimes, the OTP listed instances of murder, destruction of property, rape, and targeting installations and peacekeepers (ibid.). Similarly, the prosecution documented instances of crimes against humanity, such as persecution, forced displacement of populations, torture, imprisonment and extermination (ibid.).

For these crimes, the OTP identified some of the perpetrators with most responsibility, pointing to some government officials, and leaders of the Janjaweed militia and the Resistance Front (ibid.). Specifically, on the OTP's charge sheet were al-Bashir, Harun and Kushayb (state actors), as well as Abu Garda, Saleh Mohammed Jerbo Jamus and Abdel Raheem Muhammad Hussein (non-state actors) (ibid.).

Similarly, the ICC's intervention in Kenya's 2007/2008 post-election violence acknowledged the serious crimes committed against the population (ICC 2018b). According to the OTP, the violence led to more than 1,000 deaths, 900 acts of sexual and gender-based violence, 3,500 serious injuries and the internal displacement of 350,000 people (ibid.). The OTP specifically noted disruptions of the victims' socioeconomic conditions, psychological trauma, and falling health standards (ibid.).

As a result, the ICC listed an equal number of suspects from both sides of the conflict – the Party of National Unity (PNU) and the Orange Democratic

Movement (ODM).[10] These included Uhuru Kenyatta (deputy prime minister and minister for finance), Francis Muthaura (head of the civil service) and Mohammed Hussein Ali (police commissioner) from the PNU (ICC 2010). The ODM suspects were William Ruto (minister for education), Henry Kosgey (minister for industrialization) and Joshua Arap Sang (radio journalist) (ibid.).

Likewise, the ICC's interventions in the DRC, Mali, CAR, Uganda, Libya and Côte d'Ivoire documented the various forms of crime and the specific harm suffered by victims. Similarly, the OTP apportioned blame to particular individuals who were subsequently placed under investigation and/or subject to criminal prosecutions. Since then, a number of suspects have been convicted, and the trials of several others are ongoing. Nevertheless, the ICC's African focus generated opposition to its discretion in selecting cases.

Of great concern was the fact that opposition to the ICC's case selection was driven by some of the political elites who had been accused of crimes. For example, Sudan's al-Bashir, Kenya's Kenyatta and Ruto, as well as some Libyan authorities regularly accused the ICC of unfairly targeting Africans. Al-Bashir, for instance, argued that the ICC was an institution of injustice and a manifestation of Africa's oppression and unfair treatment, which he vowed to oppose (Xinhua 2016). In the Kenyan case, Kenyatta and Ruto formed the Jubilee Alliance, a political coalition which was used to counter-shame the ICC as neocolonial: they subsequently won the March 2013 elections and formed a government (Lugano 2017). After assuming office, the co-accused continued to propagate anti-ICC narratives on national, regional and international platforms (ibid.).

In a similar vein, some African political elites conveniently appropriated claims that the ICC was biased in efforts to undermine the Court's investigations. For example, concerned about the ICC investigating regime atrocities in the northern conflict, Uganda's Museveni regularly accused the Court of promoting imperial interests and acting unfairly against Africans (Makana 2014). In the same way, after the ICC declared its intention to commence investigations in Burundi, some of the country's political elites repeated allegations of the Court's bias against Africa, after which they passed motions to withdraw from the "unjust" institution (Ngendakumana 2016).

In sum, the ICC's "Africa problem" was used by some of the political elites who were under scrutiny as leverage to circumvent justice. In an opportunistic

10 The ODM was the main opposition party that contested the announcement of PNU's Mwai Kibaki as the winner of the presidential elections. Following international mediation, a transitional PNU/ODM power-sharing government was established that led to relative peace and stability.

way, the political actors partly shifted attention from their position as suspects of international crimes to debates on why the ICC focuses exclusively on Africa. In turn, the debates spoke to the continent's postcolonial condition, where Africans are passive recipients of colonial intellectual legacies, with the ICC being part of this inheritance (Ba 2017). Such interpretations were difficult to counter, given the West's history of colonial domination of Africa, support for the Court, dominance in the UNSC, commission of atrocities elsewhere, and the Court's inaction in other serious conflicts that some Western states engaged in (Lugano 2017).

So within individual African states there was direct opposition to the ways in which the ICC chose the cases it took action on, and at the level of the AU, the Court's focus was increasingly attacked. Given the AU's position as the vanguard of the continent's unity, sovereignty and territorial integrity,[11] the ICC's perceived bias in Africa triggered a significant chain of counter-reactions that also contributed to suppression of the justice cascade.

Chain of counter-reactions against the International Criminal Court

The belief that the ICC was reinforcing Africa's postcolonial condition prompted the AU to take a number of collective decisions: (1) not to cooperate with the ICC, (2) to establish a regional alternative to the ICC, and (3) to contemplate African states' withdrawal from the Rome Statute. Whereas decisions on non-cooperation were supposed to be implemented by individual member states, alternatives to the ICC included expanding the jurisdiction of the African Court of Justice and Human Rights (ACJHR). The option of collective withdrawal from the ICC was envisaged as the final step in Africa's opposition to the ICC's biased focus.

The ACJHR was established in 2004 after the African Court on Human and Peoples' Rights was merged with the Court of Justice of the African Union (Protocol on the Statute of the African Court of Justice and Human Rights). It has two sections – general affairs and human rights – with each having eight judges (ibid.). As stipulated under Article 29 of the Protocol to the ACJHR, cases can be brought forward to the Court by state parties to the Protocol, organs of the AU, staff members of the AU on appeal, African intergovernmental organizations, non-governmental organizations and human rights institutions, as well as individuals. The Court's jurisdiction is limited to interpreting the AU constitutive act of 2000, union treaties and

11 Constitutive Act of the African Union of 2000.

subsidiary legal instruments, international legal obligations, and regulations and decisions of the Union (ibid.). As the AU envisioned in its battles with the ICC, the ACJHR would also investigate and prosecute alleged perpetrators of international crimes in order to limit the continent's submission to the global institution (AU 2017). To date, state ratification of the expanded Protocol has been slow, given the lack of adequate political will (Kuteesa 2017).

Although the establishment of the ICC was followed by an increased number of prosecutions of alleged perpetrators of atrocity crimes in Africa, the chain of counter-reactions disrupted the justice cascade. In doing so, the AU's collective decisions had the net effect of challenging the Court's moral authority and slowing down its activities.

With the intensification of the ICC's interventions in Africa, the AU embarked on a policy of collective non-cooperation with the Court. In one of the AU's summits in 2009, member states stressed that they and the AU had the right to take appropriate actions that would safeguard and preserve "the dignity, sovereignty and integrity of the continent" (AU 2009, 3). This decision was reiterated at the 2013 summit of the AU that regretted the ICC's continued prosecution of African leaders, which undermined the "constitutional order, stability and, integrity of Member States" (AU 2013, 2). In this light, the AU went ahead to express its concerns about the ICC's "politicization and misuse of indictments" of African leaders (ibid., 1).

As a result, the AU opposed the prosecution of African leaders before any international criminal tribunal (ibid.). The AU also decided that together with African ICC member states, they were at liberty to decide on appropriate measures or actions essential to guaranteeing the dignity, security, peace, stability and sovereignty of the continent (AU 2014). Conversely, the regional institution was silent on the fate of indicted non-state actors who offered little reputational damage to their states and the AU.

Given the AU's non-cooperation, any African fugitive of justice was free to roam the continent with limited chances of their being apprehended and transferred to the ICC. For example, al-Bashir travelled through many African countries, such as Kenya, Malawi, Uganda, South Africa and Nigeria, because his safety was assured (Kaberia 2013; Reuters 2011; Hamilton 2013; Bowcott 2015; Musisi 2017). Thus, the decision of the AU not to cooperate with the ICC reduced the costs of individual AU ICC member states and indicted African leaders failing to comply with the ICC. Moreover, the decisions undermined the norm of accountability by putting many African states in a position of competing obligations to the AU and the ICC. Thus, South Africa partly explained its refusal to arrest al-Bashir when he visited the country in 2015 by rival commitments to both the AU and the ICC (Ngari 2017). Besides, the decisions stemming from the AU's non-cooperation were rationalized under customary national and international laws, under which immunity is guaranteed to sitting heads of states (AU 2013).

Indeed, the AU's promotion of immunity for sitting heads of states works directly against the justice cascade, in which the ICC has acquired more power than other institutional frameworks. The ICC leads the way in seeking the urgent prosecution of those most responsible for the perpetration of international crime with its policy of intolerance to impunity. In this regard, the Court proposes the principle of "irrelevance of official capacity" as articulated in Article 27 of the Rome Statute. According to this, the Statute applies equally to all individuals, regardless of their position in government.

But the AU's envisaged regional alternative to the ICC – the ACJHR – stresses the relevance of official capacity. The ACJHR has an immunity clause for sitting heads of states that does not fit well with the norm of accountability, since it grants shelter to those most responsible for crimes whose impunity the ICC so seeks to end.

Furthermore, the ACJHR was not necessarily considered to be based "on the interest of justice," but was a rival of, or substitute for, the ICC. In one of the AU's documents, it is expressly stated that the ACJHR would limit the ICC's involvement in Africa – a fulfilment of the mantra of "African solutions to African problems" (AU 2017, 12). Moreover, the ACJHR would add another layer of complementarity – regional criminal jurisdictions – as a recognition of the need for continental solutions and mechanisms (ibid., 13). Nonetheless, it has been proven over the years that African leaders are accustomed to impunity, hence the limited prospects of regional complementarity.

Perhaps the climax of the AU's opposition to the ICC was the decision to withdraw *en masse* from the Rome Statute. Moved by Kenya, the motion on collective withdrawal hinted at "making a powerful statement that reflects Africa's refusal to be carried along in a system that tramples on Africans' dignity" (PSCU 2016, 1). Debates on the collective withdrawal were energized by the formation of an *ad hoc* Open-Ended Ministerial Committee[12] that subsequently drafted the AU's collective withdrawal strategy (AU 2017, 2). Amongst the Committee's objectives were: countering perceptions of double standards at the ICC, striving for a fair and transparent international criminal justice system and furthering the notion of African solutions to African problems (ibid.).

12 The Open-ended Committee comprises Ministers of Foreign Affairs, and was established in 2015 following the decisions of the 25th AU Summit held in South Africa. See Allafrica.com (2015).

Decrying the ICC's selective focus on Africa, the Open-Ended Ministerial Committee denounced the prevalence of African suspects in the international criminal justice system, and reiterated the problems with prosecution discretion in selecting cases to be investigated and tried (ibid.). Furthermore, the Committee attributed these outcomes to inequities in international decision making, whereby political imbalances are reflected in the application of international law (ibid.). In this regard, the Committee further entrenched the ICC in an international politics that pitted Africa against the global system. Such eventualities deflected the agency from attending to atrocities committed on the continent, thus marginalizing voices arguing for victim-centeredness, international cooperation and complementarity, as well as the ICC's position as a court of last resort. However, many African states have since refrained from following up on the decision to abandon the Rome Statute. Perhaps this could be attributed to the general acceptance of the ICC's utility that led to the AU's calls for reforms of the global institution (AU 2017). More interestingly, Kenya has made no concrete steps to withdraw from the ICC despite leading such endeavors at the AU (Mathenge 2016). In addition, South Africa and The Gambia revoked their earlier declarations of withdrawal to the UN Secretary General (UN 2017; Saine & Jahateh 2017). Since then, only Burundi has finally abandoned the ICC, in October 2017, whereas many African states restated their commitment to the Court at the 2016 Assembly of State Parties (ASP) meeting (Keppler 2016). Nonetheless, contemplating the possibility of Africa's mass withdrawal from the Rome Statute sent a clear message to the ICC and its supporters that Africa would consider drastic measures to resist the Court's continued exclusive focus.

Conclusion

Although the ICC's interventions in several African situations have cascaded the prosecution of individual perpetrators of violence, this diffusion of a norm of accountability has been considerably slowed down by perceptions of the Court's exclusive focus. In other words, contrary to the positive features of the ICC's interventions in Africa, there are also criticisms that the Court's skewed focus perpetuates the continent's postcolonial condition in which external powers impose their hierarchies of decision making.

Consequently, the perceived connection of the ICC's interventions with Africa's postcolonialism has provided the means to contest the Court's discretion in selecting cases and triggered chains of counter-reactions against the Court. Because of this, the ICC's interventions in Africa have led to unintended consequences that are contrary to the aims of the drafters of the Rome Statute – challenging the Court's position of power and leading to a fragmentation of the norm of accountability. Given such outcomes, there is a need for vigilance about the possible knock-on effects of the African precedent of contesting the ICC's discretions.

The African political elites' resistance to the ICC is problematic, given that they do not speak for the victims who suffer atrocities. This is demonstrated in their reluctance to institute domestic proceedings for atrocity crimes, and their inability to establish a viable regional tribunal that would overcome the accusations of imperialism against the ICC. Hence, the backlash from political actors is best understood as a clever maneuver to evade the ICC's reach, whilst the victim community still perceives the Court as the only viable alternative to Africa's cycle of impunity around atrocity crimes.

Nevertheless, Africa's future relationship with the ICC will continue to be shaped by the Court's discretion about which cases it takes on. Perhaps a positive outcome would be the ICC's movement towards the universality of justice in order to overturn the growing resistance to its justice.

References

African Union, 2009. Decision on the Meeting of African States Parties to the Rome Statute of the International Criminal Court (ICC). Doc. Assembly/AU/13(XIII). Available at: https://au.int/sites/default/files/decisions/9560-assembly_en_1_3_july_2009_auc_thirteenth_ordinary_session_decisions_declarations_message_congratulations_motion_0.pdf [Accessed May 3, 2018].

African Union, 2013. Decision on Africa's Relationship with the International Criminal Court (ICC). Ext/Assembly/AU/Dec.1(Oct.2013). Available at: https://au.int/sites/default/files/decisions/9655-ext_assembly_au_dec_decl_e_0.pdf [Accessed August 2, 2020].

African Union, 2014. Decision on the progress report of the commission on the implementation of the decisions on the International Criminal Court. Doc. Assembly/AU/13(XXII). Available at: https://au.int/sites/default/files/decisions/9659-assembly_au_dec_490-516_xxii_e.pdf [Accessed October 13, 2015].

African Union, 2017. Withdrawal Strategy Document. Available at: https://www.hrw.org/sites/default/files/supporting_resources/icc_withdrawal_strategy_jan._2017.pdf [Accessed August 2, 2020].

Allafrica, 2015. *Africa: The Open-Ended Committee on ICC Meeting.* Available at: https://allafrica.com/stories/201510010723.html [Accessed August 9, 2019].

Amin, M., 2017. "Paul Kagame and Omar Bashir join hands against ICC." *Daily Nation,* December 21. Available at: https://www.nation.co.ke/news/africa/Paul-KagameRwanda-Omar-Bashir-Sudan-against-ICC/1066-4237468-akfani/index.html [Accessed April 30, 2018].

Annan, K., 2016. "State impunity is back in fashion – we need the International Court more than ever." *The Guardian,* November 18. Available at: https://www.theguardian.com/commentisfree/2016/nov/18/state-impunity-international-criminal-court-african [Accessed August 2, 2020].

Ba, O., 2017. "International Justice and the Post-colonial Condition." *Africa Today* 63(4): 44–62.

Baker, B., 2004. "Twilight of Impunity for Africa's Presidential Criminals." *Third World Quarterly* 25(8): 1487–1499.

Boehme, F., 2017. "'We Chose Africa': South Africa and the Regional Politics of Cooperation with the International Criminal Court." *International Journal of Transitional Justice* 11(1): 50–70.

Bosco, D., 2014. *Rough justice: The International Criminal Court in a world of power politics*. Oxford: Oxford University Press.

Bowcott, O., 2015. "Sudan president Omar al-Bashir leaves South Africa as court considers arrest." *The Guardian*, June 15. Available at: https://www.theguardian.com/world/2015/jun/15/south-africa-to-fight-omar-al-bashirs-arrestwarrant-sudan [Accessed April 21, 2020].

Clark, P., 2018. *Distant Justice: The Impact of the International Criminal Court on African Politics*. Cambridge: Cambridge University Press.

Clark, P. & Waddel, N., 2008. "Introduction." In Clark, P. & Waddel, N. (eds.) *Courting Conflict? Justice, Peace and the ICC in Africa*. London: Royal African Society, 37–46.

Cody, S., Stover, E., Balthazard, M. & Koenig, A., 2015. *The Victims' Court? A Study of 622 Victim Participants at the International Criminal Court*. Berkeley, CA: Human Rights Center, University of California, Berkeley, School of Law. Available at: https://www.law.berkeley.edu/wp-content/uploads/2015/04/VP_report_2015_final_full2.pdf [Accessed April 15, 2020].

Constitutive Act of the African Union of 2000.

Daily Nation, 2013. "ICC Targets Africans on Race Basis: African Union Chair," May 27. Available at: http://www.nation.co.ke/news/politics/ICC-targetsAfricans-on-race-basis-African-Union-chair/1064-1864200-3quy5fz/index.html [Accessed April 10, 2020].

Edroos, F., 2018. "Rwanda's Paul Kagame accuses ICC of bias against Africa." Available at: https://www.aljazeera.com/news/2018/04/rwanda-kagame-accuses-icc-bias-africa-180429050656022.html [Accessed April 30, 2020].

Gelvin, J., 2014. *The Israel-Palestine Conflict: One Hundred Years of War*. Cambridge: Cambridge University Press.

Hamilton, R., 2013. "Sudan President Bashir's Nigeria visit causes anger." BBC, July 1. Available at: http://www.bbc.com/news/world-africa-23313730 [Accessed April 21, 2020].

Human Rights Watch, 2017. *Burma: Methodical Massacre at Rohingya Village*. Available at: https://www.hrw.org/news/2017/12/19/burma-methodical-massacre-rohingya-village [Accessed April 21, 2020].

Mathenge, O., 2016. "ICC exit shelved as Kenya takes reforms to UN." *The Star*, May 21. Available at: https://www.the-star.co.ke/news/2016-05-21-icc-exit-shelved-as-kenya-takes-reforms-to-un/ [Accessed August 2, 2020].

International Criminal Court, 2010. *Situation in the Republic of Kenya*. ICC01/09, 1.

International Criminal Court, 2018a. *Sudan: Jurisdiction in the general situation*. Available at: https://www.icc-cpi.int/darfur [Accessed May 3, 2020].

International Criminal Court, 2018b. *Kenya: Jurisdiction in the general situation*. Available at: https://www.icc-cpi.int/kenya [Accessed May 3, 2020].

International Criminal Court, 2020. *Situations and cases*. Available at: https://www.icc-cpi.int/Pages/cases.aspx [Accessed April 29, 2020].

Kaberia, J., 2010. "Uproar over Bashir visit to Kenya." Available at: https://www.capitalfm.co.ke/news/2010/08/uproar-over-bashir-visit-to-kenya/ [Accessed April 10, 2020].

Kaul, P.H., 2011. "The International Criminal Court – Current Challenges and Perspectives." Available at: https://www.icc-cpi.int/nr/rdonlyres/289b449a-347d-4360-a854-3b7d0a4b9f06/283740/010911salzburglawschool.pdf [Accessed August 2, 2020].

Keppler, E., 2016. *African Members Reaffirm Support at International Criminal Court Meeting.* Available at: https://www.hrw.org/news/2016/11/17/african-members-reaffirm-support-international-criminal-court-meeting [Accessed April 18, 2020].

Kuteesa, H., 2017. "Africa urged on willpower to start own criminal Court." *The New Times*, August 23. Available at: http://www.newtimes.co.rw/section/read/218505/ [Accessed May 5, 2020].

Lugano, G., 2017. "Counter-Shaming the International Criminal Court's Intervention as Neocolonial: Lessons from Kenya." *International Journal of Transitional Justice* 11(1): 9–29.

Lynch, G., 2014. "Electing the 'alliance of the accused': The success of the Jubilee Alliance in Kenya's Rift Valley." *Journal of Eastern African Studies* 8(1): 93–114.

Makana, F., 2014. "Ugandan President Yoweri Museveni lashes out at ICC, wants Africa to pull out." *The Standard*, last updated 23:32 on December 12, 2014. Available at: https://www.standardmedia.co.ke/article/2000144601/ugandan-president-yoweri-musevenilashes-out-at-icc-wants-africa-to-pull-out [Accessed April 29, 2020].

Meron, T., 2011. *The Making of International Criminal Justice. A View from the Bench.* Oxford: Oxford University Press.

Musisi, F., 2017. "Security tight as Bashir arrives in Uganda." *Daily Monitor*, November 13. Available at: http://www.monitor.co.ug/News/National/Sudanese-president-Bashir-arrives-Uganda-three-days-visit/688334-4184982-tihmbi/index.html [Accessed April 20, 2020].

Ngari, A., 2017. "Clutching at straws: SA's reasons for not arresting al-Bashir." Institute for Security Studies (ISS). Available at: https://issafrica.org/iss-today/clutching-atstraws-sas-reasons-for-not-arresting-al-bashir [Accessed April 21, 2020].

Ngendakumana, P., 2017. "Burundi: Target for ICC?" *Iwacu*, November 9. Available at: http://www.iwacu-burundi.org/englishnews/burundi-target-for-icc/ [Accessed April 17, 2020].

Nouwen, S. M. H., 2011. *Complementarity in the line of fire: The catalysing effect of the International Criminal Court in Uganda and Sudan.* Cambridge: Cambridge University Press.

Plessis, M., 2013. "Universalising international criminal law: The ICC, Africa and the problem of political perceptions." Pretoria: Institute for Security Studies. Available at: https://issafrica.org/research/papers/universalising-international-criminal-law-the-icc-africa-and-the-problem-of-political-perceptions [Accessed April 11, 2020].

Presidential Strategic Communication Unit, 2013. "Speech by President Uhuru Kenyatta at the Extraordinary Session of the African Union." *The Standard*, last updated 00.06 GMT on October 13, 2013. Available at: https://www.standardmedia.co.ke/article/2000095433/speech-by-president-uhuru-kenyatta-atthe-extraordinary-session-of-the-african-union [Accessed April 22, 2020].

Presidential Strategic Communication Unit, 2016. "AU adopts President Uhuru's proposal for mass withdrawal from ICC." *The Standard*, last updated 07.31 on February 1, 2016. Available at: https://www.standardmedia.co.ke/article/2000190043/au-adopts-presidentuhuru-s-proposal-for-mass-withdrawal-from-icc [Accessed January 29, 2020].

Protocol on the Statute of the African Court of Justice and Human Rights. 2008.

Reuters, 2011. "Hague court questions Bashir's visit to Malawi." October 19. Available at: https://www.reuters.com/article/ozatp-warcrimes-bashir-20111019-idAFJOE79I0K520111019 [Accessed April 21, 2020].

Saine, P. & Jahateh, L., 2017. "Gambia announces plans to stay in International Criminal Court." *Reuters*, February 14. Available at: https://www.reuters.com/article/usgambia-justice-icc-idUSKBN15S2HF [Accessed April 21, 2020].

Schofield, V., 2010. *Kashmir in Conflict: India, Pakistan and the Unending War.* London: I. B. Tauris and Co. Ltd.

Sikkink, K., 2011. *The Justice Cascade: How Human Rights Prosecutions are Changing World Politics.* New York: W. W. Norton and Co. Ltd.

Smith, D., 2009. "The International Criminal Court: The long arm of neo-colonialim?" *International Affairs Review.* Available at: https://iar-gwu.org/2009/11/02/the-international-criminal-court-the-long-arm-of-neocolonialism/ [Accessed August 2, 2020].

Taylor, A., 2016. "The Philippine Drug Crackdown Has Claimed 2,000 Lives in Two Months." *The Atlantic,* August 30. Available at: https://www.theatlantic.com/photo/2016/08/the-philippine-drug-crackdown-has-claimed-2000-lives-in-two-months/498071/ [Accessed April 21, 2020].

Tisdall, S., 2016. "Why Yemen conflict has becomte another Syria." *The Guardian,* October 10. Available at: https://www.theguardian.com/world/2016/oct/10/why-yemen-conflict-has-become-another-syria [Accessed April 21, 2020].

United Nations, 2004. *Relationship Agreement Between the United Nations and the International Criminal Court.* United Nations General Assembly. Available at: http://legal.un.org/ola/media/UN-ICC_Cooperation/UN-ICC%20Relationship%20Agreement.pdf [Accessed April 21, 2020].

United Nations, 2017. *South Africa: Withdrawal of notification of Withdrawal.* Available at: https://treaties.un.org/doc/Publication/CN/2017/CN.121.2017-Eng.pdf [Accessed August 2, 2020].

Xinhua, 2009. "Bashir: Sudan to fight 'neocolonialism,'" August 3. Available at: http://www.chinadaily.com.cn/world/2009-03/08/content_7552449.htm [Accessed April 3, 2020].

Yeebo, Z., 2012. "The ICC debate: A pan-African perspective." *Pambazuka News,* February 8. Available at: https://www.pambazuka.org/pan-africanism/icc-debate-pan-african-perspective [Accessed April 27, 2020].

Conditions and Cultural Consequences of International Criminal Justice Intervention
The Case of Darfur[1]

Joachim J. Savelsberg

Darfur as a case study on conditions and consequences of the justice cascade

One of the first cases of mass atrocity during the early 21st century unfolded in the Darfur region of Sudan, beginning in 2003. Darfur shares important commonalities with many other instances of mass violence: the center of the country neglected and repressed the periphery. Militant rebel movements emerged and violently responded to neglect and repression. The country's government responded with massive force not just against the armed rebels, but also against the civilian population from which the rebels were recruited. Millions were displaced and hundreds of thousands lost their lives (Hagan & Rymond-Richmond 2009). The case shares one additional feature with others instances of mass violence of the late 20th and early 21st centuries: the international community responded and international criminal justice institutions filed charges, in this case the new International Criminal Court (ICC).

The case of Darfur thus lends itself to an examination of crucial questions debated by scholars and practitioners who are concerned with interventions by international criminal law. First, how do responses to mass violence in Darfur square with theses about a "justice cascade" (Sikkink 2011) in the late 20th and early 21st centuries, the substantial increase in individual criminal accountability in cases of grave human rights violations? We know that the United Nations Security Council (UNSC) and the ICC intervened. They were supported by social movements, international NGOs (INGOs) and national governments,

1 Underlying research was supported by the National Science Foundation (SES-0957946). I thank the editors for their careful reading of an earlier version. Their queries and suggestions helped me improve the text.

including all European countries and the majority of countries represented on the UNSC (the US abstained, but allowed the case to move forward). These interventions are, it seems, in line with notions of the justice cascade, its nature and its conditions. A closer look below reveals important specifications. Second, what are the consequences of international criminal justice, here ICC, interventions? While fighters for a justice cascade invest great hopes in the notion of deterrence through the threat of punishment, my concern focuses on the cultural effects of judicial interventions. Such effects are too often disregarded by scholars and practitioners, but they may well be of the greatest consequence as they contribute to the construction of delegitimizing narratives about mass violence. In other words, I am especially interested in the representational power of international criminal justice (ICJ). By representational power, I mean the chance of an ICJ institution to affect collective representations and memories, even against resistance, and thereby to impress on a global public a particular understanding of mass violence as a form of criminal violence.

Empirical findings in this chapter are gained, and conclusions drawn, from a large-scale empirical investigation. I conducted interviews with Africa correspondents and with Sudan experts in foreign ministries, one humanitarian aid NGO (MSF) and one human rights NGO (Amnesty International) in eight countries of North America (Canada, United States) and Europe (Austria, France, Germany, Ireland, Switzerland, United Kingdom). I conducted almost all interviews in 2011, in each country's capital city, but also in seats of major newspapers and INGOs; in respondents' offices and in private homes; all in person, only in four cases over the phone. In addition, my research team, supported by funding from the National Science Foundation, conducted a content analysis of a sample of 3,387 media articles on Darfur, resulting in the Darfur Media Data Set. We randomly selected reports and opinion pieces published in leading newspapers in the same eight countries, specifically one with a center-conservative and one with a left-liberal orientation (with the exception of Ireland and Switzerland, where international news is covered mostly by one dominant paper). Coders read articles and worked along a detailed coding scheme developed for this project. Intercoder-reliability was perfect for some variables and sufficient, by common statistical standards, for the others (for further methodological details see Savelsberg 2015, 16–27).

In the following, I first summarize arguments about the justice cascade. I examine subsequently how responses to the mass violence in Darfur align with these arguments. An analysis of the cultural consequences of judicial intervention follows. Findings show that the criminalizing narrative unfolds stronger representational power than its competitors do. While proponents of ICJ may draw hope from such findings, they also have to consider cautionary notes regarding internal conflict within ICJ, the intrusion of political forces into law, and country-specific receptivity to the criminalizing narrative generated by the court. An exploration of such cautionary notes for Darfur leads over to conclusions.

"Justice cascade" and the criminalization of human rights offending

Political and military leaders responsible for mass killings and atrocities were, through much of human history, celebrated as heroes (Giesen 2004). More recently, denial took the place of adoration (Cohen 2001). This shift is associated with remarkable changes throughout the 20th century. After all, its uniqueness lies not in the horrendous atrocities committed (too many past centuries can compete), but in humanity's new inventiveness and efforts toward curbing the perpetration of human rights violations (Minow 1998). Relatedly, Kathryn Sikkink (2011) portrays the late 20th and early 21st centuries as characterized by a "justice cascade," a massive increase in individual criminal accountability for grave human rights violations. Leaders of human rights movements express similar optimism (Neier 2012). These authors see strong social forces at work that contribute to the criminalization of grave human rights abuses and mass atrocities.

Sikkink (2011), while not discounting the Nuremberg and Tokyo trials, sets the stage with a discussion of challenging cases that did not result from military defeat. Her detailed studies of Greece (regime change 1975), Portugal (1974), Spain (1975) and Argentina (1985) show that regional opportunity structures had developed by the 1970s that favored transitional justice proceedings. Examples of such structures are the creation of the European Court of Human Rights in 1959 and the foundation of Amnesty International in 1961. Amnesty, soon after its foundation, became actively engaged in Greece. Its activism coincided with a supportive international legal environment, and this constellation advanced the launching of trials. The 1975 "Torture Declaration" was promulgated concurrently with the Greek torture trials. The UN General Assembly adopted it just a few months after their conclusion. Yet trials of the 1970s and 1980s occurred only after "ruptured" transitions from dictatorship to democracy (Greece, Portugal, Argentina) as opposed to "pacted" transitions that involved a significantly stronger element of negotiation between former power holders and their successors (Spain). By the 2000s onwards, however, "ruptured" transitions were no longer a prerequisite for criminal trials against human rights perpetrators, as the cases of Guatemala, Chile, and Uruguay illustrate.[2] Institutionalization of a human rights regime had progressed, and the fear of blowbacks had diminished.

Initial steps toward human rights prosecutions eventually resulted in a decentralized, interactive system of global accountability that challenged national sovereignty. Sikkink (2011, 96–125) identifies two contributors – "streams," to use her metaphor. The first stream is constituted by international prosecutions, from Nuremberg and Tokyo via the International Criminal Tribunal for the former Yugoslavia (ICTY) and its equivalent for Rwanda (ICTR) and finally on to the ICC with its jurisdiction over cases of aggression, war crimes, crimes against humanity and genocide. The second stream consists of domestic and foreign prosecutions such as those in Greece, Portugal, and Argentina in the mid-1970s and the Pinochet case of 1998–2000. In addition, a "hard law streambed" led from various conventions such as the Genocide Convention (1948), Geneva Convention (1949), Apartheid Convention (1980) and Torture Convention (1987), via the Inter-American Convention on Forced Disappearances (1996) to the Rome Statute (1998).

This spread of human rights initiatives, and their solidification in a system, was not simply the result of contagion. Instead, individuals, associations, trans-governmental networks, penetrated by an epistemic community of criminal law experts, and NGOs such as Human Rights Watch (HRW) and Amnesty, achieved the progressive institutionalization of individual criminal liability, that is, *criminalization* and *individualization* of international law. This focus on actors builds on earlier work, in which Sikkink, in collaboration with Margaret Keck, examined advocacy in international politics. Their much-cited book drew attention to transnational advocacy networks (TANs) and the engagement of TANs in information politics that tied networks together, leverage politics that shamed evildoers, and accountability politics that "tricked" nations into commitments to hold them accountable subsequently. The 1975 Helsinki Accord is just the most famous example of the latter (Keck & Sikkink 1998).

Leaders of the human rights movement, not surprisingly, share a tendency to privilege advocacy as a driving force of criminalization. Aryeh Neier, formerly Executive Director of HRW and President of the Open Society Foundation, confirms that even after the success of early truth commissions, "some in the international human rights movement continued to espouse prosecutions and criminal sanctions against those principally responsible for the most egregious offenses" (Neier 2012, 264).

2 See Sikkink (2011). For further developments in human rights trials in these country case studies compare the chapters of Sharnak (for Uruguay) and Hau (for Chile) in this edited volume.

Other analysts emphasize contributions of different types of actors. Hagan, for example, in his study of the ICTY, focuses on successive chief prosecutors, each of whom brought a new form of "capital" to bear. All of them combined innovative strategies with established legal practices: from securing international support (Richard Goldstone) to issuing sealed indictments and surprise arrests (Louise Arbour) to Carla del Ponte's charges against former President Milošević. Innovative strategies eventually become "doxa:" taken-for-granted legal standards in the emerging international criminal tribunal in The Hague. Yet elsewhere, David Scheffer (2012), former right hand of the US Secretary of State Madeleine Albright, highlights diplomats as crucial contributors to the establishment of international judicial institutions, from the ICTY to the ICC.

No matter the relative weight of each of these types of actors, their interactions contributed to the passing of the Rome Statute in 1998 and the establishment of the ICC. The ICC entered into force in 2002 when 60 countries had ratified the Statute. A decade later, the number of ratifying countries had more than doubled, and many of those charged had to face the Court. The continuation of (this) history is, of course, not yet known and difficult to forecast.

Responding to Darfur in the context of the justice cascade

The events surrounding responses to the horrifying mass violence of Darfur align well with arguments about the justice cascade. In the year 2000, around the time of the formation of the ICC, activists against Sudan's ruling elite had issued *The Black Book: Imbalance of Power and Wealth in Sudan*. Distributed widely, especially in the surroundings of mosques after Friday prayers, the *Black Book* castigated the domination of Sudan by "only one Region [Northern Region] with just over 5% of Sudan's population" (The Black Book 2003, 1). A March 22, 2004 translation, signed by "Translater," states that: "As of last year [March 2003], some of the activists involved in the preparation of the Book took arms against the government" (The Black Book 2004, 1). Indeed, February and March of 2003 saw the formation of the Sudan Liberation Army (SLA) and the Justice and Equality Movement (JEM), two organizations that led a violent rebellion against the government of Sudan. They were recruited from groups defined, increasingly rigidly, as "Black African," mostly sedentary farmers, specifically the Fur, Masalit and Zaghawa. Not explicitly aiming at secession of the Darfur region from Sudan, their declared goal was to overcome the marginalization and repression of non-Arabs in the "periphery" of Sudan. Their armed uprising was surprisingly effective. The government of Sudan, under the leadership of President Omar al-Bashir (in power after a 1989 coup, but deposed and imprisoned in a 2019 uprising), and dominated by the ruling

National Congress party, and its military responded with brute force. They were supported by Janjawiid militias, paramilitary groups that the government in Khartoum supported ideologically and materially. The Janjawiid were recruited from nomadic Arab tribes, herders that found themselves under increasing economic pressure given the advancement of the Sahara Desert into the Sahel zone and the resulting disappearance of grasslands. Growing resource scarcity resulting from ecological change thus promoted intergroup conflict, which the government of Sudan instrumentalized.

A first wave of mass killings unfolded between June and September of 2003. Targets included not just armed rebels but primarily civilian villagers, including elderly men, women and children. Following a brief cease-fire, in December 2003, President al-Bashir vowed to "annihilate" the Darfur rebels. His vow evoked a second wave of mass killings that lasted from December of 2003 through April of 2004. Massive displacements of the civilian population were the consequence. Tens of thousands of lives were extinguished as a direct result of violence and many more during the Darfuris' flight from the violence and due to problematic conditions in displaced person camps in Sudan and refugee camps in neighboring Chad.

Much of the Western world took note only after the first peak of killings (summer 2003) had subsided and when the second wave (winter 2003/2004) was under way. The first public pronouncement, a "genocide alert," was issued by the United States Holocaust Memorial Museum (USHMM) in January of 2004. It was followed by a series of op-ed pieces (opinion pieces by regular contributors of commentary) in prominent American media; a speech by UN Secretary-General Kofi Annan on April 7, 2004, on the occasion of the 10th anniversary of the Rwandan genocide, before the UN General Assembly; UNSC Resolution 1564, instituting an International Commission of Inquiry on Darfur (ICID) on September 18, 2004; delivery of the Commission's report (ICID 2005); and the UNSC's referral of the case of Darfur to the ICC on March 31, 2005. Parallel to UN interventions, a massive civil society movement evolved. In the United States, the Save Darfur movement gathered some 200 liberal and conservative organizations under its umbrella. The US Congress resolved that the violence in Darfur amounted to genocide. Secretary of State Colin Powell initiated an "Atrocities Documentation Survey," a survey of more than 1,000 Darfuri refugees in the camps of Eastern Chad. Based on findings from this survey he determined, at a hearing before the Senate Foreign Relations Committee, on September 9, 2004, that genocide was being committed.[3] President

3 The Atrocities Documentation Survey, its history, method of collection, and a more detailed analysis than that offered by Colin Powell is described by Hagan & Rymond-Richmond 2009.

George W. Bush followed suit a few weeks later. Internationally, NGOs such as Amnesty International and Human Rights Watch took strong positions.[4]

Importantly in our context, soon after the UNSC referred the case of Darfur to the ICC on March 31, 2005, the court took action.[5] After almost two years of investigation, on February 27, 2007, the ICC's chief prosecutor Luis Moreno-Ocampo applied for an arrest warrant against Ahmad Harun, then Sudan's Deputy Minister for the Interior and responsible for the "Darfur Security Desk," and against Ali Kushayb, a Janjawiid leader. On April 27, 2007, the court issued a warrant of arrest against both actors for war crimes and crimes against humanity. It took another year until the Prosecutor also applied for an arrest warrant against Sudanese President Omar al-Bashir, charging crimes against humanity, war crimes, and genocide (July 14, 2008). The judges did not initially follow this application in its entirety, but on March 4, 2009, they issued a warrant against al-Bashir for crimes against humanity and war crimes. With more than a year's delay and five years after the UNSC referral to the ICC, on July 12, 2010, the court followed up with a warrant against the President of Sudan for the crime of genocide.

In short, civil society, international NGOs, national governments, the UN and the ICC, the exact driving forces cited in the literature on the justice cascade, acted to criminalize the violence of Darfur and to initiate a legal case before the International Criminal Court, as described above. The question arises, then, if the Darfur case also justifies the optimism proponents of the justice cascade invest in its consequences. After all, none of the leading actors charged by the ICC has thus far faced the Court. Al-Bashir – after his ouster from power in 2019 – was convicted and sentenced to two years in prison. Yet he only faced a domestic court and was found guilty of corruption charges alone.

Consequences of the justice cascade: between hope and cautionary notes

Scholars as well as movement actors anticipate consequences of the justice cascade with substantial optimism. Sikkink (2011) herself draws hope from her impressive collection of data on a large number of transitional justice situations. Her statistical analyses suggest, against the skepticism of many

4 See, for example: http://www.amnesty.org/en/library/asset/AFR54/007/2013/en/9233d37f-a7da-45d5-9e34-d45232889fb88/afr540072013en.pdf [accessed April 21, 2020].

5 For relevant ICC documents see https://www.icc-cpi.int/darfur [accessed January 12, 2020].

(e.g. Pensky 2008; Snyder & Vinjamuri 2003/2004), that prosecutions of human rights perpetrators, including high-level actors, while achieving retribution, do not systematically produce counter-productive consequences. They may in fact advance human rights and democracy records, especially where trials are accompanied by truth commissions (Kim & Sikkink 2010). These findings have recently been supported by Jo & Simmons (2016), who identify reductions of government and rebel violence in the aftermath of ICC prosecutions (on rebels specifically, see Jo 2015).

Proponents of the justice cascade have typically explained positive effects through a deterrence mechanism. They assume political and military figures to be rational actors who understand that an increase in the risk of prosecution and punishment from zero to at least modest levels may reduce inclinations to commit future crimes. I argue that the sole focus on deterrence is shortsighted. It overlooks a potentially more powerful cultural or socialization mechanism. Such a mechanism is a precondition of deterrence (actors need to be aware of past punishment to be deterred), and it is a force in its own right. Building on a recent line of scholarship, I argue that collective memories created by criminal proceedings against human rights offenders potentially delegitimize violations, thus reducing the likelihood of their recurrence. Potential violations may no longer even appear on the decision tree of rational actors.

Expectations of criminal law's delegitimizing functions are supported by a new line of neo-Durkheimian work in cultural sociology. Here criminal punishment is interpreted as a didactic exercise, a "speech act in which society talks to itself about its moral identity" (Smith 2008, 16). The potential weight of this mechanism for our theme becomes clear if indeed the IMT in Nuremberg and the Universal Declaration of Human Rights initiated the extension of the Holocaust and psychological identification with the victims, as Alexander (2004) has argued. Judicial events like Nuremberg, the Eichmann trial in Jerusalem, or the Frankfurt Auschwitz trial produced cultural trauma: members of a world audience were affected by an experience to which they themselves had not been exposed. Empirical research by historians and sociologists shows that criminal trials indeed have the capacity of coloring not just narratives of recent events, but also the collective memory of a more distant past in the minds of subsequent generations (Savelsberg & King 2011).

Building on these arguments, I suggest that we explore the *representational power* of ICJ as defined above (p. 182).

Cultural consequences of intervention: empirically examining the case of Darfur

Interviews with actors from the fields of humanitarian aid and diplomacy revealed a first challenge with which ICJ has to contend. Their representations of Darfur pose a distinct challenge to the ICC's criminalizing narrative. Table 1 displays ideal typical accounts of these competing representations along a set of analytic dimensions. It is informed by the interviews I conducted with Darfur specialists in each of the three fields (for method see above). To be sure, ideal types are theoretical constructs, and empirical types always deviate from them. Nevertheless, actual knowledge repertoires at least approximate the ideal types in each of the fields under study.

Table 1. Analytic dimensions of the Darfur conflict and their use by holders of different positions in three social fields (constructed from interview transcripts)

Analytic Dimensions	Fields		
	human rights/ criminal law	humanitarian aid	diplomacy
Suffering/ Victimization	graphic accounts, high numbers for killings and rapes especially among "black African" groups	graphic accounts, high numbers for displacements, caution on death counts	caution about numbers, stress of victims on both sides of conflict
Responsible actors	GoS, SAF, Janjawiid, specified individuals	caution about identifying actors	vague reference to indirect responsibility, more on rebel side than in other fields
Origins/time	short-term	short-term	long-term
Causes of violence	ethno-political entrepreneurs	complex historical, cross-national processes	history of colonialism, center-periphery conflicts
Frame	crime, genocide	humanitarian emergency	insurgency and counter-insurgency
Policy conclusions	toward justice	toward survival	toward peace

Detailed accounts of victimization and the identification of specific actors, including high-level government officials, dominate human rights and criminal justice narratives. The humanitarian aid field instead generates representations that – highlighting forms of suffering that humanitarian aid work can address – are much more cautious about the attribution of criminal responsibility to specific individual actors. The latter pattern also applies to the diplomatic field. Contrasts between field-specific narratives are similarly stark with regard to the underlying causes, the period, the interpretive frame and appropriate policy conclusions. In addition, not only do these representations compete with that of institutions of ICJ. Those who provide competing representations, here in the fields of humanitarian aid and diplomacy, at times actually challenge interpretations of the violence as a form of criminal violence. The question then arises who prevails in the competition over the validity of competing representations. What is the ICC's *representational power* relative to that of its competitors?

The question regarding the ICC's representational power can be answered when we examine the effect of interventions on how competing representations are reflected in those media reports that provide a world audience with information about the mass violence. Consider thus the frequency of citations of the crime frame, which competed with the humanitarian emergency and armed conflict frames. Analysis of the Darfur Media Data Set, described above, demonstrates that several judicial intervention points are intensely reflected in journalistic reporting. Figure 1 displays the percentage of articles about Darfur per period that cite the crime frame, in combination with three competing frames. The graph shows that increases in citations of the crime frame follow the release of the ICID report, the application for an arrest warrant related to Darfur by the ICC prosecutor (against Harun and Kushayb), the application for an arrest warrant against al-Bashir (remaining at that rather high level after its issuing), and finally a first court appearance.

The crime frame loses ground during periods that are marked by UNSC Resolution 1564 (establishing the ICID) and the UNSC's referral of the Darfur situation to the ICC. The latter instance is of particular interest as the intervention is followed immediately by a major diplomatic event (signing of the Abuja Peace Treaty), the preparation and echo of which appear to have overwhelmed uses of the crime frame. Media reporting, reflecting diplomatic activities, favored instead the use of the civil war frame during this period as the respective lines indicate. Another, but this time surprising and unexplained, drop of the crime frame occurs after the ICC issued the first major arrest warrants (against Harun and Kushayb).

Figure 1. Competing frames over stages marked by intervention points (based on Darfur Media Data Set described above; figure adopted from Savelsberg 2015, 236)

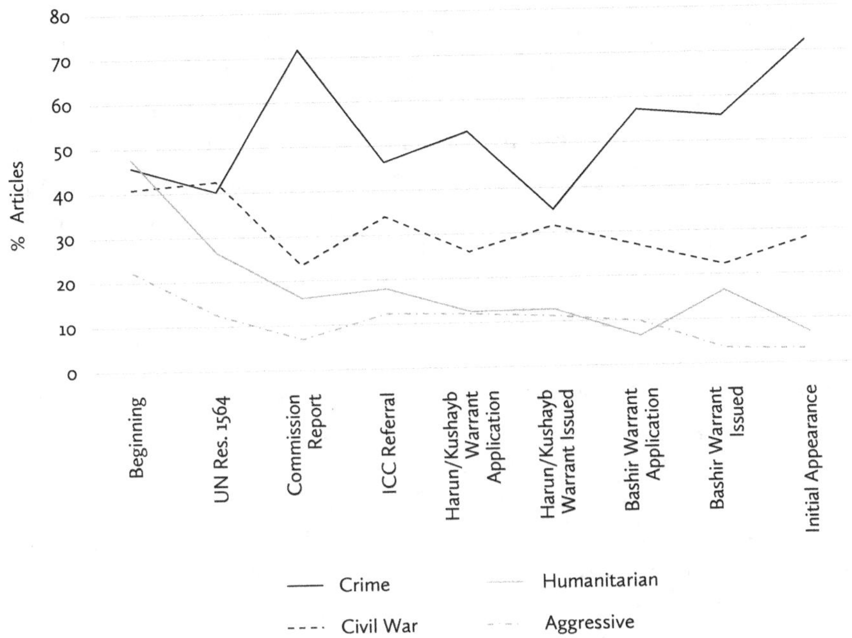

Data also show that reference to particular types of violence and crimes peaks, albeit in less pronounced ways, at similar stages as the use of the crime frame. Specifically, reporting about killings and rapes reaches its highest levels during exactly those periods in which use of the crime frame also peaks: the release of the ICID report, the prosecutor's application for arrest warrants against Ahmed Harun and Ali Kushayb, and the application for, and the issuing of, an arrest warrant against President al-Bashir. The reporting of destruction of livelihood and displacements, on the other hand, is characterized by steady declines that judicial interventions barely interrupt.

Multivariate statistical analyses of the Darfur Media Data Set, conducted by the author in collaboration with Hollie Nyseth Brehm, and presented elsewhere in detail, confirm that ICJ interventions intensify the depiction of the mass violence in Darfur as a form of criminal violence (Savelsberg & Nyseth Brehm 2015).

Cautionary notes: constraints of law's representational power

While our data suggest considerable representational power of ICJ institutions, the generation of criminalizing narratives simultaneously faces substantial constraints. They include narrative limits imposed by the institutional logic of criminal law, the political environment of international relations in which international courts operate, conflicts internal to criminal law, and varying levels of receptivity at the level of nation states toward criminalizing narratives. I address each in turn.

Internal constraints and institutional logic

Court narratives are constrained by the institutional logic of criminal law, the rules of the legal game that become part of legal practitioners' habitus in the process of legal education and professional socialization. These rules include a focus on the behavior of individuals. Structural conditions of genocide and larger cultural patterns that contribute to atrocity crimes, at the center of sociologically based narratives, are omitted. Further, criminal courts focus on behaviors defined as criminal by statutes or precedent. Actions of bystanders (and of protagonists in the world of cultural production) may well play central, enabling, roles; but they rarely enter into the criminal court narrative. In addition, criminal courts follow specific rules of evidence that differ from those used by scholars such as historians. This is appropriate in light of due process protections, but it further contributes to narrative constraints of criminal law. Finally, criminal law, even though it may recognize aggravating and mitigating circumstances, in final logic is bound to a binary logic of guilty versus not guilty. Such simplification would be shared neither by social psychologists nor even by survivors of atrocity crimes who, like Primo Levi, are mindful of shades of grey. Importantly in our context, media reports often directly translate these constraints into their own depictions, given journalists' literal reading of trials, as powerfully described by Devin Pendas (2006) for the Frankfurt Auschwitz trial (see Weinke's chapter in this volume).

The constraints resulting from the institutional logic of law are on full display in the interventions and criminal proceedings of the Darfur case. Soon after UNSC Resolution 1564, in October of 2004, Secretary-General Annan appointed the ICID, which began its work on October 25, 2004. In line with the Resolution, the Commission was charged "'to investigate reports of violations of international humanitarian law and human rights law in Darfur by all parties'; 'to determine also whether or not acts of genocide have occurred'; and 'to identify the perpetrators of such violations'; 'with a view to ensuring that those responsible are held accountable'" (ICID 2005, 9). Clearly, the mandate is framed in the terms of criminal law, specifically international humanitarian and human rights law. The selection of Commission members, their educational backgrounds, careers and positions further solidifies the placement of the Darfur issue in the field of criminal law and justice.

In light of its mission and the background of its members, the Commission report strictly follows the logic of criminal law. It categorizes legal actors ("1. Government Armed Forces"; "2. Government supported and/or controlled militias – The Janjaweed"; "3. Rebel movement groups" (ibid., 27–39)), spells out the legal rules that are binding on the Government of Sudan and on the rebel groups, identifies categories of international crimes, and associates available and legally relevant evidence with those legal concepts (ibid., 40–107). In summarizing its findings, the ICID first speaks to the *actus reus* with regard to "Violations of international human rights law and international humanitarian law." It links this evidence to the legal categories of the Rome Statute and, by identifying the acts of violence as "widespread and systematic," it determines that they amount to crimes against humanity, as defined in the Rome Statute, and thus fall under the jurisdiction of the ICC. Finally, while major parts of the report refer to organizational actors such as the Government of Sudan, militias, or rebel groups, the ICID eventually follows the logic of criminal law also by attributing responsibility to individuals. It does so in a later section of the report on the "Identification of Perpetrators." The charging documents of the ICC repeat and intensify the representational consequences of the institutional logic of criminal law, here illustrated for the ICID.

Political power and substantive rationales

A second constraint of international criminal courts results from the substantive consequences that decisions guided by formal legal procedure may generate and from the political environment of international relations in which they operate. The challenge of substantive consequences of formal justice at times results in intense internal conflicts within criminal law institutions. Within the ICC, for example, scholars find conflicting reasoning between lawyers versus technocrats (Meierhenrich 2014; Savelsberg 2017). On one side of the divide is law's formal rationality, oriented toward a system of legal criteria, for which codifications such as the Rome Statute have laid the ground; these indeed begin to revolutionize a world in which foreign affairs used to be subject to political reasoning alone. On the other side are those actors who are more concerned with substantive outcomes of court action than with formal procedure, outcomes that in the types of cases under consideration may well involve the immediate survival chances of thousands. Foreign policy makers at times back the latter side of the divide, as illustrated by the words of one of my interviewees from the foreign ministry of one large European country, an actor who specialized on issues of the ICC within his ministry's Division of International Law and who represented his country in the ICC's Assembly of States:

> As to my interlocutors in the [Foreign Ministry] ... there were constantly conflicting perceptions. I do remember quite a number of quarrels I had with my colleagues in the political department ... And the reason is that we had two different approaches. Their approach was purely political. ... Now there is a new factor, a new player on the ground [the ICC], which does not make a political assessment, but which simply applies the law. That is a new phenomenon, and I think for those who have an exclusively political approach that is difficult to accept. (Interview conducted by author 2011)

As this interview quote illustrates, foreign policy makers who work for the autonomy of international law face contending forces within their own ministries and within in the UN. In addition, the Rome Statute opens the window for substantive, political concerns to intrude into the work of the ICC, for example through its Article 16, allowing the UNSC to defer court proceedings for one year, and to do so successively. Externally, the court's vulnerability vis-à-vis political powers is enhanced as many countries have not yet ratified the Rome Statute, including such powerful actors as the United States, the People's Republic of China and Russia. Others have threatened to withdraw from the Rome Statute

Yet again, substantive, political and practical pressures are not just external to the Court. Substantive outcomes of legal decision making also matter to jurists themselves. Max Weber, in his classic work on the sociology of law, recognized how lawyers resent a notion of formal rationality that threatens to reduce them to an automaton into which one drops the facts and the fees for them to spew out the decision (and the opinion). Instead, Weber argues, lawyers seek discretion, enabling them to consider ethical maxims or practical concerns of political, economic, or geopolitical nature. The long history of criminal law speaks to this tension between formal and substantive rationality. In international criminal law, substantive considerations have particular weight, as thousands of lives may be at stake if conditions on the ground and practical consequences of legal decisions are disregarded. Applied to the case of Darfur, many foreign policy makers, including several of my interviewees, expressed concern that charges against President al-Bashir, especially on the grounds of genocide, might threaten the North–South agreement and the referendum on the independence of South Sudan. It is hard to imagine that these concerns did not touch decision makers at the ICC.

In short, despite its particular institutional logic, criminal law is no stranger to internal contradictions and conflicts. Conflicts between formal legal criteria versus substantive concerns, while dividing legal and political actors, also create ambivalences and internal tensions within the legal field. The ICC, and the case of Darfur, are no exceptions. I have elsewhere described in detail this struggle and the ICJ system's treacherous journey between the Scylla of formal-rational justice and the Charybdis of practical concerns in a highly politicized environment (Savelsberg 2017).

National contexts of reception: policy preferences and cultural sensitivities

Finally, when ICJ institutions advance a criminalizing narrative, their attempts are likely to face resistance at the level of nation states. Also in the case of Darfur, and despite the overall privileging of the crime frame, media from the eight countries differed in their preference for each of the competing narratives. Even those that embraced the criminalizing frame did so to varying degrees. And, within that frame, due to variation in policy preferences, cultural sensitivities and civil society mobilization, some were more reluctant than others to apply to category of "genocide" when reporting about Darfur (see Figure 2).

Figure 2. Use of the term "genocide" in media reports on Darfur across countries (based on Darfur Media Data Set described above; adopted from Savelsberg 2015, 253)

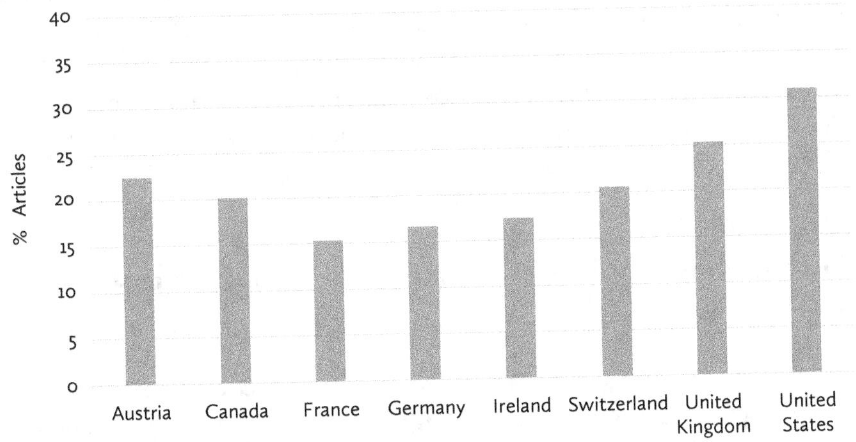

US journalists, for example, who especially favored the crime frame, also used the genocide label more often than their colleagues did from other countries. On the one hand, this may be surprising given their country's reluctance to ratify the Rome Statute, the foundation of the ICC. On the other hand, it is consistent with the broad-based mobilization and genocide rhetoric by the Save Darfur coalition, encompassing some 200 civil society organizations, liberal and conservative as well as religious and secular.

Ireland offers an interesting contrast. Its journalists were relatively reluctant to use both the crime frame and the genocide label, a reluctance they explained by their country's strong humanitarian climate. This humanitarian orientation is manifested in a pronounced aid orientation of Irish foreign policy and close cooperation between the state and humanitarian aid NGOs, including those affiliated with the Irish Catholic Church. Collective memories of the Irish potato famine and extreme poverty provide cultural support. Multivariate statistical analyses show that a national focus on aid programs is generally associated with less frequent use of the crime and genocide labels, lower victimization counts (with the exception of displacements), and a less frequent identification of the Sudanese state as a criminal organization.

To provide a final example of country-specific patterns, German media reported extensively about Darfur and generously applied the crime frame. Yet media reports and interviewees quite rarely used the term genocide; respondents explained their reluctance with their caution towards likening mass atrocities such as those in Darfur with the Shoah, not wanting to risk accusations of seeking to relativize the Holocaust.

NGO actors similarly adjusted their rhetoric to conditions of the country in which they operated. They were mindful of sensitivities of potential activists (e.g. anti-militarism in Germany and Austria); pillars of civil society organization (strong role of churches in German humanitarian aid); an intense anti-genocide rhetoric in civil society mobilization (US); aid-oriented foreign policy (Ireland); and their countries' status as former colonial powers in Sudan (UK) and in neighboring Chad (France), associated with substantial expat communities in these countries. Obviously, thus, the representational power of ICJ institutions is contingent on country-specific structural and cultural conditions.

Conclusions: conditions and impact of the justice cascade and the case of Darfur

The case of Darfur fits squarely into the logic of the justice cascade. It confirms several arguments regarding the driving forces behind the growing tendency to prosecute perpetrators of grave human rights violations. Simultaneously, studying consequences of intervention, I demonstrated ICJ's considerable representational power. The crime frame, advanced by ICJ institutions, and supported by human rights NGOs, prevails over competing frames generated in the fields of diplomacy and humanitarian aid. This is a significant finding as such representations may hammer the final nail into the coffin in which the remains of a past glorification of perpetrators of mass violence are laid to rest. Importantly, this finding is not unique to Darfur. It applies to other cases, ones of ICJ intervention, as in the case of the Yugoslav wars, and of domestic war crimes cases, as that of the My Lai massacre for the United States (Savelsberg & King 2011).

Representing mass atrocities through criminal justice, however, comes at a cost, and it faces impediments. Obstacles include the specific institutional logic of criminal law. The narrative told by criminal law focuses on few individual perpetrators, in disregard of larger structural forces and cultural patterns that sociologists would consider. It focuses on a short time frame, neglecting longer historical trajectories with which historians are concerned. It is further constrained by legal categories that leave actions of some unaddressed who causally contributed to the violence but whose actions are not covered by criminal codes. Both the dominance of judicial representations and their selectivity have been documented in other cases. They include proceedings in cases as varied as the Frankfurt Auschwitz trial (Pendas 2006), proceedings by the International Criminal Tribunal for the former Yugoslavia (Hagan 2003), and the courts martial against perpetrators of the My Lai massacre of the Vietnam War (Savelsberg & King 2011). Obstacles also include the consideration of extra-legal goals by actors outside the judicial sphere, especially diplomats, considerations that also generate conflicts within international courts (Savelsberg 2017). For example, the decision to prosecute heads of state may reduce their willingness to cede power or to cooperate in international diplomatic efforts to end the violence, to the detriment of thousands. Power relations matter in other respects as well, most noteworthy the lack of the ICC's enforcement power. The latter, combined with extrajudicial concerns of major powers, is responsible for the fact that none of the major actors charged with crimes in Darfur has been brought before the ICC to date, clearly weakening effects of the justice cascade. In addition, potential nation-level resistances to criminalizing narratives may impede the cultural effectiveness of international criminal courts. They may grow out of policy traditions, collective memories, and cultural sensitivities at the level of nation states. The text above provides examples of contrasting cases, such as the United States with its strong social movement for Darfur,

Ireland with its humanitarian orientation, and Germany with its legacy of the Holocaust.

Finally, as is true with any case study, future work should submit findings from a single case to systematic comparative analysis. As stated at the outset, the case of Darfur has many similarities with other instances of mass violence. Yet it is also marked by particularities. Decisive for international intervention was, for example, the willingness of the US administration to allow for the referral of Darfur to the ICC, despite its general resistance to the court. Its surprising willingness resulted from massive civil society mobilization in American society that cannot be taken for granted in all cases. Importantly though, when ICJ intervenes, then cultural consequences similar to those in the Darfur case have been documented by multiple studies cited above for other cases. This indeed is the central conclusion: we must avoid the mistake of paying too much attention to the explicit philosophies and manifest functions of criminal prosecution and punishment. We should instead be much more mindful of their latent function, especially their cultural effects: collective representations and memories of evil and the associated delegitimization of responsible actors and strategies that involve mass atrocities.

References

Alexander, J. C., 2004. "On the Social Construction of Moral Universals: The 'Holocaust' from War Crime to Trauma Drama." In Alexander, J. C. et al. (eds.) *Cultural Trauma and Collective Identity*. Berkeley, CA: University of California Press, 196–262.

Cohen, S., 2001. *States of Denial: Knowing about Atrocities and Suffering*. Cambridge, UK/Malden, MA: Polity/Blackwell Publishers.

Giesen, B., 2004. *Triumph and Trauma*. Boulder, CO: Paradigm.

Hagan, J., 2003. *Justice in the Balkans: Prosecuting War Crimes in the Hague Tribunal*. Chicago Series in Law and Society. Chicago: University of Chicago Press.

International Commission of Inquiry on Darfur (ICID), 2005. *Report of the International Commission of Inquiry on Darfur to the Secretary-General of the United Nations*. Available at: https://www.un.org/ruleoflaw/files/com_inq_darfur.pdf [Accessed January 12, 2020].

Jo, H., 2015. *Compliant Rebels: Rebel Groups and International Law in World Politics*. Cambridge: Cambridge University Press.

Jo, H. & Simmons, B., 2016. "Can the International Criminal Court Deter Atrocity?" *International Organization* 70(3): 443–475.

Keck, M. E. & Sikkink, K., 1998. *Activists beyond Borders: Advocacy Networks in International Politics*. Ithaca, NY: Cornell University Press.

Kim, H. & Sikkink, K., 2010. "Explaining the Deterrence Effect of Human Rights Prosecutions for Transitional Countries." *International Studies Quarterl*, 5 (4): 939–963.

Meierhenrich, J., 2014. "The Evolution of the Office of the Prosecutor at the International Criminal Court: Insights from Institutional Theory." In Minow, M., Whiting, A. & True-Frost, C. (eds.) *The First Global Prosecutor*. Ann Arbor, MI: University of Michigan Press.

Minow, M., 1998. *Between Vengeance and Forgiveness: Facing History after Genocide and Mass Violence.* Boston: Beacon Press.

Neier, A., 2012. *The International Human Rights Movement: A History. Human Rights and Crimes against Humanity.* Princeton: Princeton University Press.

Pendas, D. O., 2006. *The Frankfurt Auschwitz Trial, 1963–65: Genocide, History, and the Limits of Law.* Cambridge: Cambridge University Press.

Pensky, M., 2008. "Amnesty on Trial: Impunity, Accountability, and the Norms of International Law." *Ethics & Global Politics* 1(1–2): 1–40.

Savelsberg, J. J., 2015. *Representing Mass Violence: Conflicting Responses to Human Rights Violations in Darfur.* Oakland, CA: University of California Press.

Savelsberg, J. J., 2017. "Formal and Substantive Rationality in Max Weber's Sociology of Law: Tensions in International Criminal Law." In Gephart, W. (ed.) *Law as Culture: Max Weber's Comparative Sociology of Law.* Frankfurt: Vittorio Klostermann, 493–510.

Savelsberg, J. J. & King, R. D., 2011. *American Memories: Atrocities and the Law.* New York: Russell Sage Foundation.

Savelsberg, J. J. & Nyseth Brehm, H., 2015. "Representing Human Rights Violations in Darfur: Global Justice, Local Distinctions." *American Journal of Sociology* 121(2): 564–603.

Scheffer, D., 2012. *All the Missing Souls: A Personal History of the War Crimes Tribunals.* Princeton, NJ: Princeton University Press.

Sikkink, K., 2011. *The Justice Cascade: How Human Rights Prosecutions Are Changing World Politics.* New York: W. W. Norton.

Smith, P., 2008. *Punishment and Culture.* Chicago: University of Chicago Press.

Snyder, J. & Vinjamuri, L., 2003/2004. "Trials and Errors: Principle and Pragmatism in Strategies of International Justice." *International Security* 28(3): 5–44.

The Black Book. 2003. By Seekers of Truth and Justice (no place or publisher).

The Effects of Seeking Justice *on Behalf of* the Victim

A Critical Analysis of Criminal Trials in the Kenyan Post-Election Violence Transitional Justice Process

Valeria Vegh Weis

This chapter looks at the criminal trials that took place following the post-election violence (PEV) of 2007 in Kenya. The analysis encompasses the dynamics of these international and domestic attempts at prosecutions within the large history of human rights violations in the country. Particularly, this contribution examines the victims' role in this complex process and the potential role of victims' organizations in overcoming the legacy of impunity in what might be referred to as a *victim-driven approach* (Vegh Weis 2017).

To do so, the study incorporates an analysis of primary and secondary sources, including court files from the International Criminal Court (ICC), reports from civil society organizations (CSOs), media articles and academic scholarship. Furthermore, the research includes some input from my personal experience while working in Kenya as a research fellow between September 2016 and April 2017.

In this framework, after this introduction, section 2 briefly describes the human rights violations experienced in the country. Section 3 analyzes the (postponed) transitional justice process. Section 4 explores the different attempts to achieve accountability in domestic and international criminal courts. Section 5 analyzes the dynamics and constraints of these trials. The last section offers final thoughts on the potential insight that a *victim-driven approach* could bring to Kenya.

A brief history of human rights violations in Kenya

Kenya has experienced systematic human rights violations traversed by ethnic and power conflicts throughout its history. The roots of these ethnic confrontations can be traced back to the colonial period (1895–1963). Indeed, the colonial power, the United Kingdom (UK), not only oppressed the local population in Kenya through institutionalized racism, forced "villagization" and torture, but also fostered ethnic conflicts under the *divide and rule* approach. In other words, the UK encouraged rivalries and conflicts amongst communities by favoring one over the other, particularly in relation to land distribution. After Kenya formally achieved its independence, rivalries were never fully resolved and politics and voting trends remain largely based on ethnicity until today. The existing 43 ethnic groups form coalitions and alliances that frequently take a violent turn during the election periods, when all parties are seeking out the control of state. In most cases, the political contest is between the three largest ethnic groups: the Kikuyu, the Luo and the Kalenjin (Wachira & Sillah 2014; Ireland 2011).

These ethnic confrontations, just after independence, gave rise to the Shifta Conflict (1963–1968). Four traditionally marginalized pastoral communities, the Somali, Boran, Gabra and Rendille, started a separatist movement to which the central government responded by declaring a state of emergency and introducing forced villagization and torture (Whittaker, 2012, p. 359). Meanwhile, in the rest of the country, systematic torture of political opponents, detentions without fair trial and extrajudicial executions were a constant feature of Kenyan politics (KNCHR 2008; Wachira & Sillah 2014).

In the following decades, episodes of violence inclusive of systematic human rights violations became constant in Kenya's political system. The peak of this permanent national violence occurred 40 years after the Shifta Conflict, in December 2007, when Kenyans voted in general elections. Before the balloting began, opinion polls suggested that Raila Odinga – presidential candidate for the opposition group known as Orange Democratic Movement (ODM) and member of the Luo community – had a considerable lead over then President Mwai Kibaki, who was a Kikuyu and represented the Party of National Unity (PNU). After the elections, there were delays in announcing the results which led to deep frustration and suspicion among citizens. Security forces, informal militias and ordinary civilians-initiated violence against people from the opposite party and other ethnic groups, all of which was encouraged by their political and ethnic leaders, the media and businessmen. Supporters of the PNU, a party which is mostly comprised of people from the Kikuyu, Kisii and Kamba ethnic communities, experienced ongoing confrontations with ODM supporters, who were mostly from the Kalenjin, Luo and Luhya ethnic groups. This situation continued for several months in six of the eight Kenyan provinces (Murphy 2015, 29). Overall, more than 1,000 people were murdered, at least 900 suffered sexual violence and almost 700,000 were displaced (CIPEV 2008; HRW 2015, 4). This aforementioned violence included torture, abduction, severe ill-treatment, forced disappearances and violations of socioeconomic rights, including but not limited to the burning of houses, theft or killing of cattle, looting of property and destruction of crops (ICTJ & KNCHR 2016). These events as a whole became infamously known as the 2007 PEV.

Considering the continuity of violence that dates back to Kenya's independence, the transitional justice process that formally commenced immediately following the PEV of 2007, was not influenced by just that singular – although dramatic – episode. Instead, the transitional process was designed in response to the entire history of Kenya as an independent country from 1963 to 2007. As stated in the report of the Commission of Inquiry into Post-Election Violence (known as the CIPEV or Waki Commission because it was led by former Kenya Court of Appeal Judge, Philip Waki): "Kenya has an extremely troubled past. Its history of ethnic violence has been papered over for years until it exploded in horror during and after the 2007 elections" (CIPEV 2008, 15–16).

A postponed transitional justice process

When the African leaders, and Kenyans in particular, had to confront the human rights violations committed during the colonial and precolonial era, they tended to show readiness for reconciliation and a lack of interest in retributive justice (see e.g. Mugabe 1980). Immediately after independence, in 1963, Jomo Kenyatta, the first president of Kenya, addressed the white farmers in the Nakuru region, stating: "you must also learn to forgive one another" (Kenyatta 1963; 1968, 147). Later on, when confronting the crimes and violations committed during the Shifta Conflict (1963–1968), the Kenyan Parliament also closed the path towards trials, by passing the Indemnity Act in 1970. However, there was some hope that this would change when the National Rainbow Coalition won elections in 2002 and Mwai Kibaki assumed the presidency. In his inaugural speech, President Kibaki suggested that trials might follow:

> One would have preferred to overlook some of the all too obvious human errors and forge ahead, but it would be unfair to Kenyans not to raise

> questions about deliberate actions or policies of the past that continue to have grave consequences on the present … We want to bring back the culture of due process, accountability and transparency in public office. The era of "anything goes" is gone forever … (TJRC 2013)

In order to translate this promise into action, in 2003 Kibaki established a Task Force on the Establishment of Truth, Justice and Reconciliation Commission under the leadership of a prominent Kenyan scholar Makau Mutua (Wachira & Sillah 2014). The purpose of the Task Force was to find out if it was necessary for Kenya to establish a truth commission and, if so, to make recommendations on the type of commission that would need to be implemented. The Task Force found out that there was an overwhelming desire among Kenyans for a truth commission to focus on events that occurred during the period of 1963–2002 and to recommend redress for the victims, lustration mechanisms and prosecution (Mutua 2003). However, these efforts were postponed until the fateful 2007 general elections. Indeed, the failure of Kenyan leadership to establish the truth commission is often considered the main cause of the eruption of PEV. Regarding this concept, the then Minister of Justice, National Cohesion and Constitutional Affairs, Martha Karua said in 2008, "We failed to set up the Commission then, and we also failed to set it up throughout the last Parliament term. I believe that, as a nation we have paid for failing to act [in reference to the PEV]" (see also Kenya National Assembly Official Record 2008, 2111).

The start of the formal transitional justice process took place in 2008, when – in the midst of the PEV – the two main political parties agreed to seek mediation by a Panel of Eminent African Personalities under the Chairmanship of former UN Secretary-General, Kofi Annan. Through this mediation process, the Kenya National Dialogue and Reconciliation Agreements were signed. These agreements included four agenda items, opening the path toward transitional justice that, as mentioned before, would include the human rights violations that occurred from 1963 to 2007 (Amnesty International Report 2013, 7). Despite this progress, the government's response to the historical cycle of violence has been fragmented and incomplete. In terms of truth, the truth commission known as the Waki Commission was established in 2008 (ICTJ & KNCHR 2016). In relation to guarantees of non-repetition, President Mwai Kibaki issued an apology to victims of all historical injustices in his State of the Nation Address in 2008 and passed a constitutional reform in 2010. Concerning reparations, the creation of the Restorative Justice Fund was announced, but there is still no legal framework to implement it (Wakaya 2018; Kisika 2018). Even more alarming are the accusations of corruption surrounding the chosen destinations of the promised money (Rajab 2018). Justice through criminal trials, as we shall see, has not been fully achieved either.

Limited justice: trials at the domestic and international levels

With the goal of ensuring justice in Kenya, the first proposal came from the Waki Commission report and consisted of the creation of a hybrid Special Tribunal (CIPEV 2008, 472). The Tribunal would apply national and international law, it would be composed of a foreign prosecutor and, to avoid political interference, only one of the three judges would be Kenyan. To select the judges, the African Union's Panel of Eminent African Personalities would provide a list of qualified international officials to the Kenyan President, who would make his selection in consultation with the Prime Minister. This hybrid Special Tribunal was promoted as the best available option because it would try hundreds of alleged perpetrators, including mid- and high-ranking members of the security forces, the media, businessmen and civilians. This broader scope of who would be called to trial in the hybrid Special Tribunal proposed a solution to the problem of the small number of high-level state individuals charged at the International Criminal Court (ICC) (Brown & Sriram 2012). As a backup plan, the leader of the truth commission, Mr. Waki, handed over to UN Secretary-General Kofi Annan a sealed envelope containing the names of some 20 suspected perpetrators – presumably including people from the main political parties, high-ranking public servants and relevant people from the media – accompanied by numerous boxes of evidence (CIPEV 2008). If the government failed to create the hybrid Special Tribunal within 105 days of the publication of the Waki Report, Kofi Annan would pass on evidence to the ICC with a request that the prosecutor undertake investigations and prosecutions.

However, a problem arose concerning the crimes for which a perpetrator could be indicted. The Kenyan Parliament enacted the International Crimes Act in 2009 to incorporate the Rome Statute – already ratified in 2005 – into domestic law, defining crimes against humanity and other crimes under international law as crimes in national law (Brown & Sriram 2012). The problem was that the offenses committed before the enactment of the law could not be judged as international crimes, frustrating the basis of a hybrid Special Tribunal (Bosire & Lynchy 2014). As an alternative, civil society organizations, including Kenyans for Peace with Truth and Justice, proposed to create an International Crimes Division within the Kenyan High Court with international legal experts and Kenyan judges with a background in international criminal law (KPTJ 2013). They also proposed that the Kenyan Parliament adopt legislation to appoint prosecutors and investigators independent from the existing (and allegedly biased) Director of Public Prosecutions. However, the Parliament rejected the proposal three times (Bjorkt & Goebertustt 2011). Presumably, many parliamentarians from the two leading political parties were implicated in the crimes but were not among the "big fish" – such as Ruto or Kenyatta – and thus had little to fear, considering that the ICC would only be able to judge a few high-ranking members of the government. As a consequence, these parliamentarians obstructed the civil society's proposal and, instead, joined those who were truly skeptical of any Kenya-based court, trying to bring prosecutions to an international arena, under the slogan "don't be vague, let's go to The Hague" (Brown & Sriram 2012).

As the negotiations did not advance at the domestic level, by July 2009, Kofi Annan did hand over the Waki envelope and evidence to the ICC's Chief Prosecutor, Luis Moreno-Ocampo. On November 26, 2009, pursuant to Article 15 of the Rome Statute, the Prosecutor requested authorization from Pre-Trial Chamber II to proceed with an investigation. Following a four-month review of the Prosecutor's application, Pre-Trial Chamber II granted Moreno-Ocampo's request (Senier 2011).[1] There were two main cases involving six individuals who had been accused. Case I was carried out against the ODM members William Ruto and Henry Kiprono Kosgey, as well as the radio producer and journalist Joshua Arap Sang, related to violence committed against perceived supporters of the PNU (as said, mostly from the Kikuyu, Kisii and Kamba ethnic communities living in and around Eldoret). Case II was against Uhuru Kenyatta from the PNU, former Police Commissioner Mohammad Hussein Ali and former Head of the Civil Service Francis Muthaura, who was in charge of coordinating all public servants on behalf of the President. The accusations they were facing were related

1 This was the first ruling by an ICC Pre-Trial Chamber on a prosecutorial *proprio motu* request under the Rome Statute. The decision raised the discussion about how to interpret the contextual element of crimes against humanity in Article 7(2) of the Rome Statute. In the absence of proof of a high-level state policy within the PEV, the debate was whether the presence of an organizational policy requires state intervention or whether an amorphous or private group of individuals infringing basic human values was enough (para. 90; para. 53). Ultimately, the majority determined that many of the PEV cases were planned, directed or organized by a concert of local leaders, businessmen and politicians affiliated with the two leading parties, and on that basis essentially disposed of the organizational policy requirement to ground a finding of crimes against humanity (paras. 116–128) (Chernor 2011).

to violence committed against perceived supporters of the ODM (as said, predominantly from the Kalenjin, Luo and Luhya communities living in Nakuru and Naivasha).

After the ICC initiated investigations, the government tried to undermine the process, completely disregarding Article 5 of the International Crimes Bill (2005), which obliges Kenya to cooperate with the Court. In December 2010, the Parliament passed a non-binding motion urging the government to withdraw from the Rome Statute, repeal the International Crimes Act and establish a domestic accountability process to act in lieu of the ICC (Amnesty International 2014). In February and March 2011, the government also tried to make the UN Security Council postpone the ICC's involvement, arguing that the trials would endanger peace and security. The government also invoked Article 19 of the Rome Statute and challenged the admissibility of the cases in court. The basis of their argument was that the constitutional reform of 2010 (see next section of this chapter) was definitive proof of the governmental willingness to deal with such criminal cases at the national level (ICC 2011). However, the ICC resolved that the Rome Statute requires clear evidence of the initiation of a credible criminal process against the same alleged perpetrators and for the same crimes as the ones before the ICC. As this was not happening in the Kenyan case, the majority of the ICC Appeals Chamber rejected the government's appeal.[2]

Indeed, at the domestic level, the efforts to ensure accountability were, at least, mild. A Multi-Agency Task Force created *ad hoc* under the supervision of the (presumably biased) Director of Public Prosecutions was established, but not until 2012 (Amnesty International 2013). The mandate of the Task Force included "reviewing, re-evaluating and re-examining all Post-Election Violence pending investigations, pending trials and concluded cases" (ICC 2017, para. 13). However, the Task Force has not yet published clear information about its work (ibid., para. 14). At that point, only 24 low-level suspects were convicted out of the 6,081 cases presented by the police to the Task Force (ICC 2017, para. 16). In terms of sexual violence, there were only 23 convictions out of 900 cases (HRW 2015, 7). Moreover, the details surrounding these few convictions and the sentences issued remains unclear. The Task Force report was "compiled hastily, with little concern for accuracy" and "a number of cases included in the report have nothing to do with the election violence"

2 The case *Prosecutor v. Francis Kirimi Muthaura, Uhuru Muigai Kenyatta and Mohammed Hussein Ali* is the first ruling by the Appeals Chamber on whether national investigations must cover not only the same conduct but also the same person as a pending ICC case for the case to be declared inadmissible under Article 17(1)(a) of the Rome Statute (Stubbins Bates 2011).

or concern extremely minor offenses within the PEV, such as "handling stolen property" (KPTJ 2013b, 9). The Task Force concluded that most of the remaining cases were unsuitable for prosecution due to a lack of credible evidence, particularly enough witness statements (Amnesty International 2014). Notably, evidence gathering was particularly undermined because those who were supposed to protect the witnesses were the ones the witnesses were likely to testify against (Kiprotich 2009). This means that many civilians who were initially willing to testify were later afraid to do so because people from the military forces and the government were still in positions of power and could retaliate. In this regard, CSOs insisted on the need to strengthen witness protection because, even though there was a witness protection program under the 2006 Witness Protection Act, it lacked funding and capacity to implement its mandate (Cheptinga 2017).

As a result of the limited scope of the Task Force's work, there is "a near total lack of investigations of those who organized and financed the violence" (HRW 2011, 3) and almost no accountability for mid- and high-ranking perpetrators (ibid., 4; ICC 2017, paras. 21–23). Moreover, some of those accused of committing human rights violations were still in power or were elected to higher office. Furthermore, the broader "political and economic elite that financed much of the post-election violence is still operating and has significant influence over the justice system" (Bjorkt & Goebertustt 2011; Brown & Sriram 2012).

Confronting the lack of accountability for mid- or high-ranking agents at the national level, the ICC continued investigating the cases. On March 8, 2011, the Pre-Trial Chamber II issued a summons requiring the six accused to appear before the Court. On April 7–8, 2011, all six individuals voluntarily appeared, and between September 1 and October 5, the hearings of these charges took place.

In this context, the Kenyan government initiated a new strategy: delegitimizing the ICC as a neocolonial intervention (Lugano 2017a; Engbo 2015) and a creature of an anti-Kenyan conspiracy (USAID 2014, 1). Through this campaign, two of the defendants, Ruto and Kenyatta, effectively cast themselves as political victims of national and international plots against them and retained significant public support in their own ethnic-regional communities (Brown & Sriram 2012; Gachoka 2012). Evidence of the positive results of the strategy was that, when returning after the initial hearings in The Hague, the accused were given a public heroes' welcome (ibid.). Moreover, the accused used this anti-imperialist and victimization rhetoric not only to undermine the efforts of the ICC but also to gain more supporters for the upcoming election. Kenyatta and Ruto formed the Jubilee political party to compete in the 2013 elections while accusing the former Prime Minister and opposition leader, Odinga, of having engineered the submission of their names to the ICC (Okuku 2002). The neocolonial plot discourse was involuntarily reinforced by US Assistant Secretary of State Johnnie Carson when he said that "choices would have consequences," in reference to the possible victory of Kenyatta and Ruto (Joselow 2013; see Lugano's chapter in this book). Following these signs, some analysts suggested that the ICC might have unwittingly strengthened Kenyatta's position in the 2013 electoral process (Menocal 2013).

On top of that, the government also soaked up the support of the African Union (ICG 2012, 8–10). The Union issued a resolution demanding that Kenyatta should not appear before the ICC "until such time as the concerns raised by the AU and its Member States have been adequately addressed by the UN Security Council and the ICC" (2013, para. 10xi). On October 12, 2013, in the Extraordinary Session of the Assembly of Heads of State and Government, the African Union issued a series of decisions, stating the need to "safeguard the constitutional order, stability and integrity of member states" by ensuring that "no charges shall be commenced or continued before any International Court or Tribunal against any serving AU Head of State or Government or anybody acting or entitled to act in such a capacity during their terms of office" (ibid., para. 10i). Therefore, it decided "that President Uhuru Kenyatta would not appear before the ICC until the concerns raised by the AU and its member states have been adequately addressed by the UN Security Council and the ICC" (ibid., para. 10xi).

Overall, the scarce domestic criminal trials combined with intense anti-ICC propaganda and the undermining of the court's evidential efforts[3] created a legal environment that made it extremely challenging to continue with the initial criminal proceedings. Even though the ICC Prosecutor initially confirmed charges against Ruto, Sang and Kenyatta,[4] the newly appointed ICC Prosecutor, Fatou Bensouda, withdrew them because the available evidence was not sufficient to prove the alleged criminal responsibility beyond reasonable doubt (ICC 2014).

3 Facing challenges to evidence, the judgment in *Prosecutor v. Ruto* is the first to determine that an ICC trial chamber may summon unwilling witnesses to testify and that the Court may request that a state party to the Rome Statute compel the witnesses – if necessary by using compulsory means under its domestic law – to appear before the judges sitting in the territory of the state party or through video link to The Hague (Chernor 2015).

4 In 2012, the Pre-Trial Chamber II found that the ICC Prosecutor's evidence failed to satisfy the evidentiary threshold required in the case of Kosgey, Ali and Muthaura. The ICC Presidency constituted Trial Chamber V to conduct the Ruto, Sang and Kenyatta cases and, in a subsequent ruling, postponed Kenyatta's trial to April 2013 after the presidential election.

The dynamics and constraints of domestic and international trials

Criminal trials for the Kenyan cases have yet to be fully developed at the international or at the national level. However, the situation is complex and there are several dynamics that can be analyzed within the struggle for justice.

First, the domestic trials seemed to have weakened the rule of law. The lack of accountability with regard to mid- and high-ranking officials and businessmen configured a "half-hearted" process (HRW 2011) that harmed the legitimacy of the courts, consequentially deemed corrupt and dependent on executive power (Mbondenyi 2010). However, these constraints fostered an isolated positive outcome with the potential to produce further social change. In spite of insufficient trials, the government attempted to demonstrate signs of transformation at a national level in order to delay the ICC intervention, which resulted in their support of a constitutional reform passed in 2010 that had been on the agenda for years, even before the PEV (Akpedonu et al. 2013). In relation to the aforementioned loss of legitimacy of the judiciary, Articles 20 and 23 of the new Constitution brought hope for a possible overturn of the processes currently in place: Article 20 establishes an independent Judicial Service Commission in charge of making judicial appointments, while Article 23 claims for the enactment of legislation for the vetting of judges and magistrates and, as a result, the Vetting of Judges and Magistrates Act was passed in 2011.

Second, the ICC intervention seemed to have operated in a manner that caused the loss of the victims' confidence in the rule of law and the legitimacy of international criminal justice. Some major factors contributing to this were the lack of opportunities for victims to raise their voices and be heard at the court, the confusion around the scope of the court intervention, and the rapid dismissal of the criminal charges.

Concerning the restricted space for victims' intervention, Tenove (2013, 57) points out that many victims expressed frustration that ICC or CSO staff collected information from them, but that these consultations did not lead to meaningful feedback or action: "The ICC always comes here to consult with us. We always give them the information they want. They go and do not come back, denying us the opportunity to know what is happening" (male participant, FGD in Barlonyo village, Lira district, Lango sub-region). Many victims were willing to participate at the ICC but failed to do so because their Common Legal Representatives faced major challenges and lacked the necessary resources to communicate effectively with their clients and to reach out to all victims within the scope of the cases (Amnesty International 2014,

1). Overall, as stated in the Victims' Response to the "Prosecution's notice of withdrawal of the charges against Uhuru Muigai Kenyatta" (ICC 2014b): "Despite every setback, [the victims] never gave up on the Court. But in the end, the Court gave up on them."

In terms of the lack of clarification of the court's role, a major discrepancy arose from the fact that victims expected the ICC would be responsible for ensuring that their material needs were met. As Bjorkt & Goebertustt (2011) express: "locals referred to lack of water, lack of food, lack of housing, corruption in the political class and lack of political accountability as the type of problems they expected the ICC to solve." Amnesty International (2014) received victims' statements with similar expectations: "If the ICC would assist us, they can assist us to start our own business." The ICC Common Legal Representatives also noted that, despite efforts to clarify their roles in their meetings with victims, many victims still view them – and more broadly the ICC – as capable of providing material assistance and compensation (ibid.).[5]

In relation to the resolution of the case, the majority of Kenyans once believed that the leaders of the two parties that contested the election in 2007 would have been prosecuted at the ICC (Tenove 2013, 9/17; Brown & Sriram 2012; Mwanzia & Kanina 2009). Victims were confident that the main perpetrators of the committed crimes would be unable to influence the procedures of the ICC, despite having been successful at influencing trials in the domestic sphere. One survivor interviewed by Amnesty International (2014) expressed: "I have a lot of hope that the success of the ICC will bring some change on what is happening in Kenya." However, the dismissal of the charges by the ICC Prosecutor severely harmed the victims' confidence in the system (see, in comparison, Lugano's chapter in this book). As a result, even in 2012, the support for the ICC among Kenyans has been steadily declining (Akpedonu et al. 2013).

In spite of these downsides, the legal process before the ICC itself was useful in requiring the powerful elite to appear in court for the first time in Kenya's history (Lugano 2017b; Akpedonu et al. 2013). As said in the local newspaper *Daily Nation*, the point was now made that no person is untouchable, and no Kenyan is a "sacred cow" – in reference to Hindu sacred consideration of this animal (Ogenga 2013). Under the same logic, a victim added: "The Rome Statute shows there is someone beyond the leader that people can fall back to" (Amnesty International 2014).

Third, the trials did not seem to improve, or even address, the complex issue of ethnic rivalries. Notably, even if demanding retributive justice before

5 The ICC can only award reparations to victims harmed by a person convicted by the Court.

the ICC, many Kenyans changed their position when a leader from their ethnic group was persecuted, as they perceived it as a witch-hunt against their ethnicity (Bosire & Lynchy 2014). In particular, opinion about the ICC shifted after the two confronting candidates during the 2007 election, Kenyatta and Ruto, decided to join in a new party and voiced the anti-Court campaign. Some victims, particularly from the ethnic groups of the two leaders mentioned above, then understood that this political union was enough to ensure peace and lost interest in and support of the ICC's efforts to move forward with prosecutions (Amnesty International 2014).

Fourth, neither the domestic criminal trial nor the ICC intervention seemed to have contributed to efforts to avoid the repetition of violence, although they did help to reduce tensions. As a result of the ICC's intervention, and as said before, Kenyatta and Ruto – former opponents – joined forces in the 2013 elections, which had a dramatic impact in defusing confrontations between the two ethnic groups of these political leaders that were the main confronters in the PEV. Nevertheless, the violence throughout the nation did not subside. In the general polls of 2017/2018, Kenya's electoral commission declared President Kenyatta the winner of a second term, in spite of formal criminal accusations of fraud and excessive use of force by the police (HWR 2018). The opposition candidate Odinga challenged the results, which led to the Supreme Court nullifying the election, but Kenyatta's party responded by threatening and intimidating the judges. When the new election took place, violence spread once again and Odinga ended up withdrawing from the competition and desisting from the legal challenges he had brought against Kenyatta. Overall, 100 people were killed during this prolonged electoral dispute. Following that, the government refused to acknowledge the murders and, on the contrary, praised the police for the work done (HRW 2018). This demonstrated that neither the timid apology from 2008 nor the constitutional reform dating back to 2010 made any substantial progress in avoiding the repetition of violence surrounding elections. The government has yet to bring charges against any security officers, even after a government probe into the murders of a nine-month-old baby and a nine-year-old girl found at least five senior police commanders and other government officials responsible (HRW 2020).

Fifth, the intervention of the ICC coupled with Kenya's response stirred the attitudes of many African countries with respect to their view of and respect for international criminal law. In 2008, when Sudanese President al-Bashir was indicted, the African Union called for its member states to implement a policy of non-cooperation (Murithi 2013). The charges against Kenya redoubled the hostility and the belief that the Court only focused on the

African continent. Indeed, aside from the underlying pursuit of impunity by some heads of state, the African Union's suspicions regarding the potentially unfair discretional case selection of the ICC might stand on reasonable grounds. When confronted with these accusations, the former ICC Prosecutor Ocampo indicated to interlocutors that he could not apply the same remit of justice to cases in Chechnya, Iraq and Afghanistan because this would be politically difficult (Okuku 2002) due to the political interests involved, including the participation of the United States and Western Europe in the human rights violations. The situation between the African Union and the ICC finally escalated when, on June 30, 2014, the Annual Summit of the Assembly of Heads of State and Government issued the Malabo Protocol, extending the jurisdiction of the African Court of Justice and Human Rights to cover international crimes, along the lines of the Rome Statute, in order to make the ICC dispensable. Within this context, the Ugandan president Museveni referred to the ICC as "a bunch of useless people" and the Rwandan president Kagame said the Court was never about "justice but politics disguised as international justice" (Kuwonu 2017). In 2016, the Presidents of Burundi, The Gambia and South Africa expressed their intention to leave the ICC and Burundi enforced the decision one year later (*The Guardian* 2017).

What went wrong? Could a victim-driven approach help achieve justice in Kenya?

The chapter has described the several episodes of human rights violations experienced in Kenya and the incomplete and limited efforts to pursue accountability. It has specifically analyzed the domestic and international legal responses to the PEV and the effects they had in terms of the rule of law, legitimacy of the domestic judiciary and the ICC and violence prevention.

A general overview of the Kenyan process shows, then, that little attention has been paid to the victims. They have been relegated to second place while CSOs, INGOs and the government have been the main agents of the transitional justice process. Most of the survivors are not involved in any autonomous initiative to overcome the human rights violations they have suffered nor are they involved in any initiatives that would support them in demanding updates from their representatives. This means that most Kenyan survivors remain isolated and are passive recipients within hierarchical relations with experts. Meanwhile, the few existing victims' organizations have been mostly acting as satellites of CSOs and INGOs rather than as independent entities.

From a psychological and collective perspective, this representation mechanism seems to have obstructed the path toward victims' empowerment which, ideally, would make them more aware of their rights and less vulnerable to potential human rights violations. Many Kenyan CSOs have expressively chosen to avoid involving the victims "to prevent possible frustrations" if the outcomes of the process were not as expected, perpetuating a paternalistic strategy that further enhances disempowerment. As a CSO leader from the Somali region of Kenya whom I interviewed expressed it: "When the TJRC initiative was launched, we had a meeting to discuss who would provide testimony and how. Then, I was told that people would expect reparations from those calls because I was calling them to declare. So, I stopped doing that." Also at the ICC level, representatives of Kenyans for Peace with Truth and Justice expressed that they have been careful not to raise victims' hopes (Tenove 2013, 24).

Specifically, prosecutions have mostly been initiated "on behalf of" or "for the benefit of" victims, without close attention being paid to the actual views and concerns of these individuals (Pena & Carayon 2013). Most focus group participants in Kenya were unaware of the role that the ICC could play in victim assistance and reparations (Tenove 2013, 24). Even more striking might be the fact that several media outlets questioned the victims' lawyer and the CSOs' representatives about their impressions of the ICC and *their* opinion of the victims. They were also questioned about what the victims had said with respect to the outcome of the criminal process, but barely any *victims' voices* appeared in the media reports (Nzwllli 2016). The victims' lawyer was the one who said: "*Many of them* are disappointed" (emphasis added) (qiraatafrican 2016). Also, Wainaina Ndung, Director of the International Center for Policy and Conflict, was the one who said: "I *think* the *victims are* in triple jeopardy" (emphasis added) (ibid.). The position of Morris Odhiambo, President of the Civil Society Congress, was as follows: "*He says* he suspects that *victims* may not see justice soon" (ibid.). In the same logic, Elizabeth Evenson, senior international justice counsel at Human Rights Watch, was quoted as saying, "the outcome is a blow *to those* who had wanted greater accountability" (ibid.). Another example follows: "Mr Midiwo [member of the Kenyan government] said *victims of post-election violence want* resettlement and justice" (emphasis added) (Barasa 2010).

The most problematic aspect of these experts' centrality – acting not in support, but rather in *lieu,* of the victims – is that in situations like the current one, when justice has been blocked at both the national and international level, victims remain in despair. When those representatives decide that more cannot be done (e.g. ceasing to file appeals in court or ending negotiation efforts with the government to achieve reparations), victims have to accept the decision as final because they do not have a voice in the decision-making process. Moreover, this situation makes re-victimization more likely as they remain in a situation of high vulnerability that it is being neither materially nor psychologically changed.

This situation might raise the question about the possible role of a more active victims' movement in order to achieve justice. In other words, is it reasonable to propose that attaining justice might require overturning the current situation of CSOs and international organizations acting on behalf of affected individuals? A *victim-driven approach* (Vegh Weis 2017) understands that survivors have the right to be familiar with the possibilities of the transitional justice process as well as be aware of the eventual challenges, thus providing them with the agency to experience both positive and negative outcomes while still being able to make informed decisions. A victim-driven approach relies on strengthening the marginalized communities by giving them a voice in the political sphere and allowing them to change their condition on their own whilst overcoming their personal grief through a collective strategy. The victim-driven approach might also be a feasible path to work towards the resolution of historical problems that perpetuate disempowerment and stigmatization, such as ethnic confrontations, by conceiving of victims as part of the same struggle for rights enforcement. Indeed, even the Kenya Transitional Justice Network (2015) states: "The TJRC further noted that there is a need for a 'bottom-up' approach."

Following this logic, the victim-driven approach changes the focus from victims' *participation* to *leadership* in public policy. "There is a critical difference between going through the empty ritual of participation and having the real power needed to affect the outcome of the process … [P]articipation without redistribution of power is an empty and frustrating process for the powerless … It maintains the status quo" (Arnstein 1969). As the Kenyan Transitional Justice Network (2015) observed when raising the question "will the recommendations be implemented considering the current lack of political will?": "county governments and civil society organizations can also take up some of the recommendations. Victim groups can decide to lobby locally for implementation." The victim-driven approach is desirable because if victims occupy leadership positions, the process is more likely to be *pertinent, effective* and *transformative*. It is likely to be *pertinent* because victims' leadership in the design of transitional justice strategies results in these strategies being more likely to respond to the unique needs and challenges of each community. In turn, community ownership plays a facilitating role in disrupting harmful norms and practices (Michau & Nakur 2003, 13–14). A victim-driven approach is also more likely to be *effective* because victims and communities are more inclined to support initiatives that they themselves took part in developing and implementing. "A growing body of public health research has demonstrated that community interventions which are multilevel, community-based and culturally situated are more likely to create a long-term community impact" (Freccero et al. 2011). Furthermore, CSOs and international bodies are more likely to accept a negative outcome, while those biographically crushed by the human rights violations might have deeper emotional and material reasons to continue seeking justice despite the severity of the struggle. Finally, *a* victim-driven approach is more likely to be *transformative* because victims' and communities' involvement has the potential to address the loss of self-esteem and confidence that can result from victimization, opening the path of transformative change in the lives of individuals and in the ability of marginalized communities to engage more meaningfully with political and legal processes. In turn, the transformation of individuals and communities is likely to "compel the public and government actors to see them as human beings with dignity, agency and a drive to be treated on the basis of equal opportunity" (USAID 2014).

Kenya has relevant victims' organizations that could be supported in spearheading the process on their own, including the National Victims and Survivors Network (which brings together the victims of all types of human right violations), the IDP network (which gathers those displaced from their lands), the Grace Agenda (which unites female victims of sexual violence), Nyayo House Torture Victims (which unites victims of torture), and the Wagalla Foundation (which gathers Somali victims from Wagalla massacre). A victim-driven approach relies on the strengthening of these organizations and on the coming together of the isolated victims on the ground to allow them to speak on their own behalf, connecting with the international organizations and disputing decision-making processes with government representatives. Even though the extension of this chapter may be sufficient to provoke thoughts about specific ways in which a victim-driven approach can be encouraged in Kenya, it is important to touch upon potential courses of actions. Building local, national and international networks with other victims' organizations, human rights associations, social movements, the media and the general population might be suitable paths to achieving comprehensive justice.

With that being said, it is also relevant to point out that Kenyan victims must deal with socioeconomic burdens and devastating rates of inequality and poverty as well as ethnic rivalries that undermine their potential empowerment. Most of the victims remain in an extremely vulnerable economic situation, while survivors of sexual violence tend to end up in even more execrable situations as many have been blamed by their partners for provoking the sexual attack, expelled from their houses and marginalized in their communities (HRW 2015). As of today, except for individual civil cases and some governmental support for the displaced people, Kenyan victims have received no economic or symbolic compensations at either the international or national levels and yet they continue to suffer the medical, social and economic consequences of the human rights violations they suffered. The remaining high levels of poverty, including significant hunger, and lack of access to health services (HRW 2015, 9/55) are so striking that victims are confined to focusing all of their energy on daily subsistence, leaving them without the time and resources needed to continue the push for criminal trials. This situation does not imply, however, that victims are not concerned about criminal justice and it definitely does not imply that Kenya should prioritize reparations over justice. As it has been repeatedly expressed, a comprehensive transitional justice process must include both complementary elements, in addition to truth and guarantees of non-repetition (De Greiff 2011; 2015). Concluding that in cases of generalized poverty, criminal justice is not a priority would be against international law and ethically questionable, as it could imply that retributive justice is only possible for non-poor victims.

To this it is added that gender inequality is still alarmingly relevant (Tamale 2009). Ndonga & Muddell (2019) noted that acts of sexual and gender-based violence had been commonly used during the Shifta Conflict, the PEV and other episodes of systematic human rights abuse, and at times as a weapon to stop women from taking active political roles. This fact weakens women's possibilities of empowerment in Kenya, leaving them mostly alienated from the struggle for justice.

Aside from the economic and health difficulties and gender inequality, ethnic conflicts among the 43 different ethnic groups undermine the possibility of a unified struggle for justice (Mureu 2017). As said before, when bringing accused people before court, the different ethnic groups tend to defend their own kind and also perceive the prosecution of their leaders as a witch-hunt against their ethnicity (Bosire & Lynchy 2014). This means that there is oftentimes an unwavering loyalty to the members of the ethnic group in spite of the crimes that they might have committed. Under the same logic, many Kenyans were won over by the call to support local leaders, despite the criminal accusations, rather than viewing the so-called "imperialist" ICC intervention objectively (see Lugano's chapter in this book). As a curse of the colonial legacy, the ethnic divisions continue to cement and solidify the struggle for power, thereby obstructing the existence of legitimate and comprehensive justice that could set Kenya on a path towards no repetition.

Overall, the process in Kenya shows that when victims are made invisible, the path toward impunity is more likely to occur without resistance. Placing those who have been personally traversed by human rights violations on the front line of the struggle for justice might be a better alternative.

References

Amnesty International, 2013. "Police reform in Kenya: 'a drop in the ocean.'" Available at: https://www.amnesty.nl/content/uploads/2016/11/kenya_afr_32_001_2013.pdf?x62907 [Accessed April 19, 2020].

Amnesty International, 2014. "Crying for Justice Victims' Perspectives on Justice for the Post-Election Violence in Kenya." Available at: https://www.amnesty.org/en/documents/AFR32/001/2014/en/ [Accessed April 19, 2020].

Arnstein, S., 1969. "Ladder of Citizen Participation." *Journal of the American Institute of Planners* 35(4): 216–224.

Barasa, L., 2010. "Mutula to Ocampo, quit Kenyan probe." *Sunday Nation*, September 18. Available at: https://www.nation.co.ke/news/politics/Mutula-to-Ocampo-Quit-Kenyan-probe-/1064-1013680-1178qd2/index.html [Accessed April 19, 2020].

Bjorkt, C. & Goebertustt, J., 2011. "Complementarity in Action: The Role of Civil Society and the ICC in Rule of Law Strengthening in Kenya." *Yale Human Rights and Development Journal* 4(1): 205-230.

Bosire, L. & Lynchy, G., 2014. "Kenya's Search for Truth and Justice: The Role of Civil Society." *The International Journal of Transitional Justice* 8: 256–276.

Brown, S. & Sriram, C., 2012. "The big fish won't fry themselves: Criminal accountability for post-election violence in Kenya." *African Affairs* 111(443): 244–260.

Cheptinga, M., 2017. Personal communication, April 22.

Chernor, C., 2011. "Situation in the Republic of Kenya." *The American Journal of International Law* 105(3): 540–547.

Chernor, C., 2015. "Prosecutor v. Ruto." *The American Journal of International Law* 109(3): 610–616.

Commission of Inquiry into the Post-Election Violence (CIPEV), 2008. Report. Available at: https://reliefweb.int/report/kenya/kenya-commission-inquiry-post-election-violence-cipev-final-report [Accessed April 19, 2020].

De Greiff, P., 2011. "Some thoughts on the Development and Present State of Transitional Justice." *Journal for Human Rights* 5: 98–128.

De Greiff, P., 2015. Report of the Special Rapporteur on the Promotion and Protection of All Human Rights, Civil, Political, Economic, Social and Cultural Rights, including the Right to Development, delivered during the 27th session of the Human Rights Council,16, UN Doc. A/70/XXX, October 21.

Engbo, G., 2015. "Justice Tides: How and When Levels of ICC Involvement Affect Peace Processes." *International Journal of Transitional Justice* 9(3): 428–448.

Freccero, J., Harris, L., Carnay, M. & Taylor, C., 2011. *Responding to sexual violence: community approaches sexual violence & accountability project*. Berkeley, CA: Human Rights Center, University of California.

Gachoka, T., 2012. "Diatribe against Uhuru and Ruto is a conspiracy to stop them running." *Daily Nation*, July 30.

Human Rights Watch (HRW), 2011. *Turning pebbles: Evading accountability for post-election violence in Kenya*. Nairobi: Human Rights Watch.
Human Rights Watch (HRW), 2015. *"I just Sit and Wait to Die." Reparations for Survivors of Kenya's 2007–2008 Post-Election Sexual Violence*. Nairobi: Human Rights Watch.
Human Rights Watch (HRW), 2018. *Kenya: Fresh Evidence of Election-Period Abuses*, February 25. Available at: https://www.hrw.org/news/2018/02/25/kenya-fresh-evidence-election-period-abuses [Accessed April 19, 2020].
Human Rights Watch (HRW), 2020. *World Report. Country Chapter: Kenya*. Available at: https://www.hrw.org/world-report/2020/country-chapters/kenya [Accessed April 19, 2020].
International Center for Transitional Justice (ICTJ) & Kenyan National Commission on Human Rights (KNCHR), 2016. *Concept Note: Experts Group Meeting to Discuss Regulations on Restorative Justice Fund for Historical Injustices*, December 6–7.
International Crisis Group (ICG), 2012. "Kenya: Impact of the ICC proceedings." *Africa Briefing* 84.
Ireland, C., 2011. "Justice for Kenya's Mau Mau. Historian Helps Make the Case that Aged Veterans Deserve Justice," September 1. Available at: https://news.harvard.edu/gazette/story/2011/09/justice-for-kenyas-mau-mau/ [Accessed April 19, 2020].
Joselow, G., 2013. "US Official Says Kenya's Elections Have 'Consequences.'" *Voices of America*, February 7. Available at: https://www.voanews.com/africa/us-official-says-kenyas-elections-have-consequences [Accessed April 19, 2020].
Karua, M., 2008. Address to the Kenyan National Assesmbly. Official Record (Hansard), July 24, Cols. 2111–2128.
Kenya National Commission on Human Rights (KNCHR), 2008. *On the Brink of the Precipice: A Human Rights Account of Kenya's Post-2007 Election Violence*. Available at: http://www.knchr.org/Portals/0/Reports/KNCHR_REPORT_ON_THE_BRINK_OF_THE_PRECIPE.pdf [Accessed April 19, 2020].
Kenyans for Peace with Truth and Justice (KPTJ), 2013a. "A Luxury Victims Cannot Afford Meaningful Participation at the International Criminal Court." *Truth and Justice Digest* 07/09.
Kenyans for Peace with Truth and Justice (KPTJ), 2013b. *Securing justice. Establishing a domestic mechanism for the 2007/8 post-election violence in Kenya*. Available at: http://africog.org/new/wp-content/uploads/Securing_Justice.pdf [Accessed April 19, 2020].
Kenyata, J., 1963. East African Standard 1963.
Kenyata, J., 1968. *Suffering without bitterness*, Nairobi: East African Publishing House.
Kiprotich, A., 2009. "Will witness protection law work?" *The Standard*, July 26. Available at: https://www.standardmedia.co.ke/article/1144020062/will-witness-protection-law-work [Accessed April 19, 2020].
Kisika, S., 2018. "Bill seeks to create agency to pay victims of injustices." *The Star*, March 29.
Kuwonu, F., 2017. "ICC: Beyond the threats of withdrawal." *Africa Renewal*, May–July.
Lugano, G., 2017a. "Counter-Shaming the International Criminal Court's Intervention as Neocolonial: Lessons from Kenya." *International Journal for Transitional Justice* 2: 9–29.
Lugano, G., 2017b. Personal communication, March. 22.
Mbondenyi, M., 2010. "The place of the judiciary in democratic transitions in Africa: A comparison of post-apartheid South Africa and post-authoritarian Kenya." *Judiciary Watch Report* 9.
Menocal, A., 2013. "Kenya's peaceful election doesn't make it a healthy democracy." *Foreign Policy*. March 22. Available at: https://foreignpolicy.com/2013/03/22/kenyas-peaceful-election-doesnt-make-it-a-healthy-democracy/ [Accessed April 19, 2020].
Michau, L. & Nakur, D., 2003. "Mobilising Communities to Prevent Domestic Violence: A Resource Guide for Communities in East and Southern Africa." *Raising Voices*: 13–14.

Mugabe, R., 1980. "Prime Minister Elect Address to the Nation." Zimbabwe Department of Information, March 4.

Mureu, M., 2017. "Why Kenya is proud of only one tribe." *The Standard*, February 10. Available at: https://www.standardmedia.co.ke/ureport/article/2001228930/why-kenya-is-proud-of-only-one-tribe [Accessed April 19, 2020].

Murithi, T., 2013. "The African Union and the International Criminal Court: An Embattled Relationship?" The Institute for Justice and Reconciliation, 8. Available at: https://www.africaportal.org/publications/the-african-union-and-the-international-criminal-court-an-embattled-relationship/ [Accessed April 19, 2020].

Murphy, K., 2015. *Learning from our Past. An Exploration of Truth, Justice, and Reconciliation in Kenya*. Nairobi: International Center for Transitional Justice.

Mutua, M., 2009. *Human Rights NGOs in East Africa: Political and Normative Tensions*. Philadelphia: University of Pennsylvania Press.

Mwanzia, M. & Kanina, A., 2009. "Kenyans Want Poll Chaos Tried in The Hague." *The Standard*, July 19. Available at: https://www.standardmedia.co.ke/business/article/1144019651/kenyans-want-poll-chaos-suspects-tried-at-the-hague [Accessed April 19, 2020].

Ndonga, A. & Muddell, K., 2019. "Ending Gender Violence in Elections," ICTJ Briefing. Available at: https://www.ictj.org/sites/default/files/ICTJ_Briefing_Kenya_Women_Inclusion_Web.pdf [Accessed April 19, 2020].

Nzwllli, F., 2016. "As ICC dismisses Kenya case, victims of 2008 violence feel left behind." *The Christian Science Monitor*, April 6. Available at: https://www.csmonitor.com/World/Africa/2016/0406/As-ICC-dismisses-Kenya-case-victims-of-2008-violence-feel-left-behind [Accessed April 19, 2020].

Ogenga, F., 2013. "The Media Coverage of the Hague Trials and the Construction of New Ethnic Subjectivities in Kenya." *African Conflict and Peacebuilding Review* 3(1): 158–174.

Okuku, J., 2002. "Civil Society and the Democratisation Processes in Kenya and Uganda: A Comparative Analysis of the Contribution of the Church and NGOs." *African Journal of Political Science/Revue Africaine de Science Politique* 7(2): 81–97.

Pena, M. & Carayon, G., 2013. "Is the ICC Making the Most of Victim Participation?" *International Journal of Transitional Justice* 7(3): 518–535.

Qiraatafrican, 2016. "As ICC dismisses Kenya case, victims of 2008 violence feel left behind", April, 11.Available at: http://qiraatafrican.com/en/new/as-icc-dismisses-kenya-case-victims-of-2008-violence-feel-left-behind#sthash.wvECs4pL.dpbs [Accessed April 19, 2020].

Rajab, R., 2018. "Implement TJRC report, deliver Sh10b restorative fund pledge, KNHCR asks Uhuru." *The Star*, March 20.

Senier, A., 2011. "Introductory note to the International Criminal Court: Situation in the Republic of Kenya." *International Legal Materials* 50(4): 494–502.

Stubbins Bates, E., 2011. "Introductory note to the International Criminal Court Appeals Chamber: Prosecutor V. Francis Kirimi Muthaura, Uhuru Muigai Kenyatta and Mohammed Hussein Ali." *International Legal Materials* 51(1): 17–43.

Tamale, S., 2009. "Law, Sexuality, and Politics in Uganda: Challenges for Women's Human Rights NGOs." In Mutua, M. (ed.) *Human Rights NGOs in East Africa: Political and Normative Tensions*. Philadelphia: University of Pennsylvania Press, 51–74.

Tenove, C., 2013. "International Justice for Victims? Assessing the International Criminal Court from the Perspective of Victims In Kenya And Uganda." Africa Portal Research Paper.

Truth, Justice and Reconciliation Commission of Kenya (TJRC), 2013. *Final Report of the TJRC*. Available at: https://www.knchr.org/Portals/0/Transitional%20Justice/kenya-tjrc-summary-report-aug-2013.pdf?ver=2018-06-08-100202-027 [Accessed April 19, 2020].

The Guardian, 2017. "Burundi becomes first nation to leave international criminal court," October 28.

USAID, 2014. *Community participation in transitional justice: a role for participatory research.* Available at: https://www.usaid.gov/sites/default/files/documents/1866/CPTJUSAID.pdf [Accessed April 19, 2020].

Vegh Weis, V., 2017. "The Relevance of Victims' Organizations in Transitional Justice Processes. The Case of Grandmothers of Plaza de Mayo in Argentina." *Intercultural Human Rights Law Review* 12: 1–70.

Wachira, G., Kamungi, P. & Sillah, K., 2014. *Streching the Truth: The Uncertain Promise of TRC's in Africa's Transitional Justice.* Nairobi: Nairobi Peace Initiative.

Wakaya, J., 2018. "Restorative Justice Fund not created 3 years after directive." *The Star*, March 19.

Whittaker, H., 2011. "Forced Villagization during the Shifta Conflict in Kenya, ca. 1963–1968." *The International Journal of African Historical Studies* 45(3): 343–336.

UN Resolutions

UN Doc. S/PRST/2002/41.
UN Doc. E/CN.4/2004/88.
UN Doc. S/2000/915, 22.

Laws

Kenyan Indemnity Act, June 4, 1970

Cases

African Union, 2013, Decision on Africa's Relationship with the International Criminal Court, EXT/Assembly/AU/Dec.1

ICC, 2011. Pre-Trial Chamber, *Prosecutor v. Francis Kirimi Muthaura, Uhuru Muigai Kenyatta and Mohammed Hussein Ali,* Decision on the Application by the Government of Kenya Challenging the Admissibility of the Case Pursuant to Article (19)(2)(b) of the Statute, May 30, 2011, ICC-01/09-02/11-96.

ICC, 2014a. Trial Chamber V(B), *Situation in the Republic of Kenya in the Case of the Prosecutor v. Uhuru Muigai Kenyatta,* December 5, 2014, ICC-01/09-02/11-983.

ICC, 2014b. Victims' Response to the "Prosecution's notice of withdrawal of the charges against Uhuru Muigai Kenyatta" within Situation in the Republic of Kenya in the Case of the Prosecutor v. Uhuru Muigai Kenyatta, December 9, 2014, ICC-01/09-02/11.

ICC, 2017. *Situation in the Republic of Kenya in the Case of the Prosecutor v. William Samoei Ruto and Joshua Arap Sang,* February 2, 2017, ICC-01/09-01/11. Available at: https://www.icc-cpi.int/CourtRecords/CR2017_00533.PDF [Accessed April 19, 2020].

Concluding Reflections
Towards the End of Impunity? The Scope and Impact of Human Rights Trials

Rosario Figari Layús and Ulrike Capdepón

Through the 10 contributions that make up this volume we have sought to address critical issues in the field of human rights prosecution by drawing on the experiences of a variety of countries covering three world regions. While the local historical and political contexts of violence and conflict differ significantly, the studies address a range of common issues around such trials (e.g. strategies for promoting accountability, social, political and victim impact, as well as resistance to, and limitations of, prosecutions), which are crucial for advancing or impeding the quest for justice through the courts. The book benefits from a wide-ranging comparative approach, offering perspectives on certain regional trends and transregional or global insights into key factors, an understanding of which is essential if countries are to learn from each other's experiences, from both the activist and the policy-maker point of view. In what follows, these final reflections will outline some of the main findings revealed in the different chapters.

The question that opened this book was: "Do human rights trials make a difference, and if so, of what kind?" However, the experiences documented in the chapters that followed have shown that there is no easy answer. Their impact varies from one context to another, yet it is not at all a matter of indifference whether a country that aspires to be inclusive and democratic decides to prosecute those responsible for gross human rights violations than to hold them immune. The establishment of accountability for human rights violations can help cultivate a "culture of rights" (Laplante 2014, 75) and reinforce the democratic principle that all are *equal before* the law. Equal access to the courts is decisive if the victims in post-conflict and post-authoritarian contexts are to enjoy full citizenship. Justice policies that discourage, hamper or prevent the prosecution of the perpetrators of human rights crimes cast doubt on the citizenship and democracy supposedly enjoyed under the new dispensation. The conduct of human rights trials represents a fundamental factor in ensuring the acknowledgement and institutional, legal, political and social inclusion of victims.

In certain contexts where the judicial system is generally viewed as operating to the benefit of political and economic elites (O'Donnell 1998), the non-prosecution of major state criminals is understood, as the Kenya chapter shows, as another manifestation of their privilege and power. Impunity for acts of state repression – a vertical, top-down type of violence – is an unambiguous expression of the unequal application of law to the benefit of those who hold power. Judicial recognition and sanction, on the other hand, serve as mechanisms of control over the behavior of the state and its agents. While impunity simply reproduces the unequal application of law, human rights trials thus operate as a means of democratization, as well as serving the ends of victim recognition and inclusion, as witnessed by the experiences of Chile, Argentina and Peru. This recognition that human rights trials can make a difference and play a decisive role in strengthening trust in institutions and the rule of law does not, of course, mean that they have the same scope and impact in all contexts. As the contributions in this volume make clear, human rights prosecutions around the world are not homogeneous, but encompass a great diversity of difficulties, effects and implications for victims, politics and civil society.

Taken together, the 10 chapters reveal certain shared patterns as well as context-related differences. In doing so, they highlight problematic aspects of current human rights trial practices that should be of great interest to justice system actors, activists and policy makers. This work will therefore hopefully contribute to the introduction of changes that may better support the pursuit of justice, enhancing the rule of law and better protecting victims' rights.

Factors in the continuum from impunity to accountability

The different country cases in this volume reveal how a variety of social and political factors play a crucial role, influencing the conduct and impact of human rights trials at the local level. While these factors may differ in the intensity or modality of their effects, they all appear to play a fundamental role in advancing or impeding human rights prosecutions or diminishing or enhancing their positive impact on victims and society. The key factors identified are (a) the continuing power of perpetrators or their supporters and/or elite patrons under the current regime; (b) the degree of institutional and governmental support for prosecutions; (c) the legitimacy and independence of the instances responsible for prosecution and trial; (d) the role and agency of victims or their representatives (relatives' associations and human rights organizations) in the demand for justice; (e) social attitudes towards measures of accountability; and (f) the passage of time since the violence occurred. These critical factors, discussed in greater detail below, have a crucial influence on the development and impact of criminal accountability for human rights violations and offer a general analytical framework for the study of human rights trials in post-violence situations.

a) The continuing power of perpetrators

The conducting of human rights prosecutions, as well as their course and their eventual shortcomings, are all the outcome of struggles between different political and social interests, not only within the country in question but also at the international level. One of the particularities of human rights trials is that they address and prosecute state crimes and public servants. This means that unlike most ordinary criminal trials, the defendants are people who had, and may still have, a certain degree of power within society, whether as political actors or as state functionaries. In many situations, the prosecution of key actors responsible for armed conflict or authoritarian rule is by no means a foregone conclusion but a matter of political contestation and public debate.

The fact that direct victims or their relatives have to struggle for justice for years reflects in many countries an asymmetry in the application of criminal law, stringent with regard to marginalized sectors of the population but lenient to members of the elite and to state officials, military personnel, entrepreneurs and other powerful groups in society (Wacquant 2009). As can be seen in the chapters on Chile, Argentina, Peru, Uruguay and Kenya here, those responsible for serious crimes have been highly influential in impeding justice. In a number of Latin American and African countries, there is a history of vacillation between immunity and accountability that reflects the fluctuation of power relations and the struggle of political interests in the government and wider society in question.

Though human rights prosecutions should properly follow from the ordinary application of law, in most cases they are the outcome of a shift or loss of power by perpetrators, on the one hand, and years of campaigning by victims and human rights organizations, on the other. In societies where perpetrators still hold significant power or where the victims' movement is not very strong and lacks institutional support, trials are less likely to take place, for those who hold power are those who determine when and how the law will be applied. As documented in the respective chapters, "pacted" transition processes, as in Spain after the Franco regime, or indeed "dictated" transitions, such as followed the formal end of the Pinochet dictatorship in Chile, are direct expressions of the continuing power and influence of the elites that sponsored the dictatorship, allowing them to impose modalities of political change that ensure immunity through amnesty laws for perpetrators while institutionalizing and securing their own political influence.

As Vegh Weis's chapter shows in the Kenyan case, relative impunity can also derive from perpetrators' own continuing power. One of the main obstacles to domestic prosecutions in Africa is the fact that many of those responsible for systematic human rights violations and mass atrocities – notably members of national, regional or local elites that supported political violence, financially or politically – remain powerful actors embedded in the political and judicial systems of their countries. In analyzing the attempts to prosecute organized political violence in the aftermath of the 2008 presidential elections in Kenya, Vegh Weis clearly demonstrates how domestic constraints and power relations can make local and even international prosecutions very difficult, thus reproducing structural impunity through time.

Power relationships are reflected in the unequal application of the law not only at the national level but also at the international level. Geoffrey Lugano's chapter echoes a strand of Vegh Weis's argument in its discussion of the role of the International Criminal Court and how it is perceived: as it turns out, only defendants from the Global South, all of them African, have ever been arraigned before it (ICC 2020). The system of international justice can also thus be seen to operate on the basis of historical asymmetries of power.

b) Institutional and governmental support for prosecution

While the possibility of mounting human rights prosecutions depends on the general relationships of power in a society, the state itself is constituted by social and political power relations and sustains the legal order, which is never neutral (O'Donnell 1993, 3). As can be seen in most of the cases discussed in this volume, the support afforded to prosecutions by the state has been crucial wherever these have taken place. The relationship holds true, in reverse, where impunity has prevailed. There, the lack of support and of political will has led to the denial of justice, by preventing or impeding prosecution *de jure* or *de facto*. Denial of justice can occur by action or omission, while institutional support for serious human rights prosecutions requires an active process of legal, political and economic decision making and policy implementation.

Accountability is rejected *de jure* when the executive, legislative and judicial branches act to pass and uphold amnesty legislation. This is a strong and active form of official denial (Cohen 2001) that operates as a legal barrier to action against the perpetrators. Amnesty laws are the fruit of a political decision that blocks the "normal" course of events, which would see the ordinary criminal justice system intervene to punish crimes. Likewise, the legislative repeal or judicial abrogation of such laws, most generally occurring after a change of regime, reflects a political will to offer victims equal access to justice.

As is seen in the case of the prosecutions of Nazis in the Federal Republic of Germany, government policy for dealing with the human rights crimes of the recent past initially involved overturning the convictions imposed by the Allies and closing ongoing investigations into Nazi crimes, culminating in the Laws of Immunity until the mid-1950s, and later again in 1968–1969. Weinke's chapter reveals a great reluctance – both legal and political – to prosecute human rights crimes committed under the Nazi regime in Western German domestic trials during the postwar years. This official rejection abated somewhat only in 1979, when the Bundestag finally voted to repeal the statute of limitations.

The degree of official political support for prosecutions is reflected in government attitudes to prosecutions, victims and perpetrators and the categorization of the violence that has taken place. Official attitudes, whether of support, rejection and even indifference, find expression both in policy on the initiation and resourcing of proceedings and in the way official discourse refers to them.

One mark of political support is the public apology for state crimes. Governments that publicly apologize for the crimes of their predecessors are generally much more likely to prosecute the crimes of the past than those that deploy a discourse of denial or reconciliation, typical of contexts where human rights violations go unpunished. Such apology expresses the contemporary state's attitude toward the wrongdoings of the past, acknowledging the state's responsibility for those crimes. This assumption of responsibility is a significant symbolic act that lends legitimacy to the quest for accountability measures while also providing a basis for official support of the prosecution of the crimes in question. The condemnation of past state crimes marks a rupture with the former regime or the political circumstances that led to the violence. At the same time, as we see in the chapter on Argentina, the Macri government's discourse on the crimes of the dictatorship and their victims reflects a significant ideological turn away from the more critical and more human-rights-oriented reading of the past offered by the *Kirchnerismo* that went before.

As documented in that chapter and elsewhere in this collection, the proper conduct of human rights prosecutions with due regard for the rights and needs of victims calls for not only political but also economic support. Even where trials may count on the political support of government, lack of adequate material and human resources can represent a serious impediment to justice.

The possible consequences of inadequate funding are manifold. A lack of staff (judges, prosecutors, legal administrators) is one of the main causes of delay in investigation and trials. It is also frequently associated with a lack of appropriate training. Fluency in the law of human rights is an obvious requirement for judges and lawyers, while an official understanding of the needs of victims is essential if survivors and witnesses are to be treated with respect and consideration in court, and not further traumatized or dehumanized.

In this circumstance, funding too is essential. For it is needed to support programs of psychological support and protective security for those testifying, as well as for meeting expenses to ensure the participation of victims who do not live conveniently near the place of trial.

Indeed, meeting personal expenses is one of the greatest obstacles encountered by victims in their quest for justice. In the case of the Argentine Complaint, complainants, victims and activists had to pay their own travel expenses as they flew from Spain to Buenos Aires to testify. Victims from among rural populations or indigenous communities far from the urban centers where trials take place are often excluded from access to justice when no public funding is available to cover travel and accommodation, as is illustrated by the chapter on Peru. There, many of the victims of the armed conflict are Quechua speakers who live in rural regions, far from the capital, Lima, where the trials are held. These victims' lack of both resources and government support places limitations on their participation in proceedings. Finally, adequate political and financial backing for prosecutions entails publicizing their existence, course and outcome, ensuring that the facts they reveal enter public awareness and the historical narrative.

c) The legitimacy and independence of the instances responsible for prosecution and trial

The local legitimacy enjoyed by the institutions responsible for prosecution and trial is crucial to the social impact of proceedings. Varying with the historical and political context, the efficiency and thus credibility of domestic or international tribunals play a significant role in the perceptions and attitudes of victims and of society more generally. The Latin American and African case studies included in this volume testify to a clear regional difference in this respect: in a number of Latin American countries, recourse to foreign tribunals and the intervention of the Inter-American Court of Human Rights have been seen by victims and human rights groups as a way of prompting and supporting domestic prosecutions, and rulings of foreign and international courts have become a central source of jurisprudence for domestic judges.

As Hau's chapter on Chile shows, rulings by the Inter-American Court of Human Rights have been a key driver for triggering domestic trials (Collins, García-Godós & Skaar 2016; Roht-Arriaza 2005; Engstrom 2009), giving rise to a "justice cascade" (Sikkink 2011; 2017, 134–135). Likewise, the invocation of universal jurisdiction to prosecute crimes against humanity abroad – as in the cases of the former Chilean dictator Augusto Pinochet in Spain and the proceedings against members of the Argentine military in several European countries at the end of the 1990s – have been crucial to ending impunity and staging domestic trials.

Yet, as Lugano's chapter in this volume reveals, the justice dispensed by the International Criminal Court has met with strong criticism in many African countries. Nor has it been seen as a means to further the quest for domestic justice. As both Lugano and Vegh Weis show, perceptions of the ICC and its role tend to be negative in African countries. Several African governments have rejected the Court, on the grounds that it perpetuates neocolonialism, even calling for a collective withdrawal from the Rome Statute. At the same time, the possibility of ICC interventions has been instrumentalized by certain governments to close the door on local accountability, thus maintaining impunity.

However, it is important to stress that continents or regions are not homogeneous blocs. There can be strong differences within them in terms of local opinion and support for international courts and their decisions. Not all Latin American countries, for example, have seen significant domestic advances following from judicial proceedings abroad. While transnational complaints and proceedings in European countries had repercussions on the judicial process in Chile and Argentina, this has not been the case in Uruguay. Despite the country's implication in the transnational human rights crimes that were the subject of the Operation Condor trial concluded in neighboring Argentina in 2016, the verdicts there do not seem to have had a strong impact on Uruguay's judicial system or its government's policy on dealing with the crimes of its own dictatorship until now. The ruling in the case of *Gelman v. Uruguay* (IACtHR 2011) also confronted considerable judicial and political resistance. Though the Uruguayan state did in fact comply with some of that Court's recommendations, including holding a public apology in its parliament, others still need to be addressed (CEJIL 2019). As Sharnak's chapter shows, transnational prosecutions seem even to have had a negative effect on support for trials in Uruguay's domestic courts, to some extent calling into question the idea of a "justice cascade." This also demonstrates the importance of the local power structures that in Uruguay have hampered the progress of human rights justice over the years.

d) The role and agency of victims and human rights organizations

One of the most important factors in advancing accountability for human rights violations is the ongoing struggle and mobilization of local victims' associations and human rights organizations. As the scholarly literature indicates (Collins 2010; Bonacker & Safferling 2013; García-Godós 2013), a strong civil society and the presence and pressure of victims' associations increase the likelihood of accountability efforts. As documented, notably, in the chapter on Chile, the relatives of the disappeared offer irrefutable proof that power and legal structures can always be challenged. The state and the justice system represent spaces of political and social contestation between conflicting group interests and values whose outcomes are of great symbolic and material consequence for society. Survivors and relatives of victims killed or disappeared have been crucial actors for change, challenging impunity and demanding their rights. In the process, they refute the customary construction of "the victim" as a passive, suffering and apolitical subject (Bouris 2007; also discussed in Capdepón's chapter).

Yet it is problematic that victims and human rights organizations so often have to take on much of the work that ought to be done by the state, seeking out evidence and identifying witnesses, ensuring coverage of trials in the press and supporting victims and relatives when such tasks should fall to the public authorities. This is a problem found in many contexts, where civil society organizations take on the responsibilities that ought to be the state's (Mihr 2017). Important as these organizations' activities are, it is very convenient for the state to abandon its responsibilities to others, and if this comfortable *laissez-faire* is allowed to extend over time it only reinforces the passivity of the state, which gets away without making the needed institutional changes.

Where prosecutions have been deemed highly unlikely, human rights groups have deployed an array of innovative and risky strategies in an effort to obtain justice at home or even abroad. Where domestic prosecutions have been initiated, they have continued to support and press them forward in different ways, giving testimony in court, supporting witnesses during hearings, gathering and marshalling evidence, pressing the authorities for funding, and publicizing trials, findings and verdicts in the press and in educational institutions such as schools.

e) Social attitudes towards accountability

A key issue in understanding the scope and impact of trials is the degree to which they enjoy majority support in the society in question. As a number of chapters of this edited volume reveal, while victims in most cases will demand justice when they can, the societies they belong to do not always support their claims. However, the massive public demonstrations against impunity organized in countries like Argentina and Chile after the end of the dictatorships were able to count on substantial social support. It is not that prosecutions did not have their opponents in those countries: they are always to be found. But where opposition is confined to a minority, the balance of pressure on governments increases the chances of their supporting prosecutions. The question then arises of whether prevailing social attitudes towards justice reflect the attitudes of the majority of the populations during the repressive period of state-sponsored violence. Their collaboration, resistance, ignorance or fear at the time indeed has long-lasting consequences and may be the occasion of much dispute. Even under totalitarian regimes that waged systematic terror, generating fear and social paralysis, there were sectors of society that collaborated more actively with the regime, perhaps from conviction and shared values. Support, complicity and collaboration are features of dictatorships (Figueroa Ibarra 2001).

f) The passage of time

The length of time between the occurrence of human rights violations and their formal investigation can be another factor in the scope and impact of prosecutions. This varies significantly across the countries studied, depending in part on the type and level of violence that must be addressed. It is especially a factor when investigations take place decades after the commission of violence, as witnessed by the relatively recent prosecutions of Nazis in the reunified Germany discussed in Weinke's chapter. As she discusses, in 2004 Germany's Federal Court of Justice overturned the conviction of Friedrich Engel, a 93-year-old former head of the SS Security Service, finding that murder was not proven although Engel had ordered the execution of captives. Another case in this volume is presented by the Argentine Complaint in the chapter on Spain, a number of whose central complainants have died in the coronavirus pandemic, as did the notorious torturer González Pacheco, known as Billy the Kid, very shortly before being officially stripped of his military decorations (*El País* 2020). The chapters on Chile and Romania provide other examples. There the eventual or impending death of untried perpetrators and likewise the death of witnesses and victims, with the loss of testimony that this entails, have proven to be a major impediment. Indeed, in Chile and Argentina, many defendants have died of old age in the course of their trials. After 30 years of impunity, the "race against time" is a central factor in the shaping of prosecutions and is crucial in determining their scope. There can be no trial without complainants, witnesses, defendants or evidence.

The scope and impact of trials

As discussed in the introduction, by "impact" we mean some kind of change, or the emergence of a new dynamic, in social, legal and political conditions. Though it is not easy to quantify the impact of human rights prosecutions on a society, the contributions assembled here allow us to identify at least three different types of outcomes or effects that they may bring about: (a) reparation to victims in the form of legal acknowledgement; (b) resistance to human rights prosecutions; and (c) changes in the construction of collective memory.

a) Legal acknowledgement and reparation

The prosecution of human rights violations can expand the traditional notion of retributive justice to incorporate restorative elements. As can be seen in the chapters on Argentina, Darfur, Romania and Peru, criminal justice shares many features with restorative initiatives, blurring the boundaries between restorative and retributive justice in practice. This recognitive and reparative dimension of criminal justice is well illustrated in the cases of Argentina and Romania, where it has restored victims' access to justice and legitimated their narratives, earlier often denied.

Some scholars have stressed the importance of judicial narrative in nourishing the historical record of the past (Wilson 2005; Douglas 2001). The construction of history and the struggle for control of the past take place in a variety of cultural and political spheres or sites, among them education, mass media, memorials, demonstrations and intergenerational conversation within the family. Judicial narrative has joined these as an institutional context within which historical narratives are reconstructed and legitimated.

The symbolic power of law (Bourdieu 1987), an apparently neutral and universalizing discourse, operates as a criterion of recognition and truth (Foucault 2007). The judicial acknowledgement of victimhood weakens other accounts circulating in society. It was said in Argentina, for example, that the disappeared had gone abroad or were otherwise responsible for their own disappearance, thus denying the crime and devaluing the victims. As a result, many survivors and relatives look to the judicial system for official acknowledgement of the truth. There, as in Romania, complainants and the relatives of victims see the courts as the legitimate authority that will provide a detailed account of official crimes and of the systematic character of state violence. Victims and others may also see the courts as the appropriate institution to counter earlier official denial. As Avram reports in the chapter on Romania, the access to truth and the possibility of giving public testimony and being heard by an institution of the state that was afforded by the "Romanian Nuremberg Trial" of 2016 was felt to be very important by victims and their relatives, even decades after the events in question.

The historical reconstruction that trials afford can contribute to a more profound understanding of *historical* justice, having an impact on historical dialogue by changing the dominant frameworks of interpretation over the long term. Legal proceedings can help to legitimate information and make it available to a wider public. Moreover, the public availability of the trial record (documenting public hearings, rulings and verdicts) serves also to document the crimes, thus countering silence or denial. Given the widespread acceptance of the judicial process and the national and official character of judicial institutions, criminal trials can confer heightened legitimacy on the facts laid down in the judicial record. As well as access to more information on the circumstances of the crimes and in certain cases on the whereabouts of the disappeared, the investigative tools deployed in prosecutions (the gathering of fresh testimony, the disclosure of documents, exhumations, searches of property, etc.) may provide certainty regarding crimes unacknowledged for years. For many surviving victims and relatives of the murdered or disappeared in Argentina and Romania, it has been important and reparative to hear testimony and to see evidence that officially confirms the crimes committed.

b) Resistance

As shown in different chapters of this volume, not all campaigns against impunity, efforts at accountability or prosecutions of human rights crimes find a supportive echo in local society, politics or institutions. The reasons for this are many: the continuing power of perpetrators, rejection by elites, general social disapproval due to a collective silencing and oblivion of past violence or even complicity with crime at the time of its commission or indeed in the present, disdain for victims, victims' own lack of interest in prosecutions, the lack of institutional or financial resources, etc. By "resistance" here, we do not necessarily mean the armed, or violent resistance or the threat of it on the part of perpetrators or their allies (O'Donnell & Schmitter 1995), but rather a spectrum of social, political and legal attitudes, ranging from indifference or lack of support for prosecutions at one end to explicit rejection and concrete obstruction of judicial proceedings at the other. Nor does resistance necessarily mean a complete rejection – or lack – of demands for justice within a society. In fact, it is in these contexts that the struggle of human rights groups and victims' collectives becomes more relevant and risky for such actors. The term "resistance" accounts for a strong confrontational dynamic process of advances and setbacks, expressing a power struggle of different sectors (or part of them, e.g. older and conservative judges and politicians) within each society. The results of this process are reflected in the judicial system across different governments and periods of time.

This resistance and disregard for human rights justice can be seen, to varying degrees, in many of the different contexts discussed in this book. Weinke's chapter on the prosecution of Nazis in Germany documents a general reluctance to investigate that prevailed in the political, legal and public discussions of the predominantly self-exculpating society of West Germany, a reluctance that faded only slowly, being maintained for the most part until the inception of the Auschwitz trials in the 1960s and even beyond. Weinke notes, furthermore, that international humanitarian law has never been invoked in the prosecutions of Nazis in the reunified Germany, the major human rights conventions not being treated as pertinent to the judicial treatment of Nazi war crimes and crimes against humanity even today.

Sharnak's chapter on Uruguay shows how a majority of Uruguayans decided in two consecutive plebiscites to uphold the amnesty law for the crimes of the country's former dictatorship, first in 1989 and then in 2009. These were not, however, the only setbacks victims have had to deal with in their long struggle for justice. The verdicts in Argentina's Operation Condor trial in 2016, which found that country to have collaborated with the Uruguayan authorities in the commission of crimes against humanity some 40 years earlier, did not have the repercussions in Uruguay that victims and human rights organizations might have expected. As Sharnak explains, while the Argentinian verdict was seen as a hopeful sign by those campaigning for domestic trials, such optimism was dispelled by a series of setbacks and worrying developments over the following years, with threats and attacks on victims and on lawyers, human rights groups and scholars working on the prosecutions. Such attacks on human rights defenders have also gone unpunished, for justice is certainly not undisputed in Uruguay. Despite the current constraints, several sectors of Uruguayan society keep on supporting the human rights movements, and victims continue filing cases and demanding justice.

To acknowledge such resistances, or what might be considered the "negative impacts" of human rights trials more generally, is not by any means to justify any failure to conduct prosecutions. On the contrary, an analysis of these setbacks offers an image of the power relations prevailing at a given time and place. This should serve to understand and address the underlying causes of such antidemocratic developments, so as to overcome these obstacles and ensure victims the access to justice.

c) The construction of memory

Their impact on the construction of collective memory is a crucial aspect of human rights prosecutions, which can have very powerful effects in changing the officially legitimated narratives regarding state-sponsored violence and repression. The quest for criminal justice can thus have significant repercussions beyond the courtroom, prompting other forms of symbolic and social recognition of victims, such as the creation of sites of memory in the form of monuments, memorials or museums. The case of Peru shows how the visibility afforded to victims of the armed conflict by criminal trials led to a variety of artistic or symbolic initiatives. Of these, the inauguration of a memorial site known as the "Sanctuary of Memory," dedicated to the thousands of disappeared from the Ayacucho region, offers a striking example of how legal proceedings can lend resonance to victims' claims and impact collective memory through enduring symbolic representations.

The Argentine Complaint has had very significant consequences for the victims of the Franco dictatorship, in the sense of supporting the emergence of a new historical narrative after many years of denial. The transnational investigation has fostered not only increased public visibility but also further differentiation among victim groups, notably between the still surviving victims of the late Franco regime and others, as described in Capdepón's chapter. On the one hand, then, the Argentine proceedings have offered a certain public acknowledgement and recognition to certain groups of victims by questioning the accepted account of a "shared guilt" narrative regarding the violence or the Spanish Civil War, a less violent late Franco regime and a peaceful transition process. On the other hand, this very success has contributed to competition among victims, leading to conflicts over strategy between the different associations involved. A positive consequence, however, has been an unprecedented intensification of pressure on Spain's political parties and judicial system to end impunity and mount domestic prosecutions, with that putting the topping on how to deal with the Francoist legacy in the political agenda.

Savelsberg's chapter offers an innovative perspective on the ICC's investigation of the situation in Darfur. Analyzing what he terms the "representational power of international criminal justice" (e.g. how it helps form collective representations and memories), he traces its impact by comparing the media discourse on Darfur in different countries and documenting the response of associations, trans-governmental networks, criminal law experts, and NGOs at the international level. Though none of the major actors charged with crimes in Darfur has actually been arraigned before the ICC, thus casting doubt, at least in this case, on the notion of the "justice cascade," Savelsberg highlights the importance of the international debate for collective representations – and thus how legal proceedings influence "social frameworks of memory" (Halbwachs 1992) and their effects on local mnemonic cultures. In examining the discursive impact of representations of evil and their delegitimizing effect, Savelsberg's approach goes much further than the customary analysis of international criminal law in simple terms of its deterrent effect, instead of highlighting its effects on memory narratives in different countries.

Are prosecutions enough?

As the findings discussed above reveal, the meaning and relevance of human rights prosecutions for victims may differ greatly not only from one country to another but also within any one society, where their outcomes may be subject to varying and indeed opposed interpretations. While the demand for retributive justice has been a high priority for the human rights movement and victims' groups in Latin America, and in the Southern Cone more particularly as witnessed by the chapters on Argentina and Chile, this does not always appear to be the case in other contexts. According to a number of scholars, the socioeconomic status of victims is a factor influencing the meaning that trials may have for them (Uprimny & Saffon 2007). As Vegh Weis explains in her consideration of the case of Kenya, where victims are often highly marginalized and living in extreme poverty, retributive justice does not seem to be their first priority. In societies with high levels of inequality, where social exclusion and poverty are a crucial causal factor in political violence and armed conflict, the victims of human rights violations usually belong to the poorest and most excluded sectors of the population. For them, retributive justice as a means of symbolic reparation, although important, would likely prove insufficient, doing nothing to remedy the marginalization and social exclusion that characterized their condition even before they suffered violence. And it would likely worsen them in turn. In such cases, public policies addressing basic social rights such as housing, health and education may be called for as a complement to – and not a replacement for – reparation by way of retribution. Prosecution in itself is often not enough to provide redress.

However, without denying the significance of victims' socioeconomic status as a factor influencing their perceptions of and attitudes towards retributive justice, it would be wrong and reductive to believe that only middle- and upper-class victims demand it. The fact that criminal justice is not the first priority for some does not mean that it is not valued by them as a right. As shown by the chapter on Peru, where prosecutions concerning the internal armed conflict have been taking place for some years now, most of the victims demanding justice and the right to a hearing belong to marginalized indigenous populations. There are similarly victims from middle- or upper-class backgrounds for whom justice in the courts is not the most important demand, or for whom that is not seen as a means of reparation. In Uruguay, for instance, efforts to end impunity by repealing the Amnesty Laws were long held to be relatively unimportant by middle- and upper-class victims. Similarly, the explicit demand for justice for and by the victims of the Spanish Civil War and of the ensuing Franco dictatorship was something that emerged only relatively recently, especially with respect to the crimes of the late Franco regime, committed in the 1960s and 1970s (Capdepón 2019; Alija-Fernández & Martín Ortega 2018). In both Uruguay and Spain, a "pacted" transition process has seen amnesty laws remain in force until today.

An agenda for future research: "double standards" in human rights and international criminal law

Surveying the scholarship on international human rights prosecutions and even transitional justice, one is usually confronted by a familiar landscape. Violence occurs in the Global South, while the legal "solutions" for dealing with the consequences of mass atrocities come from the "civilized" Global North. Human rights scholars and practitioners have tended to reproduce this hypocritical view of southern "victims" and northern "saviors" (Makau Mutua 2001). However, the complicity of the Global North in the incidence of dictatorship, violent conflict and even bloody civil wars in the South cannot be denied, testifying to an evident double standard in the application of human rights and international criminal law. Without denying the South's own responsibility in such violence, the fact alone that the ICC has initiated few prosecutions and secured no convictions of any head of state from the Global North for the commission of such crimes against humanity as military intervention, torture, targeted killings or extraordinary rendition is symptomatic of a wider imbalance, reflecting a "double standard" (Kaleck 2015). In this respect, we find that novel initiatives such as that of the Argentine Complaint, whereby victims from the Global North sought accountability in the Global South for crimes committed in Spain, deserve further study and analysis in all their complexities and ramifications.

The application of universal jurisdiction to courts in countries located in the Global South is an interesting development not only regarding North–South relations but also South–South justice advances: one of the most important African cases in this context was that held against the former dictator of Chad, Hissène Habré, after a decade-long transnational fight for justice on the part of victims and survivors. The Extraordinary African Chambers was created by the African Union and Senegal to try Habré for ordering the wrongful arrest, torture and killing of Chadian citizens during his presidency from 1982 to 1990. In a 2016 African collaboration, a historic ruling in the special court in Senegal's capital, Dakar, finally sentenced Habré to lifelong imprisonment. In the same year, as illustrated in Sharnak's chapter, 15 high-ranking military officers were sentenced in Buenos Aires for crimes against humanity within the "Operation Condor" dictatorships' network of secret services between Chile, Argentina, Bolivia, Uruguay, Paraguay and Brazil – a network that also tracked and persecuted leftist political dissidents in other countries in the 1970s and 1980s.

On the other hand, more recently, in April 2020, the world's first trial of a member of the Syrian military for war crimes and crimes against humanity got under way in Koblenz (Germany) for crimes of torture perpetrated against political enemies of the Assad regime held at the Damascus base of the Military Intelligence's Branch 251. In 2020 as well, an Iraqi was investigated in a court in Frankfurt am Main on the grounds of universal jurisdiction, accused of participating in an Islamic State-led campaign to exterminate the Yazidi religious minority. However, as discussed before, Germany was not always keen on combating impunity. In fact, German law for a long time prohibited prosecutions of Nazi-era perpetrators unless it could be demonstrated that they were directly linked to specific murders. This approach to criminal law allowed many Nazi suspects to go unpunished. Only in the 2009 case against the Nazi guard John Demjanjuk did a German court finally accept that those who knowingly participated in the death machinery should be put on trial.

Research into the domestic and international possibilities for the prosecution of those responsible, North or South, for violations of human rights such as those committed at Guantanamo, Abu Ghraib and more recently in Syria, would represent an important contribution to the study of human rights accountability. A more equal and symmetric application of international human rights law would provide it with greater credibility, acceptance, legitimacy and potential of reaching the goals it proclaims to achieve such as the guarantee of non-repetition, the substantive fulfillment of human rights and redress for victims worldwide.

References

Bonacker, T. & Safferling, C. (eds.) 2013. *Victims of International Crimes. An Interdisciplinary Discourse*. The Hague: Asser.

Bourdieu, P., 1987. "The Force of Law: Toward a Sociology of the Juridical." *Hastings Law Journal* 38(5): 817–818.

Bouris, E., 2007. *Complex Political Victims*. Bloomfield: Kumarian Press Inc.

Capdepón, U., 2019. "La 'Querella Argentina' y la represión franquista: memorias locales, procesos de justicia transnacionales y 'efectos rebote.'" In Eser, P., Schrott, A. & Winter, U. (eds.) *Transiciones democráticas y memoria en el mundo hispánico. Miradas transatlánticas: historia, cultura, política*. Frankfurt am Main: Peter Lang, 115–131.

Centro por la Justicia y el Derecho Internacional (CEJIL), 2019. "Uruguay reconoció ante la Corte Interamericana de Derechos Humanos el incumplimiento de la sentencia del caso Gelman," September 6. Available at: https://www.cejil.org/es/uruguay-reconocio-corte-interamericana-derechos-humanos-incumplimiento-sentencia-del-caso-gelman [Accessed April 29, 2020].

Cohen, S., 2001. *States of Denial. Knowing about Atrocities and Suffering*. Cambridge: Polity Press.

Collins, C., 2010. *Post-Transitional Justice: Human Rights Trials in Chile and El Salvador*. Philadelphia: Pennsylvania State University Press.

Collins, C., García-Godós, J. & Skaar, E. (eds.) 2016. "Introduction. The Accountability Challenge." In id. (eds.) *Transitional Justice in Latin America: The Uneven Road from Impunity*. New York: Routledge.

Douglas, L., 2001. *The Memory of Judgment. Making Law and History in the Trials of the Holocaust*. New Haven/London: Yale University Press.

El País, 2020. "Muere por coronavirus Billy el Niño, el policía franquista acusado de torturador," May 7.

Engstrom, P., 2009. *Argentina and the Inter-American Human Rights System*. Human Rights Consortium, November 11.

Foucault, M., 2007. *La verdad y las formas jurídicas*. Barcelona: Gedisa.

García-Godós, J., 2013. "Victims' Rights and Distributive Justice. In Search of Actors." *Human Rights Review* 14(3): 241–255.

Halbwachs, M., 1992. *On Collective Memory*. Chicago: University of Chicago Press.

Inter-American Court of Human Rights (IACtHR), 2011. *Case Gelman v. Uruguay*. Available at: www.corteidh.or.cr/docs/casos/articulos/seriec_221_ing.pdf [Accessed April 29, 2020].

International Criminal Court (ICC), 2020. 45 defendants. Available at: https://www.icc-cpi.int/defendants [Accessed April 29, 2020].

Kaleck, W., 2015. *Double Standards. International Criminal Law and the West*. Berlin: Torkel Ophsal.

Laplante, L., 2014. "The Plural Justice Aims of Reparation." In Buckley-Zistel, S., Koloma Beck, T., Braun, C. & Mieth, F. (eds.) *Transitional Justice Theories*. New York: Routledge, 66–84.

Makau Mutua, S., 2001. "Victims and Saviors: The Metaphor of Human Rights." *Harvard International Law Journal* 1: 201–245.

Mihr, A., 2017. "Human rights, non-governmental organizations in conflict transformation." In Fuentes Julio, C. & Drumond, P. (eds.) *Human Rights and Conflict Resolution. Bridging the Theoretical and Practical Divide*. New York: Routledge.

O'Donnell, G., 1993. "On the State, Democratization and Some Conceptual Problems: A Latin American View with Glances at Some Post-communist Countries." *World Development* 21(8): 1355–1369. https://doi.org/10.1016/0305-750X(93)90048-E.

O'Donnell, G., 1998. "Las poliarquías y la (in)efectividad de la ley en América Latina." In Méndez, J. E., O'Donnell, G. & Sérgio Pinheiro, P. (eds.) *La (in)efectividad de la ley y la exclusión en América Latina*. Buenos Aires: Paidós.

O'Donnell, G. & Schmitter, P. C., 1995. "Transitions From Authoritarian Rule: Tentative Conclusions About Uncertain Democracies." In Kritz, N. J. (ed.) *Transitional Justice: How emerging democracies reckon with former regimes*, Vol. 1. Washington D.C: United States Institute of Peace Press, 57–64.

Roht-Arriaza, N., 2005. *The Pinochet Effect. Transnational Justice in the Age of Human Rights*. Philadelphia: University of Pennsylvania Press.

Sikkink, K., 2011. *The Justice Cascade: How Human Rights Prosecutions Are Changing World Politics*. New York: W. W. Norton.

Sikkink, K., 2017. *Evidence for Hope: Making Human Rights in the 21st Century*. Princeton: Princeton University Press.

Uprimny, R. & Saffon, M. P., 2007. *Uses and Abuses of Transitional Justice*. Bogota: Dejusticia.

Wacquant, L., 2009. *Punishing the poor. The Neoliberal government of social insecurity*. Durham/London: Duke University Press.

Wilson, R. A., 2005. "Judging History: the Historical Record of the International Criminal Tribunal for the Former Yugoslavia." *Human Rights Quarterly* 27(3): 908–942.

Index

www.ingramcontent.com/pod-product-compliance
Lightning Source LLC
Chambersburg PA
CBHW071732210526
45486CB00032B/1382
9789462702493